Wayne Pa...

The London Government Handbook

Cassell Publishers Limited
Artillery House, Artillery Row
London SW1P 1RT

First published 1988

British Library Cataloguing in Publication Data

The London government handbook.
    1. London. Local government
    I. Hebbert, Michael   II. Travers, Tony, *1953–*
    352.0421

    ISBN 0–304–31574–5

Typeset by Inforum Limited, Portsmouth
Printed and bound by Biddles Limited, Guildford

The London Government Handbook

edited by Michael Hebbert and Tony Travers

GREATER LONDON GROUP

London School of Economics and Political Science

Cassell

CONTENTS

ACKNOWLEDGEMENTS

The preparation of this Handbook was made possible thanks to generous support from the Staff Research Fund of the London School of Economics towards Tom Clegg's contribution, and from the Nuffield Foundation, through its core funding for the Greater London Group.

The basic structure of the book took shape in 1986–7 during the regular Monday afternoon meetings of the Greater London Group. We benefitted from detailed and frank briefings from many leading actors in the post-G L C reorganisation, among them Sir Godfrey Taylor, Stephen Grigson, Paul McQuail, A. C. O. Brian Robinson, Gerald Oppenheim, Stephen Hughes and John Ferguson. Many more people, whom we cannot name individually, took pains to answer written questionnaires on the structure and operation of their organisations, endured repeated rounds of follow-up interviews on the telephone, and checked the final entries for their organisations prior to printing. Paul McQuail kindly read and commented on the full draft of Chapter 1, in so far as it describes the Departments of Environment and Transport. The very few officers (most from centrally appointed Boards) who responded ungraciously to our requests for information only served to put into relief the kindness and patience of the majority. Of course, those mentioned carry no responsibility for any remaining errors of fact or interpretation in the text, and we cannot emphasise too strongly the inevitability of error in descriptive accounts of a system so complex and so fluid.

Our task was eased thanks to the groundwork laid by various other guides to the new system of London government, to which we would like to acknowledge our thanks. One of the Greater London Council's more useful death-bed legacies to Londoners was a *Directory of GLC Services*, with the names and telephone numbers of successor authorities for each service, issued on the back of the invitation to its Farewell Festival. After abolition, the Association of London Authorities produced a looseleaf *Directory* in a ring folder, comparable with the *Factsheets on London Government* of the London Boroughs Association. The fullest compendium so far prepared, and one which we found particularly helpful, was a spiral-bound publication by the late London Strategic Policy Unit entitled *London Government Now*. Our thanks to the anonymous compilers of each of these ephemeral guides.

We encountered surprising difficulty in preparing the maps. Many agencies simply do not possess a straightforward and publicly available map of their areas. The editors owe an immense debt to the indefatigable research efforts of Susan Horsfall, who compiled the maps, and to Jane Pugh and Gary Llewellyn of the Drawing Office in the Department of Geography at L S E, who drafted them to a tight schedule.

Lastly, a special word of thanks to Alma Gibbons for advising on the word-processing of our long and complicated manuscript, and to Christine Gazely and Angela Barnes who keyed it all in so promptly and accurately. We could not have wished for a more helpful and supportive editor than Diana Russell at Cassell.

The London government system continued to evolve even as we worked on the Handbook. Because of the elaborate and shifting character of the arrangements here described we must give especial emphasis to our disclaimer clause. Though every effort has been made to ensure it, the Greater London Group cannot formally guarantee the correctness of any information contained in this Handbook.

THE GREATER LONDON GROUP

The Greater London Group is a Research Centre of the London School of Economics and Political Science. It was founded in 1958 by the late William Robson, Professor of Public Administration, himself a notable authority on the problems of big city government, who saw the scope which the L S E offered for impartial study of and comment on the case of London.

The Group aims to maintain a centre of information and documentation on London government, to comment on major policies relating to the capital, to carry out and disseminate research on policy issues, and to provide an independent location for discussion and debate. It has a publications series for research monographs and discussion papers, *The Greater London Papers*.

The current membership of the Greater London Group is given below, with details of the chapters and sections of the Handbook contributed by individual members:

Robert J. Bennett
Professor of Geography

Tom Clegg   Chapters 2, 3 and 4 and all
Research Assistant   of Chapter 5

Derek R. Diamond   Maps
Professor of Geography with Special Reference to
Urban & Regional Planning; Chairman, Greater
London Group

Patrick Dunleavy   Chapter 2
Reader in Government

Stephen Glaister   London Regional
Cassel Reader in Economics with Special   Transport
Reference to Transport

Howard Glennerster
Professor of Social Administration

Alain Guyomarche   Metropolitan Police
Research Assistant

Michael Hebbert
Lecturer in Planning Studies, Research
Secretary, Greater London Group

Introduction, Chapters 2, 3
and 10 and Maps

Christopher Husbands
Senior Lecturer in Sociology

All of Chapter 8

Richard Jackman
Senior Lecturer in Economics

George W. Jones
Professor of Government

All of Chapter 1

Martin Loughlin
Lecturer in Law

London Residuary Body

Patrick McAuslan
Professor of Public Law

Brendan O'Leary
Lecturer in Public Administration

All of Chapter 9

Michael Synnott
London River Authority

London Waste Regulation
Authority

Tony Travers
Senior Research Fellow; Director of Research,
Greater London Group

Introduction, Chapters 2,
3, 4, 7 and 10 and
Directory

Carol Vielba
City University Business School

All of Chapter 6

The Greater London Group
London School of Economics and Political Science
Houghton Street
London WC2A 2AE
England
Tel: (01) 405 7686
Telex: 24655 BLPES G
Fax: (01) 242 0392

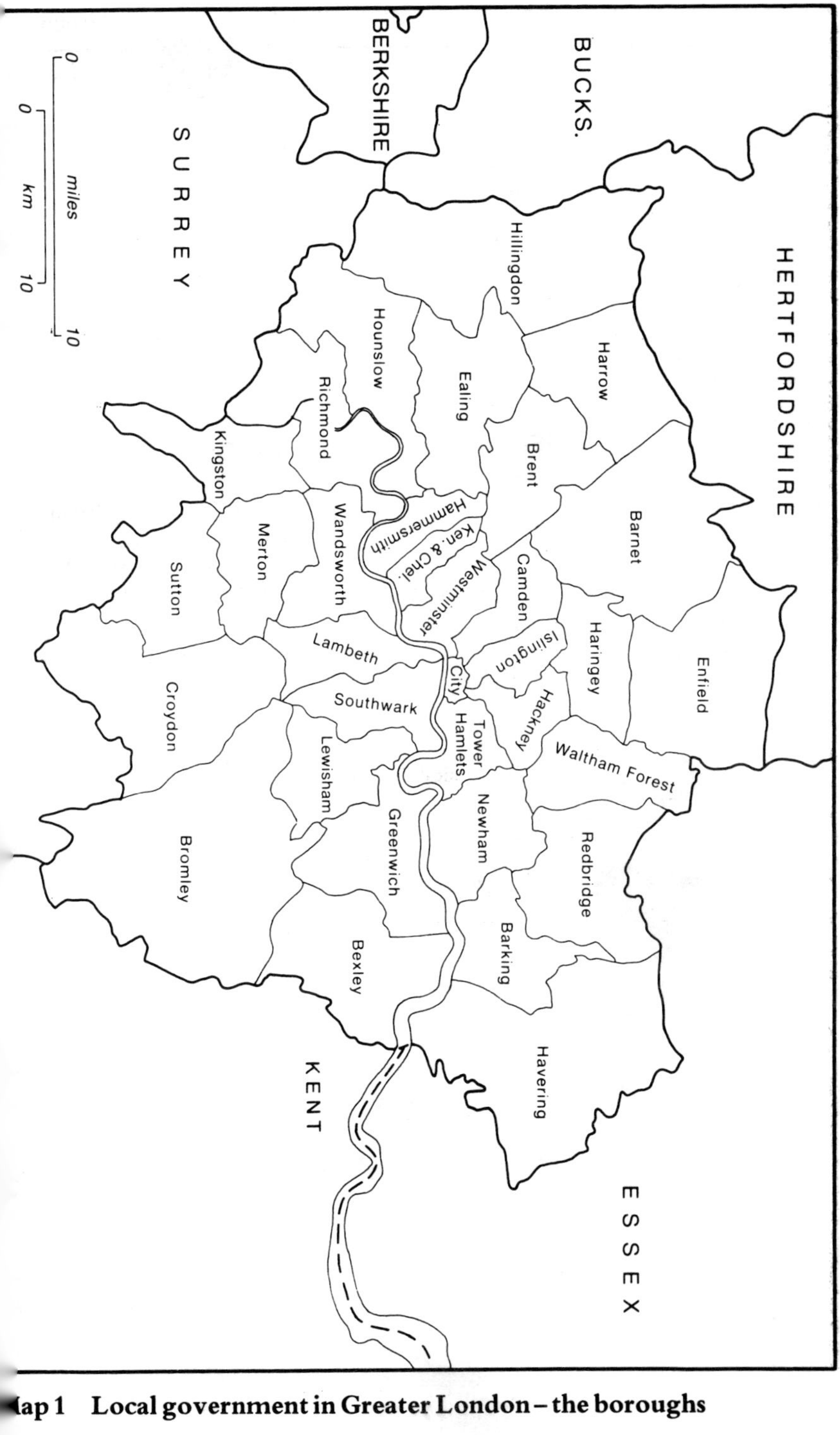

Map 1   Local government in Greater London – the boroughs

ESSEX

HERTFORDSHIRE

BUCKS.

BERKSHIRE

SURREY

KENT

% change
+5.2
+2.0
+1.0
-1.0
-2.0
-6.4
-11.1

London average: -0.4

Havering

Barking

Redbridge

Waltham Forest

Newham

Bexley

Greenwich

Lewisham

Bromley

Enfield

Haringey

Hackney

Tower Hamlets

City

Southwark

Croydon

Islington

Lambeth

Sutton

Barnet

Camden

Westminster

Wandsworth

Merton

Brent

Ken. & Chel.

Hammersmith

Kingston

Harrow

Ealing

Hounslow

Richmond

Hillingdon

0   miles   10

0   km   10

Source: O P C

Map 2   Population change by borough (1981–86)

This map, based on the mid-year estimates compiled by the Registrar General, shows how the populations of the London boroughs changed between 1981 and 1986. After four decades of decline the total population of Greater London has levelled off in the 1980s at rather over 6¾ millions. There is much internal variation. The population levels of several boroughs, such as Hammersmith and Fulham and Brent, have moved from decline to stability. Some inner city boroughs have been experiencing marked increases. Tower Hamlets, through the combination of Docklands development and a flourishing Bengali population, grew by more than 5 per cent and Hackney, Islington and Camden also had increases. In contrast to this northern arc, the populations of Lambeth (−3.2 per cent) and Westminster (−6.4 per cent) have continued to decline. Among the outer boroughs there were also some notable contrasts. The total population rose in Barnet, Enfield, Harrow and Bexley, but fell in Hounslow and Havering.

These variations are not easy to explain. Many factors influence demographic change – in- and out-migration, births and deaths, the operation of local housing markets, and changes in the physical stock of dwellings. Their combined effect has stabilised London's population overall while opening out wide variations from borough to borough, and within boroughs. These fluctuations pose many challenges for London government, perhaps most immediately in education provision.

Map 3   Unemployment by borough (1986)

This map shows the marked contrast that exists in the unemployment levels of
the London boroughs, and the clear geographical pattern of high unemployment
in the heart of the metropolis. In 1986 the overall unemployment rate of fourteen
contiguous boroughs in the middle was 17.1 per cent (a total of 226,000 persons).
The nineteen boroughs around the edge had 188,000 unemployed residents,
with an overall rate of 8.7 per cent, almost exactly half that of inner areas.
Hackney with 22.7 per cent and Tower Hamlets with 22.2 per cent were the
worst-hit boroughs, while Kingston, Sutton, Richmond and Hillingdon form the
top group, with a rate close to 6.0 per cent. The worst ward for unemployment
was Angel in Lambeth (36.1 per cent), the best, Woodcote ward in Sutton where
less than 3 per cent of the workforce were unemployed in 1986.

The high rates of unemployment in inner London reflect both a long-term
decline in the local availability of work (manufacturing and service), and the weak
competitive position of residents in the labour market. While the contrast of
inner and outer areas is far from new, London's high levels of unemployment and
the gap between best and worst areas are post-1980 phenomena. In 1966 Outer
London had between 1.5 and 2.5 per cent unemployment, while Inner London
boroughs ranged from 2.5 to 3.5 per cent.

BERKSHIRE

BUCKS.

HERTFORDSHIRE

SURREY

Hillingdon
Harrow
Hounslow
Ealing
Brent
Barnet
Richmond
Kingston
Hammersmith
Ken. & Chel.
Westminster
Camden
Haringey
Enfield
Merton
Wandsworth
Islington
Hackney
Sutton
Lambeth
City
Waltham Forest
Croydon
Southwark
Tower Hamlets
Newham
Lewisham
Greenwich
Redbridge
Bromley
Barking
Bexley
Havering

KENT

ESSEX

no data available ★

% economically
active population

	22.7
	18.0
	13.0
	11.0
	7.0
	5.9

London average: 11.9

0   miles   10
0   km   10

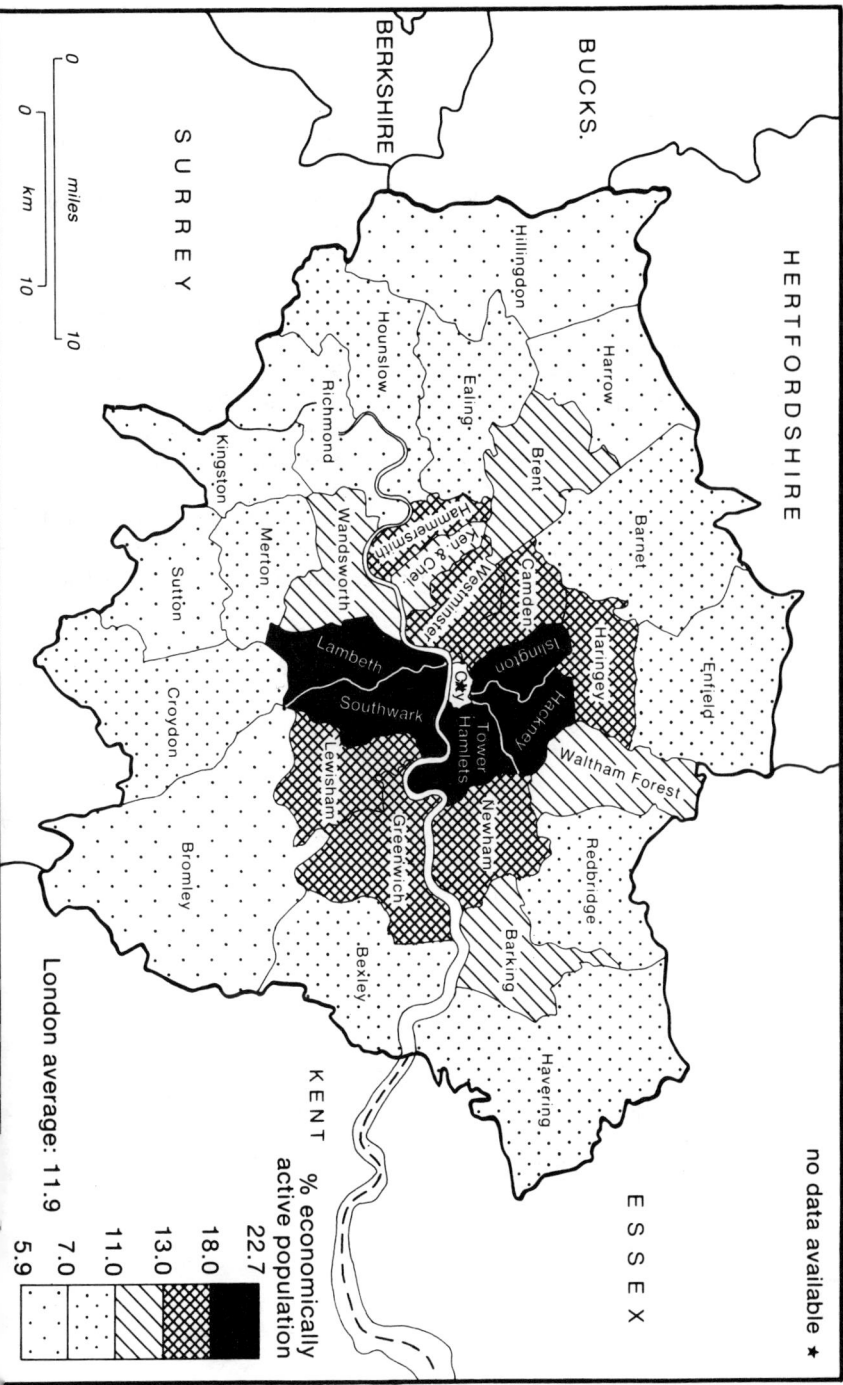

Source: London Research Centre

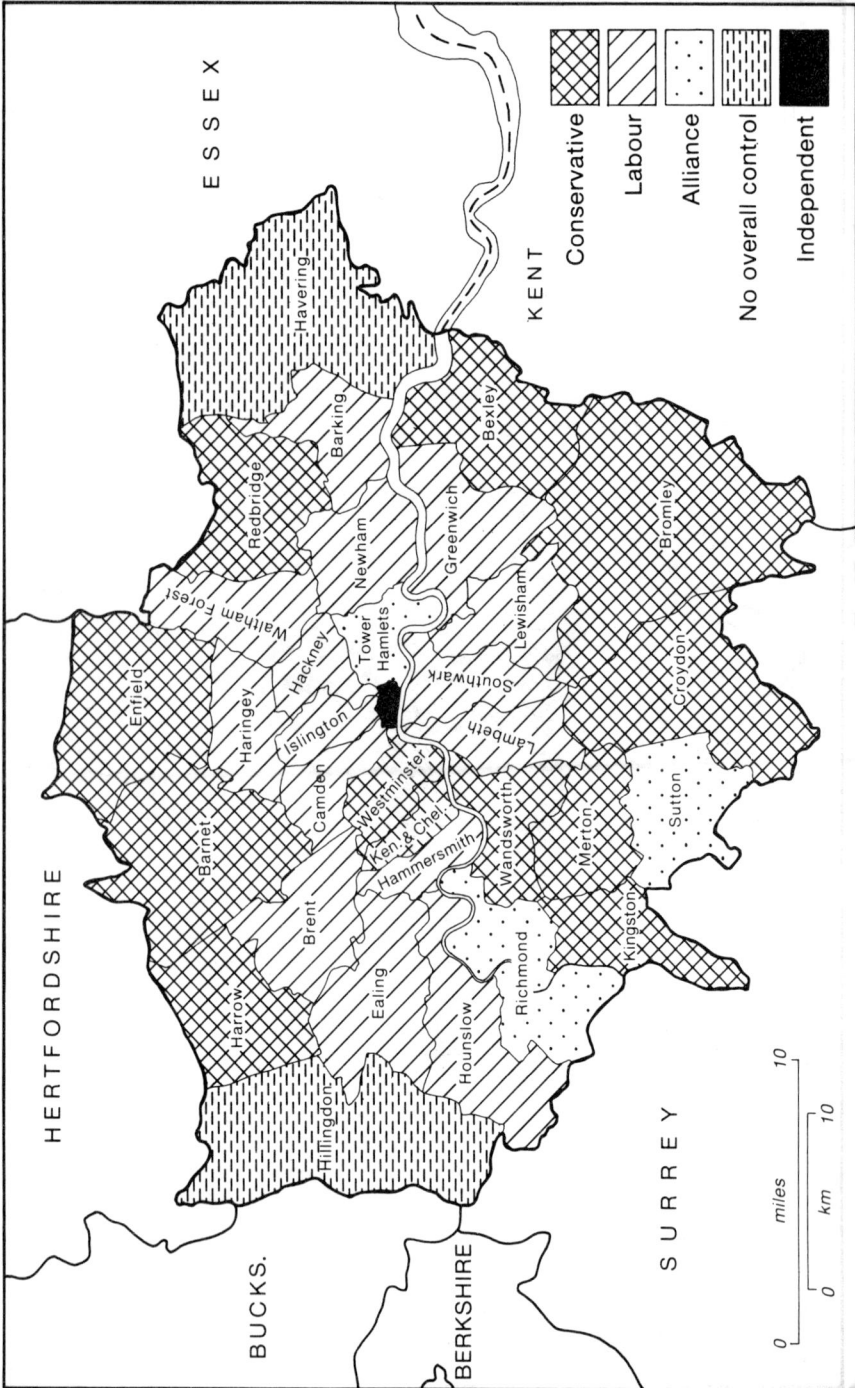

Map 4   Political control of London boroughs

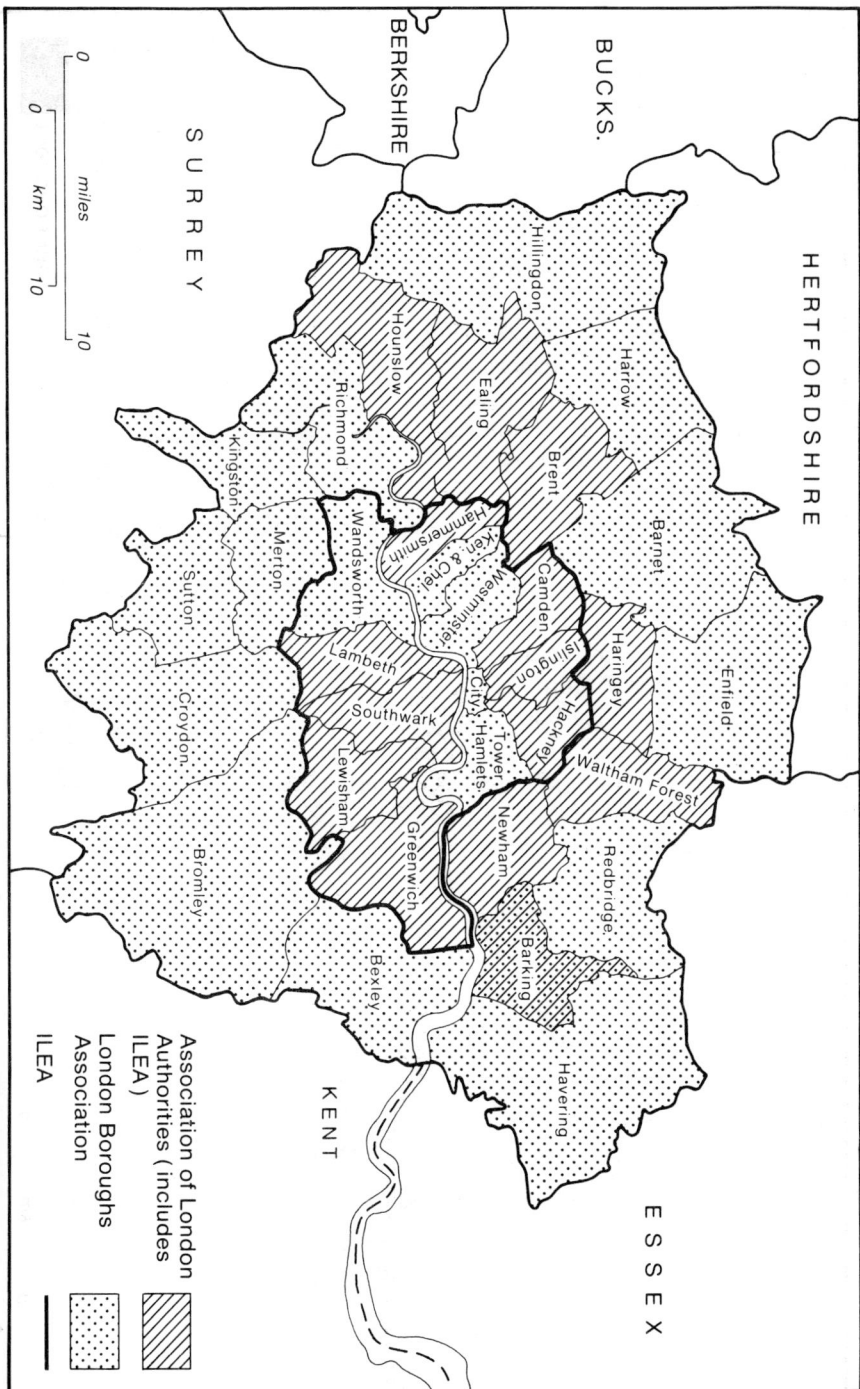

Map 5 Local authority associations

Association of London
Authorities (includes
ILEA)

London Boroughs
Association

ILEA

BERKSHIRE

BUCKS.

HERTFORDSHIRE

SURREY

ESSEX

KENT

Hillingdon

Harrow

Barnet

Enfield

Hounslow

Ealing

Brent

Richmond

Hammersmith

Ken. & Chel.

Westminster

Camden

Islington

Haringey

Hackney

Kingston

Merton

Wandsworth

Lambeth

City

Tower Hamlets

Newham

Waltham Forest

Redbridge

Havering

Sutton

Croydon

Southwark

Lewisham

Greenwich

Barking

Bexley

Bromley

0

0

km

miles

10

10

Map 6   Lead boroughs for joint committees

1. London Strategic Policy Committee
2. London Boroughs Transport Committee
3. London Planning Advisory Committee
4. London Housing Unit
5. London Area Mobility Scheme
6. London Welfare Benefits
7. London Boroughs Disability Committee
8. London Boroughs Nuclear Policy Committee
9. London Advisory Panel on Transport
10. London Boroughs Grant Scheme
11. East London Waste Authority
12. North London Waste Authority
13. West London Waste Authority
14. Western Riverside Waste Authority
15. London Research Centre
16. London Boroughs' Children's Regional Planning Committee
17. Technical Services Joint Committee
18. Docklands Consultative Committee
19. London Canals Committee
20. London River Authority
21. Croydon, Bexley, Bromley Panel of Guardians
22. Havering, Barking, Dagenham Panel of Guardians
23. Sutton, Kingston, Merton, Richmond Panel of Guardians
24. South London Lorry Ban Committee

BUCKS.

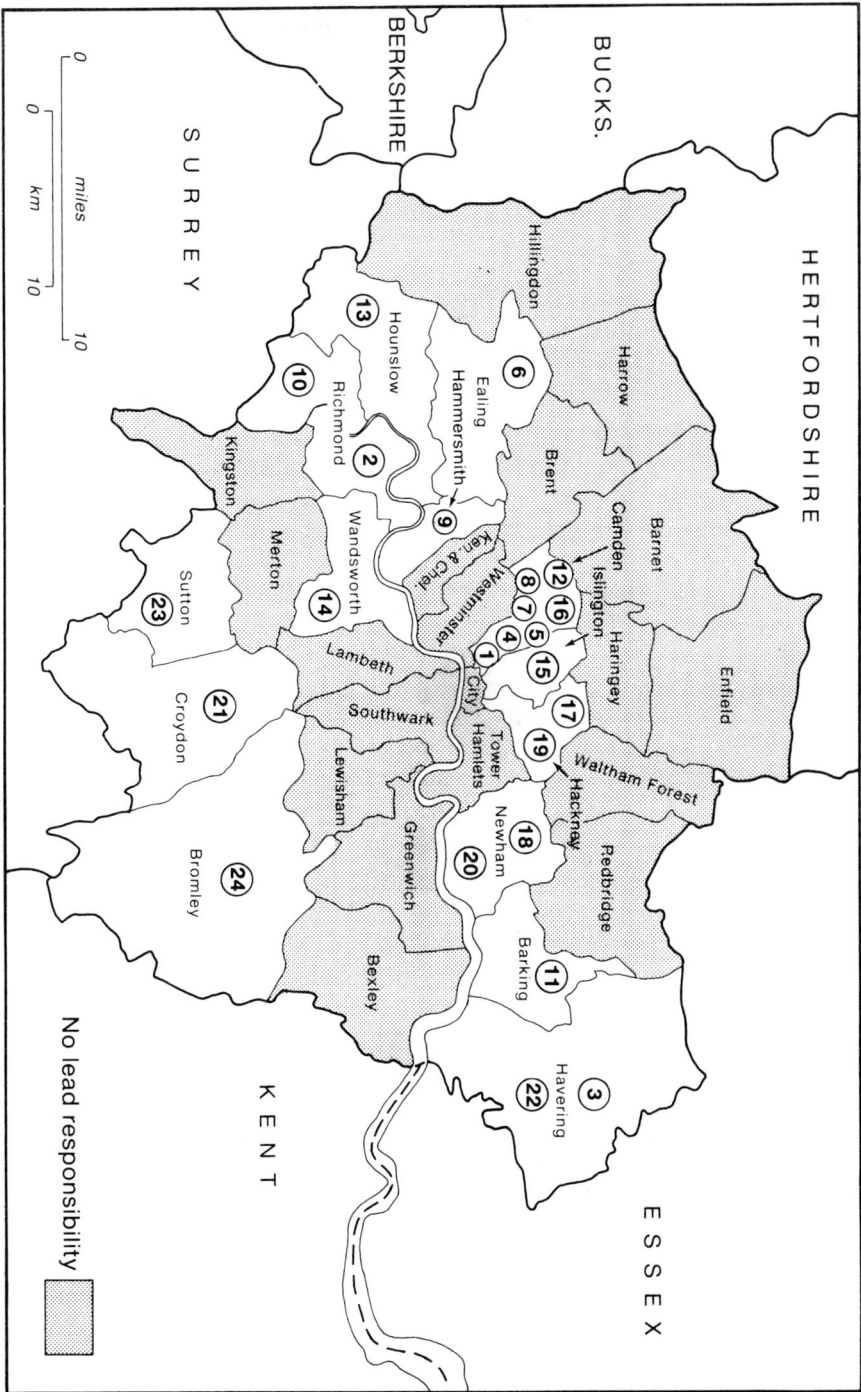

HERTFORDSHIRE

SURREY

ESSEX

KENT

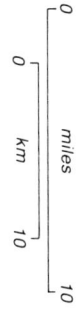

No lead responsibility

0   miles   10
0   km   10

Hillingdon

Harrow

Hounslow

Ealing

Hammersmith

Brent

Barnet

Enfield

⑬ ⑩ ⑥

Richmond

② ⑨

Ken. & Chel.

Camden

Islington

⑫ ⑯

⑧ ⑦ ⑤

④ ⑮

Westminster

Haringey

Kingston

Merton

Wandsworth

⑭

Lambeth

① City

⑰

Waltham Forest

Sutton

⑳

Croydon

Southwark

Tower Hamlets

⑲

Hackney

Redbridge

⑱

Newham

Barking

⑪

Lewisham

Greenwich

Bromley

Bexley

⑳

② ⑪

Havering

③ ㉒

Sutton ㉓

Croydon ㉑

Bromley ㉔

Newham ⑳

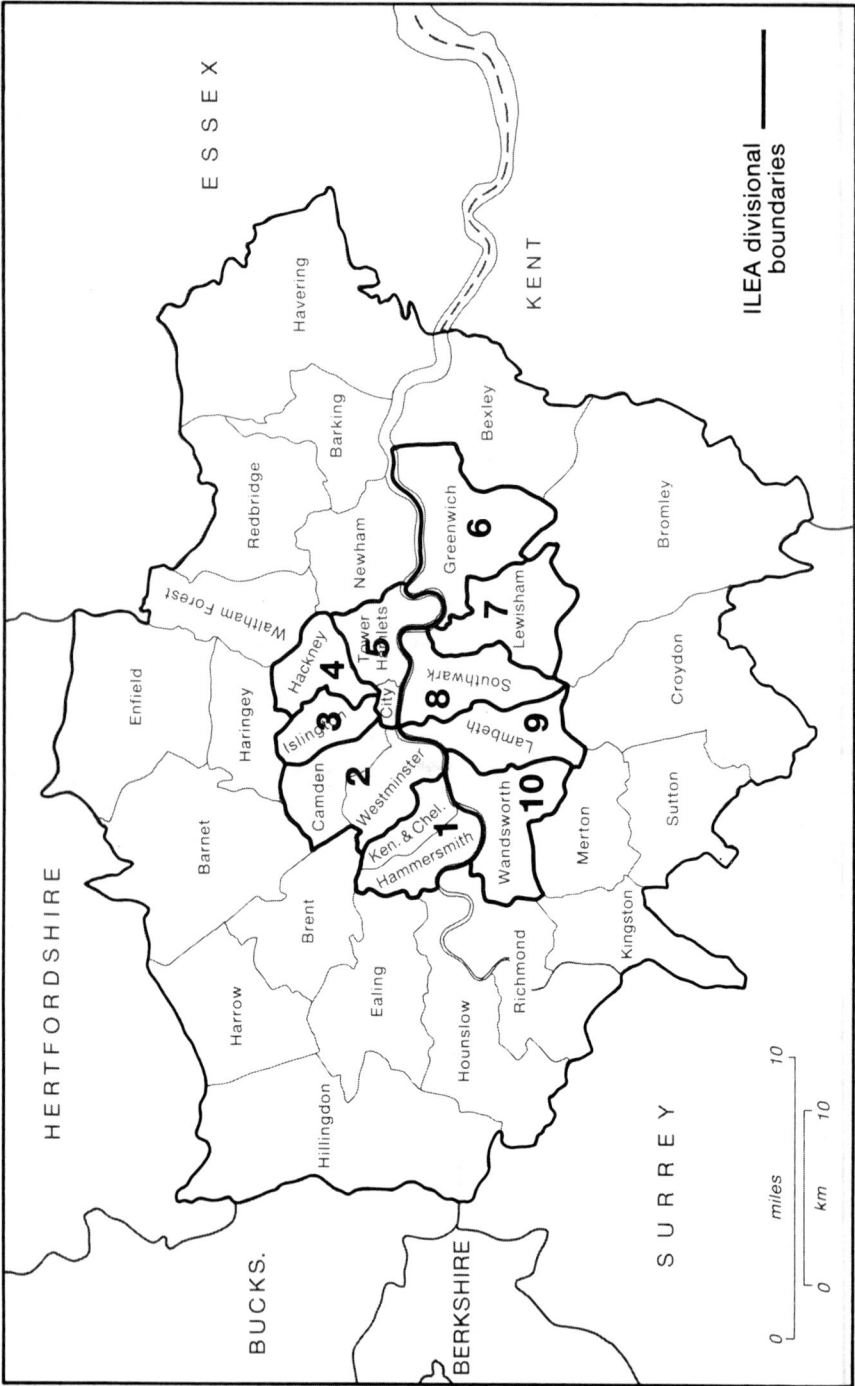

Map 7   The Inner London Education Authority

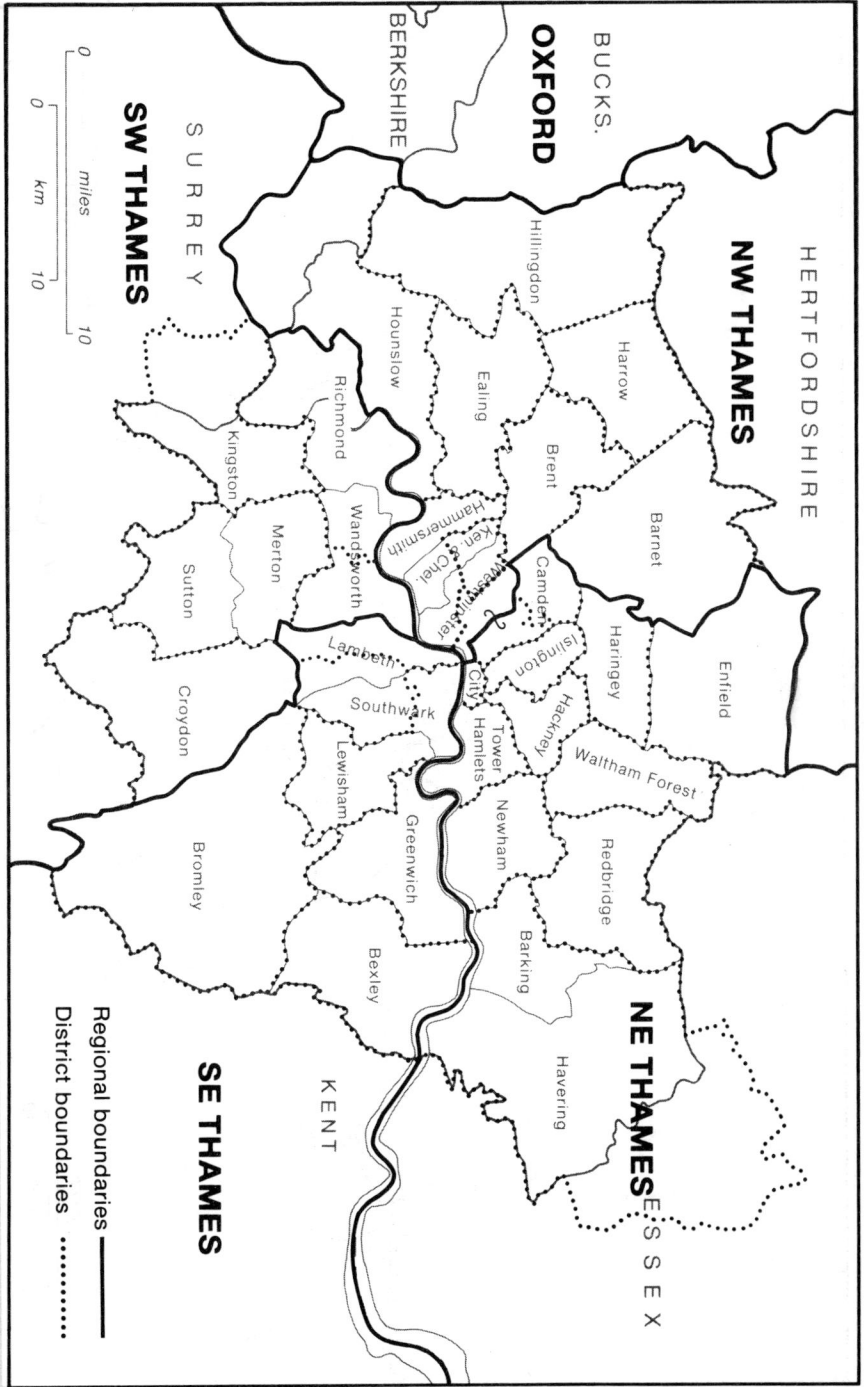

Map 8a   NHS Regions and Districts

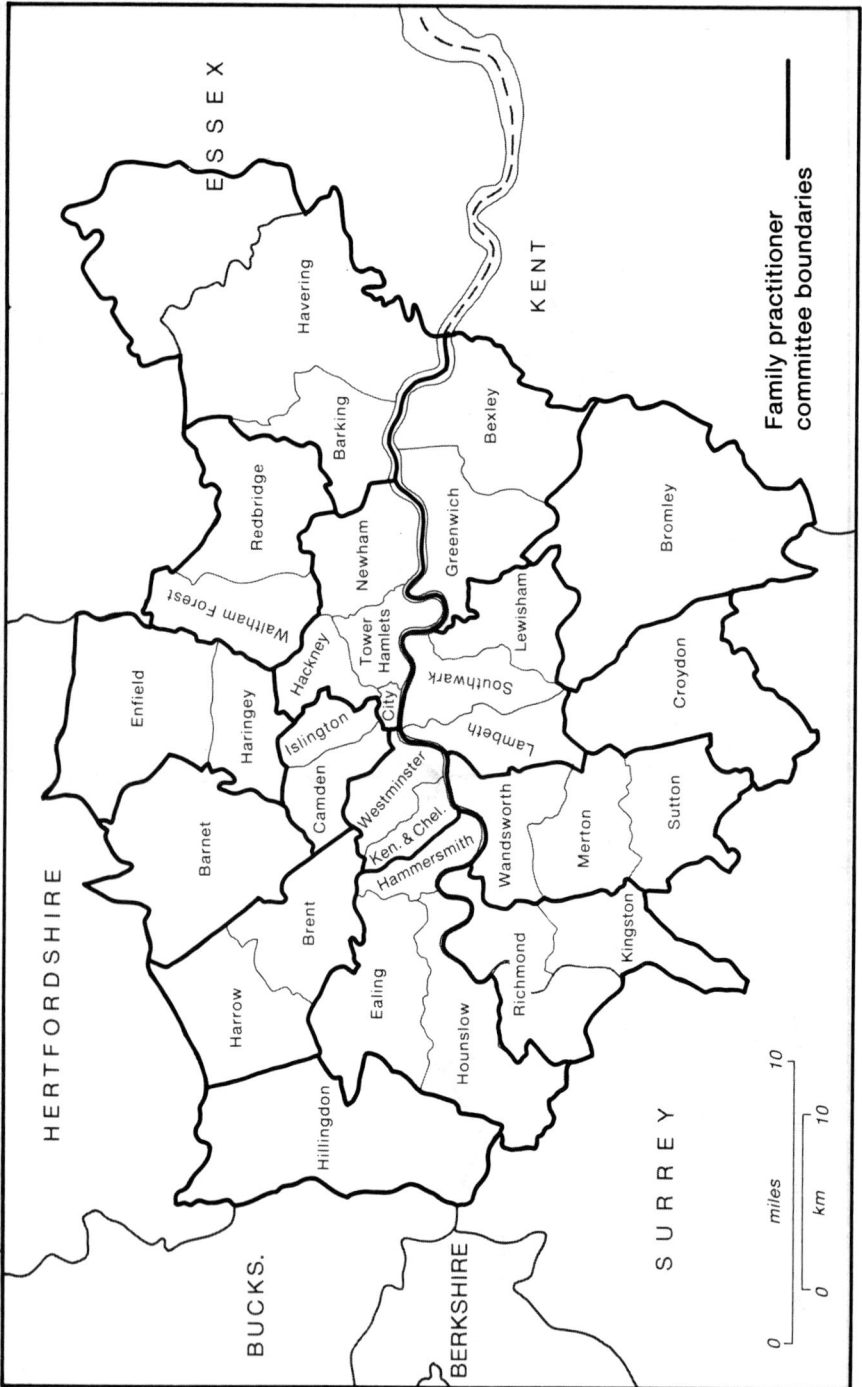

Map 8b   NHS Family Practitioner Committees

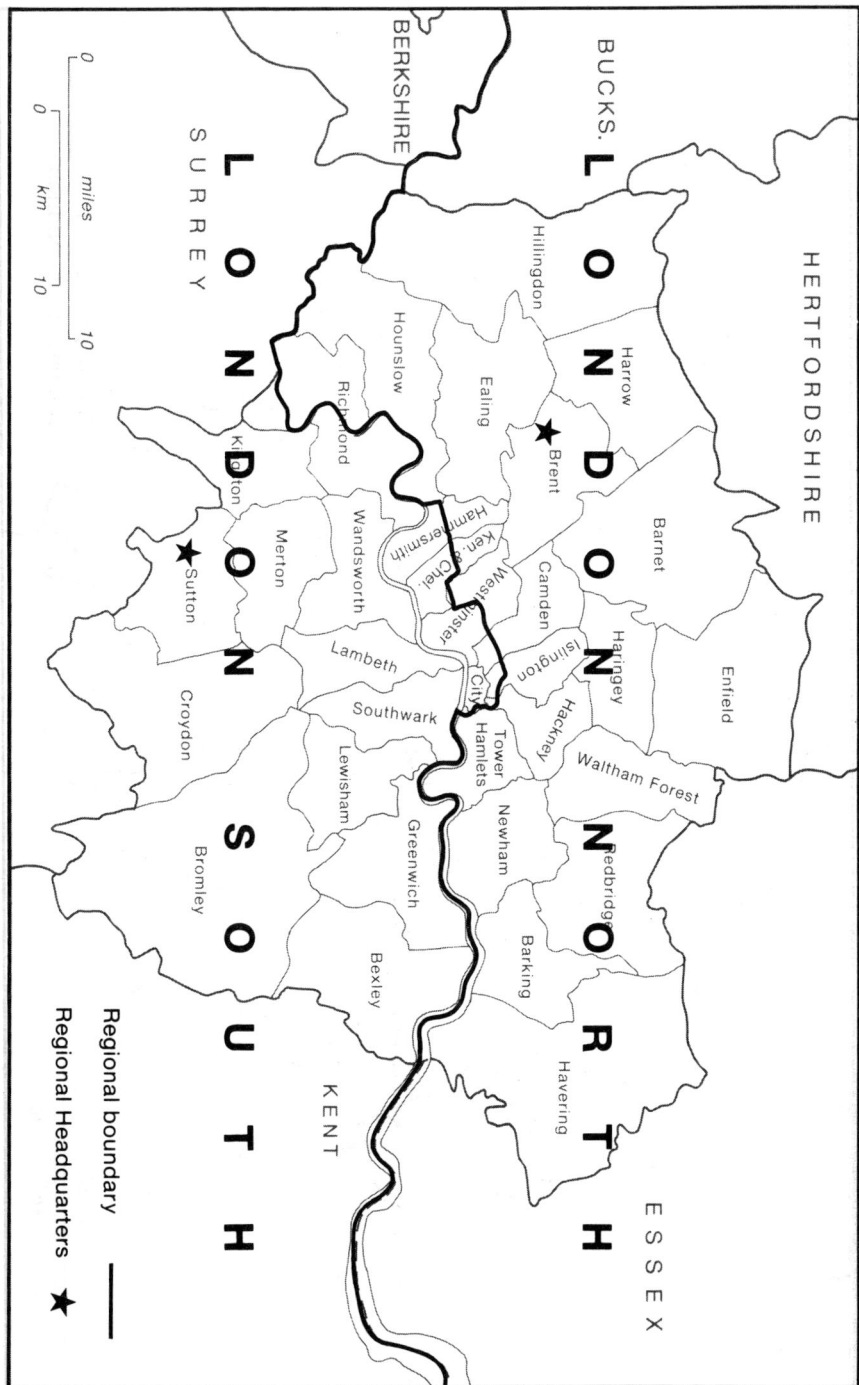

Map 9   DHSS social security regions in London

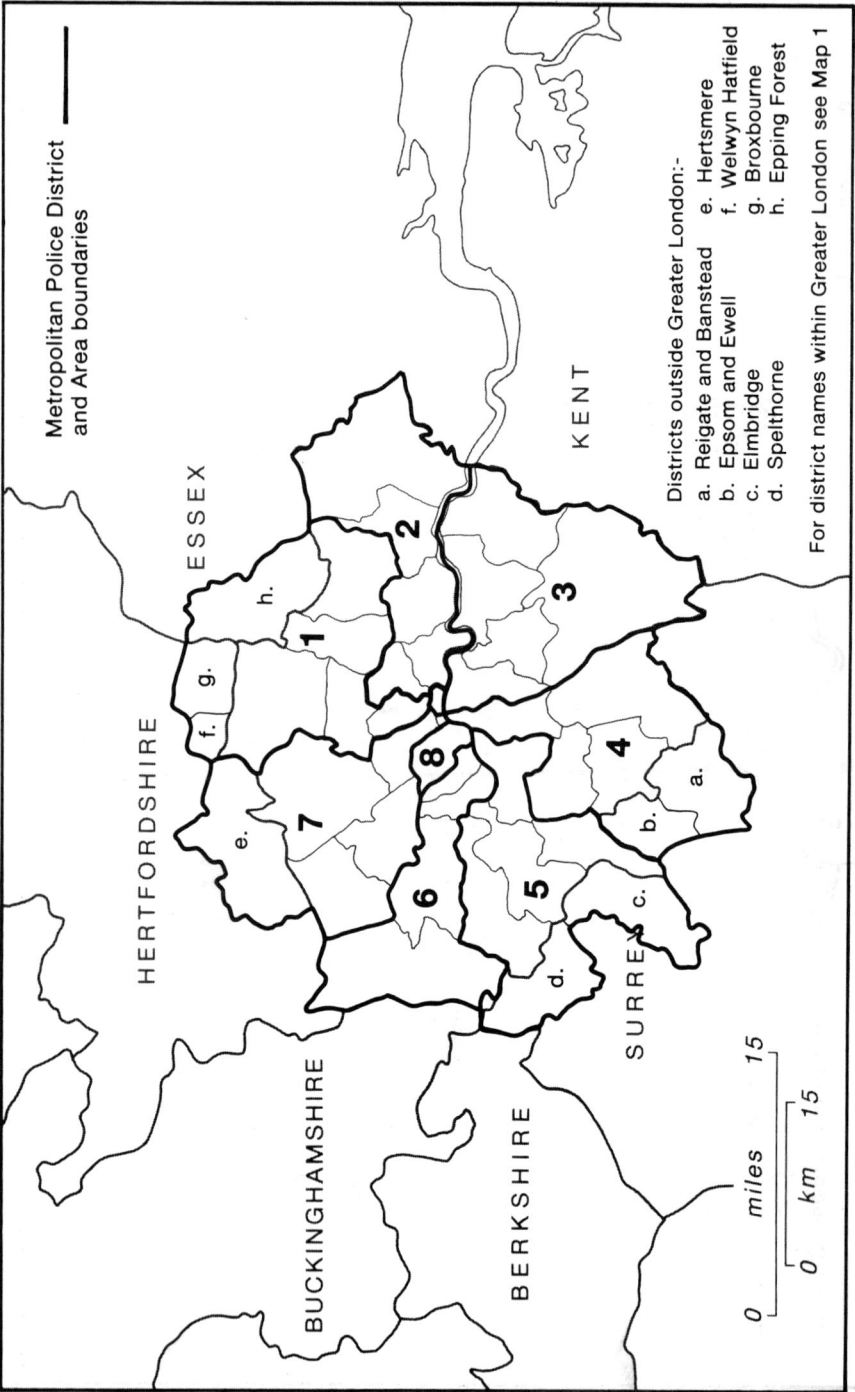

Map 10 The Metropolitan Police District

Metropolitan Police District
and Area boundaries

Districts outside Greater London:-
a. Reigate and Banstead   e. Hertsmere
b. Epsom and Ewell   f. Welwyn Hatfield
c. Elmbridge   g. Broxbourne
d. Spelthorne   h. Epping Forest

For district names within Greater London see Map 1

ESSEX

KENT

HERTFORDSHIRE

BUCKINGHAMSHIRE

BERKSHIRE

SURREY

0   miles   15

0   km   15

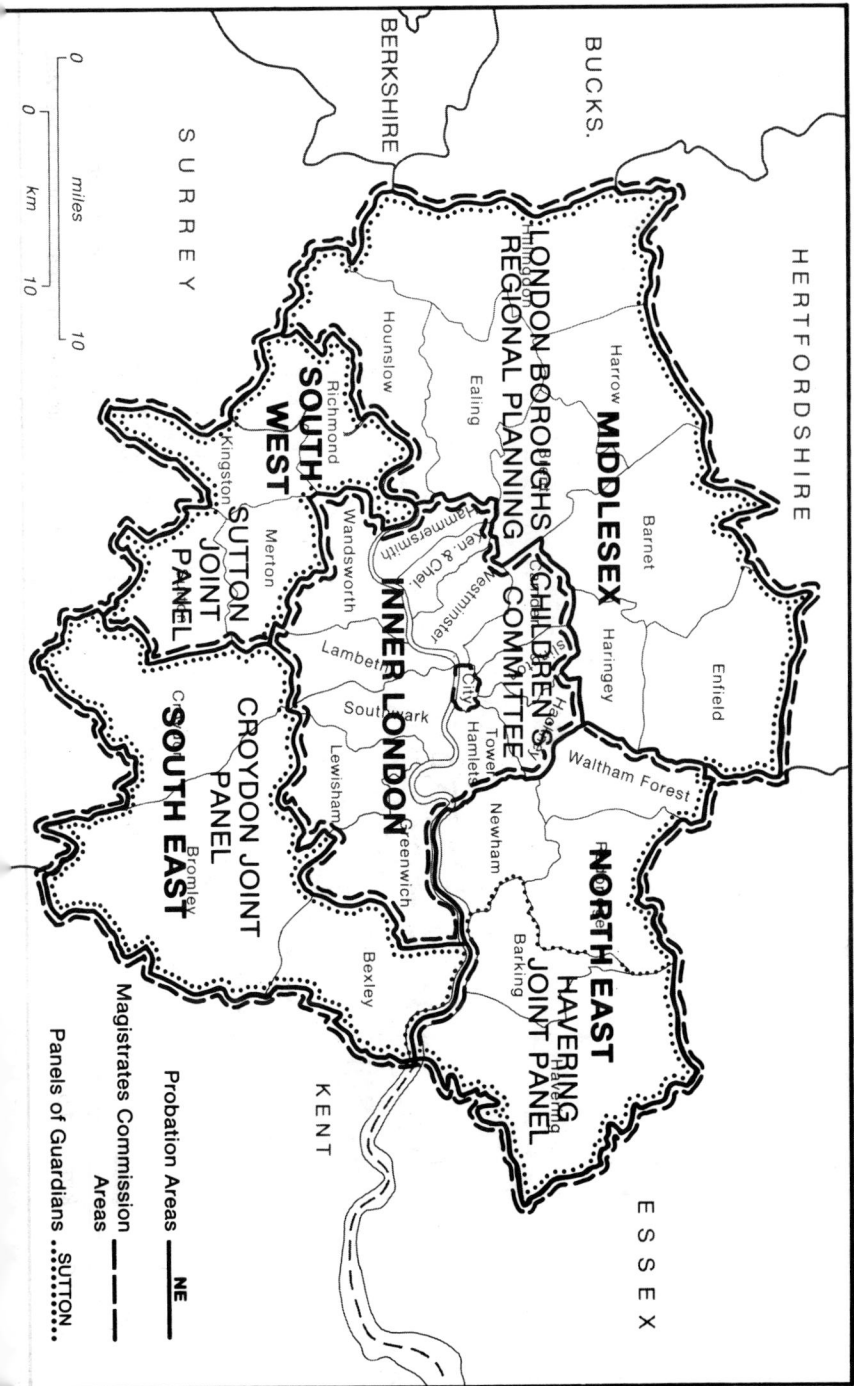

Map 11   Courts, probation and child care

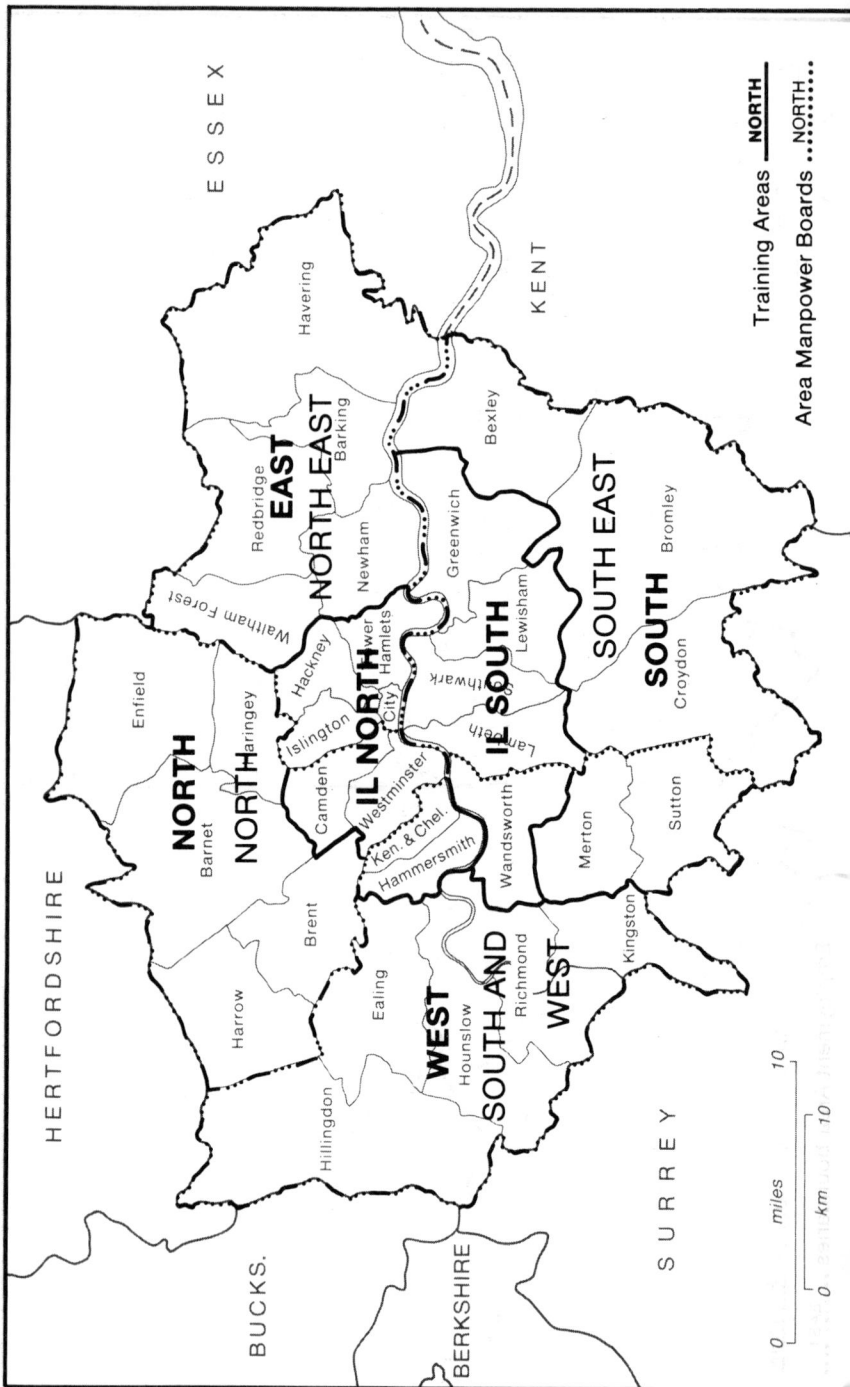

Map 12   The Manpower Services Commission

Training Areas — **NORTH**
Area Manpower Boards ······· NORTH

ESSEX

KENT

EAST
NORTH EAST

SOUTH EAST

SOUTH

Havering

Barking

Bexley

Bromley

Redbridge

Newham

Greenwich

Croydon

Waltham Forest

Hackney

Lewisham

Enfield

Haringey

Tower Hamlets

City

Southwark

Lambeth

NORTH
NORTH

Islington

Camden

Westminster

Barnet

Ken. & Chel.

Wandsworth

Merton

Sutton

HERTFORDSHIRE

Brent

Hammersmith

Harrow

Ealing

Richmond

Kingston

Hillingdon

Hounslow

WEST
SOUTH AND
WEST

SURREY

BUCKS.

BERKSHIRE

IL NORTH

IL SOUTH

miles

km

0   10

0   10

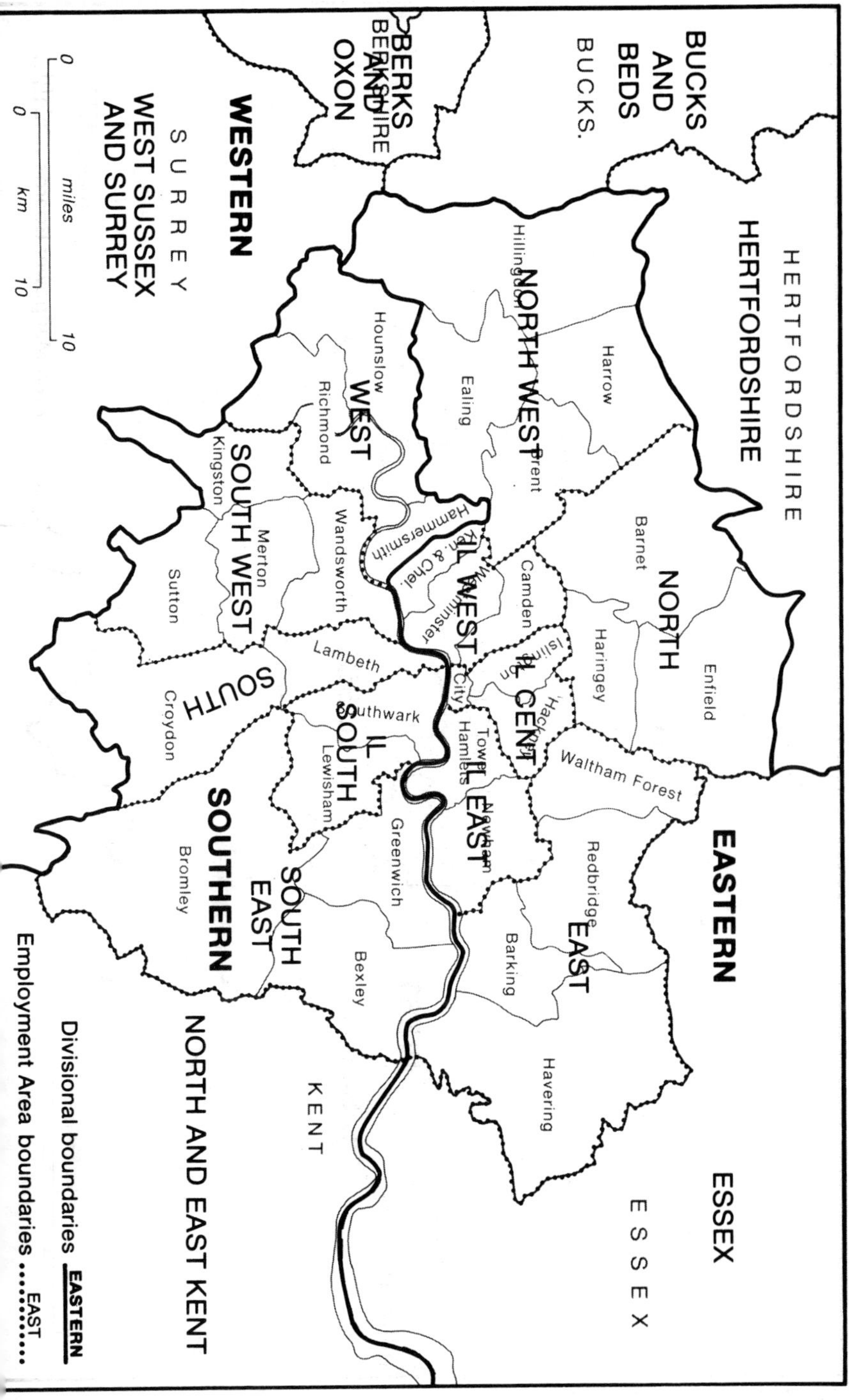

Map 13   The Employment Service

Divisional boundaries ——— **EASTERN**
Employment Area boundaries ••••••• EAST

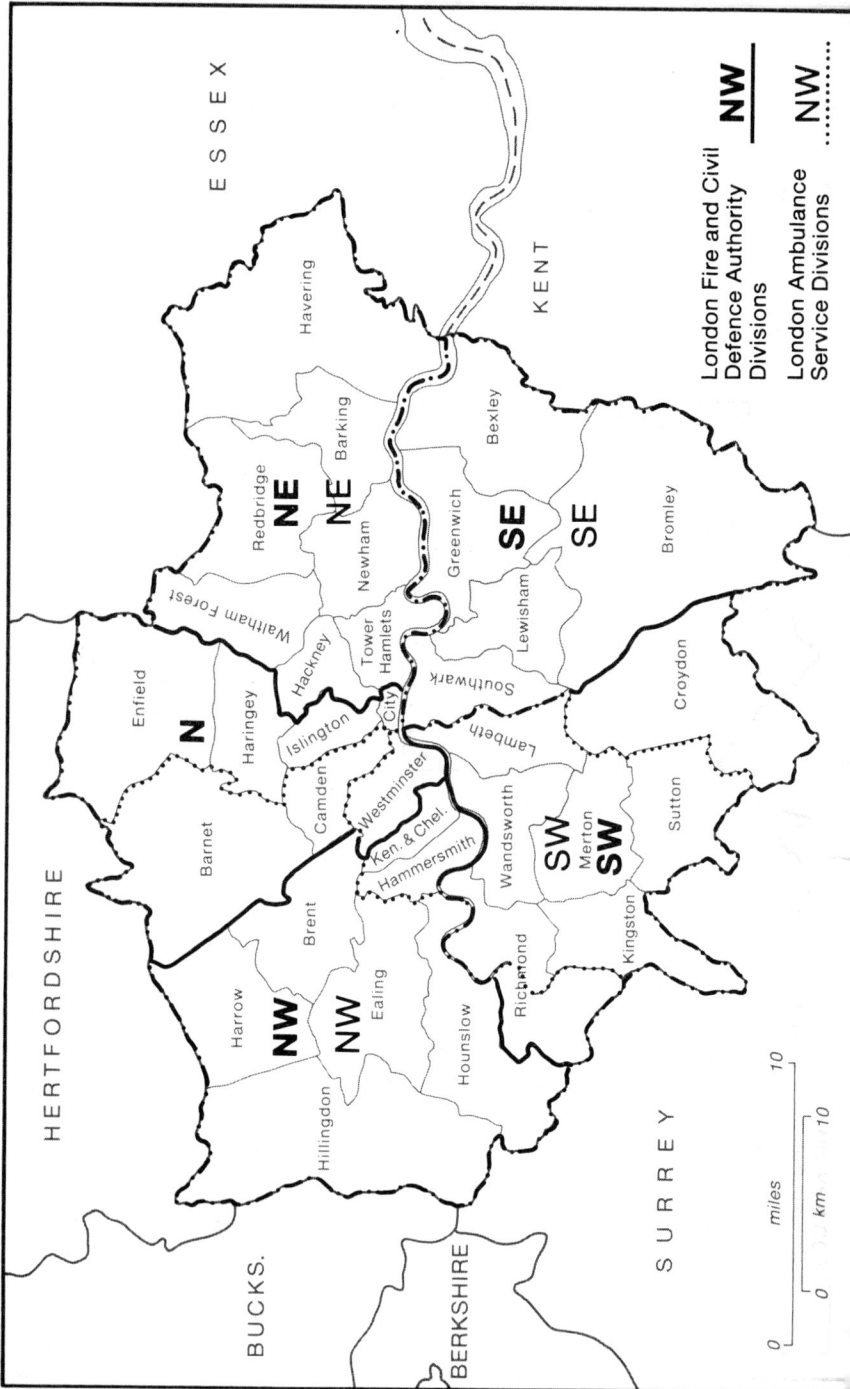

Map 14   Fire, ambulance and civil defence services

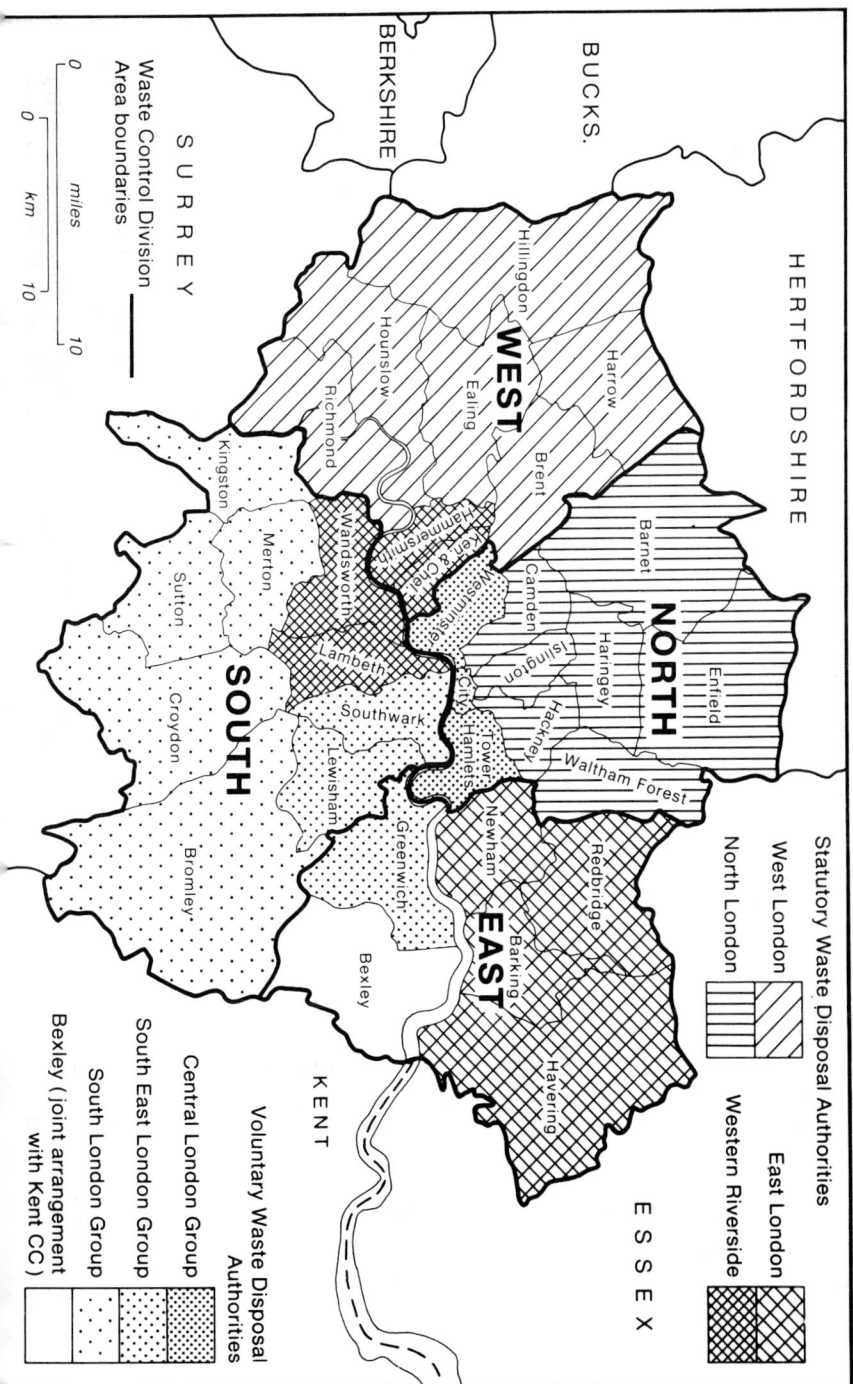

Map 15   Waste disposal and its control by the London Waste Regulation Authority

Waste Control Division
Area boundaries ———

0   miles   10
0   km   10

SURREY

BERKSHIRE

BUCKS.

HERTFORDSHIRE

ESSEX

KENT

Statutory Waste Disposal Authorities
- West London
- North London
- East London
- Western Riverside

Voluntary Waste Disposal Authorities
- Central London Group
- South East London Group
- South London Group
- Bexley (joint arrangement with Kent CC)

WEST

NORTH

SOUTH

EAST

Hillingdon, Hounslow, Richmond, Ealing, Harrow, Brent, Barnet, Kensington & Chelsea, Hammersmith, Westminster, Camden, Islington, Haringey, Enfield, Hackney, Waltham Forest, City, Tower Hamlets, Kingston, Merton, Sutton, Wandsworth, Lambeth, Southwark, Lewisham, Croydon, Bromley, Greenwich, Newham, Redbridge, Barking, Havering, Bexley

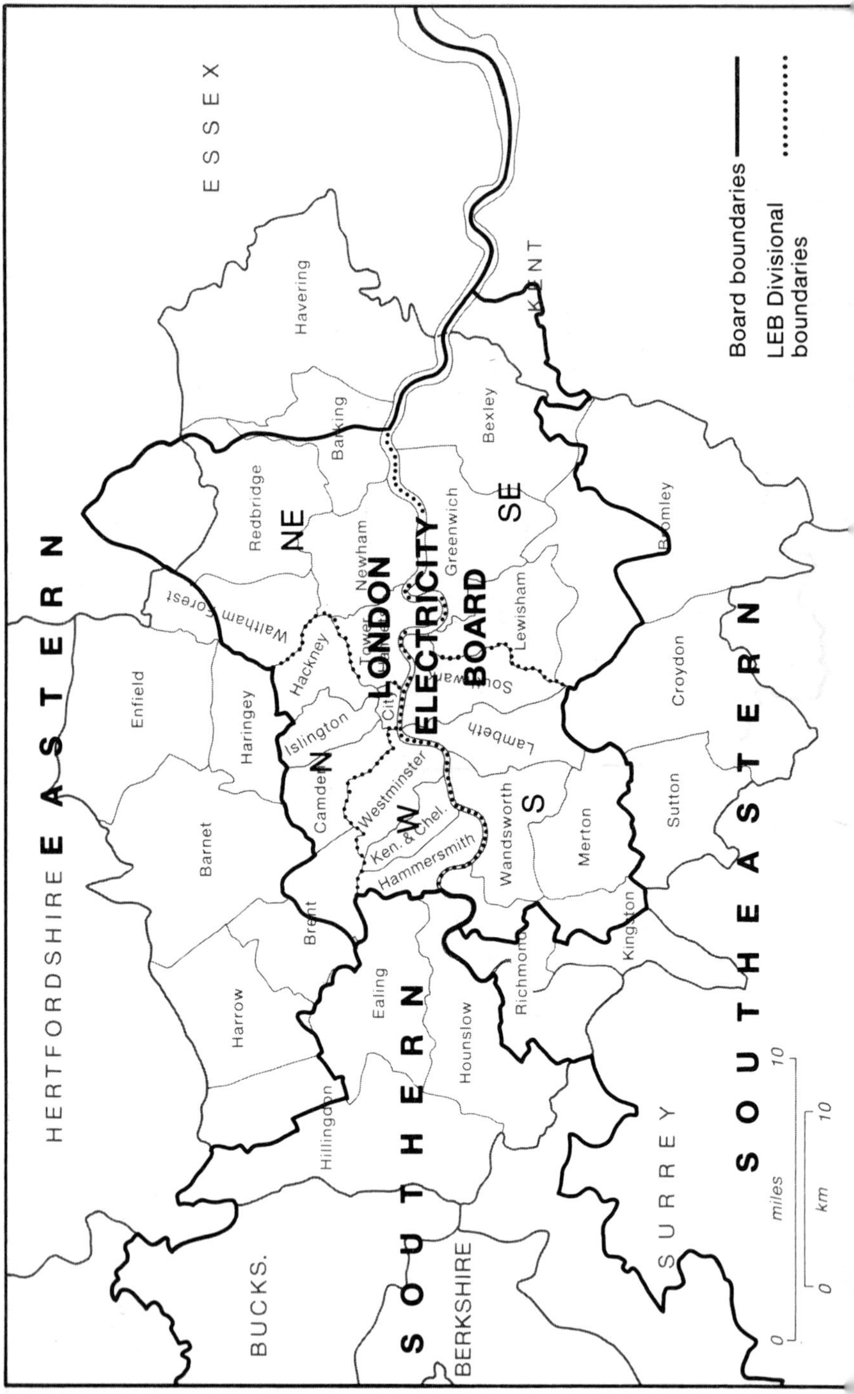

Map 16 Provision of electricity

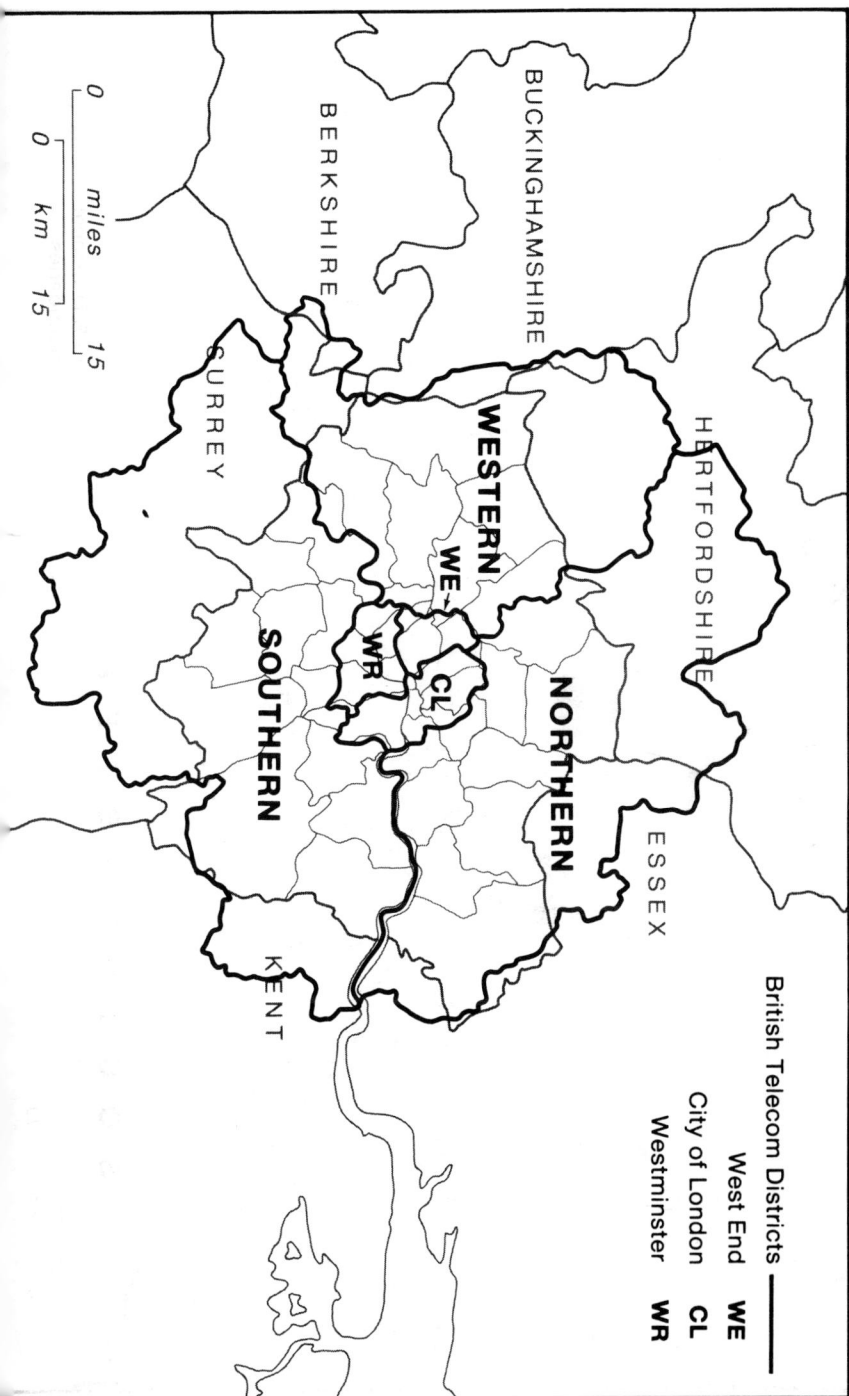

Map 17a   The telephone service: London region

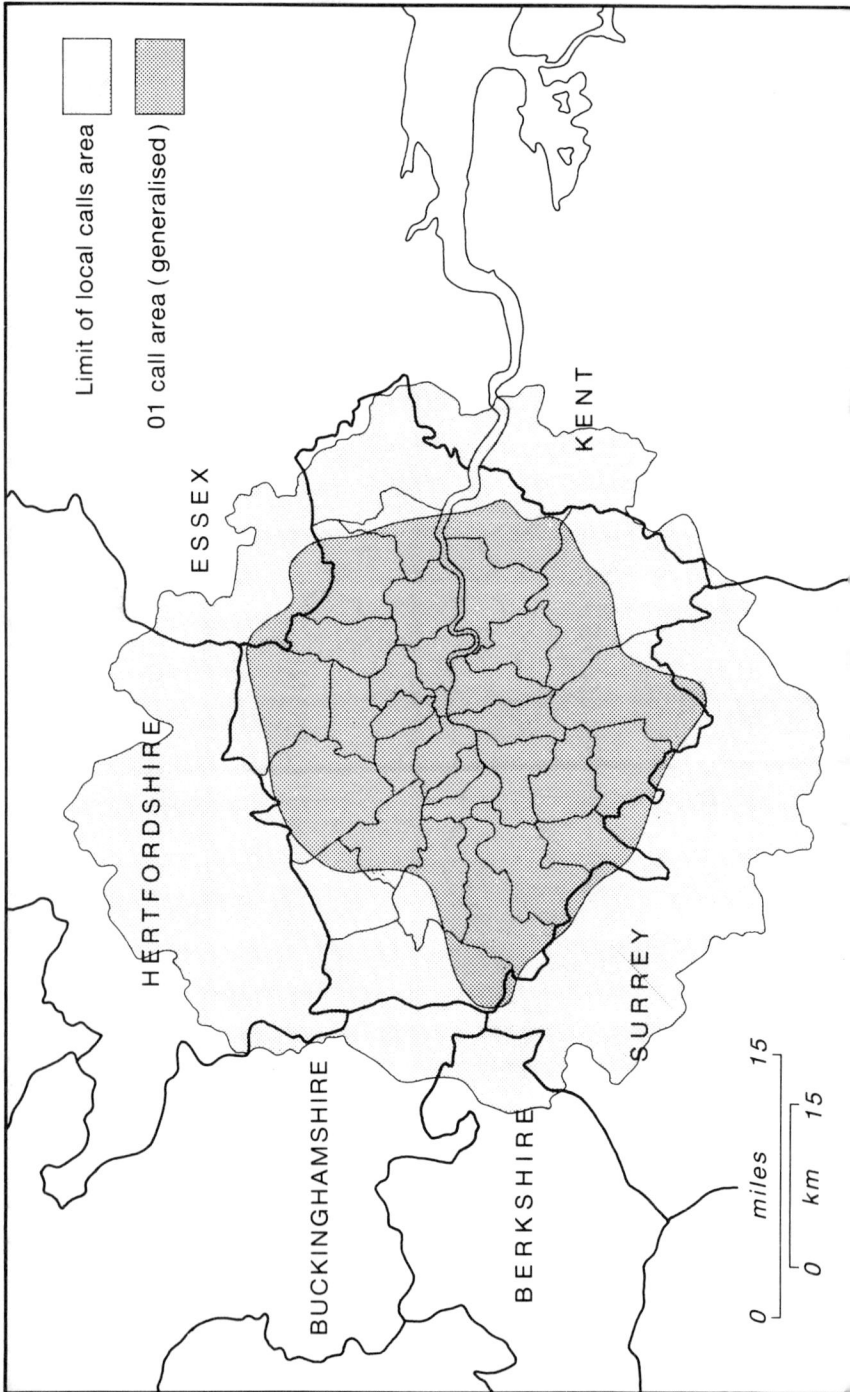

Map 17b   01 and local call areas

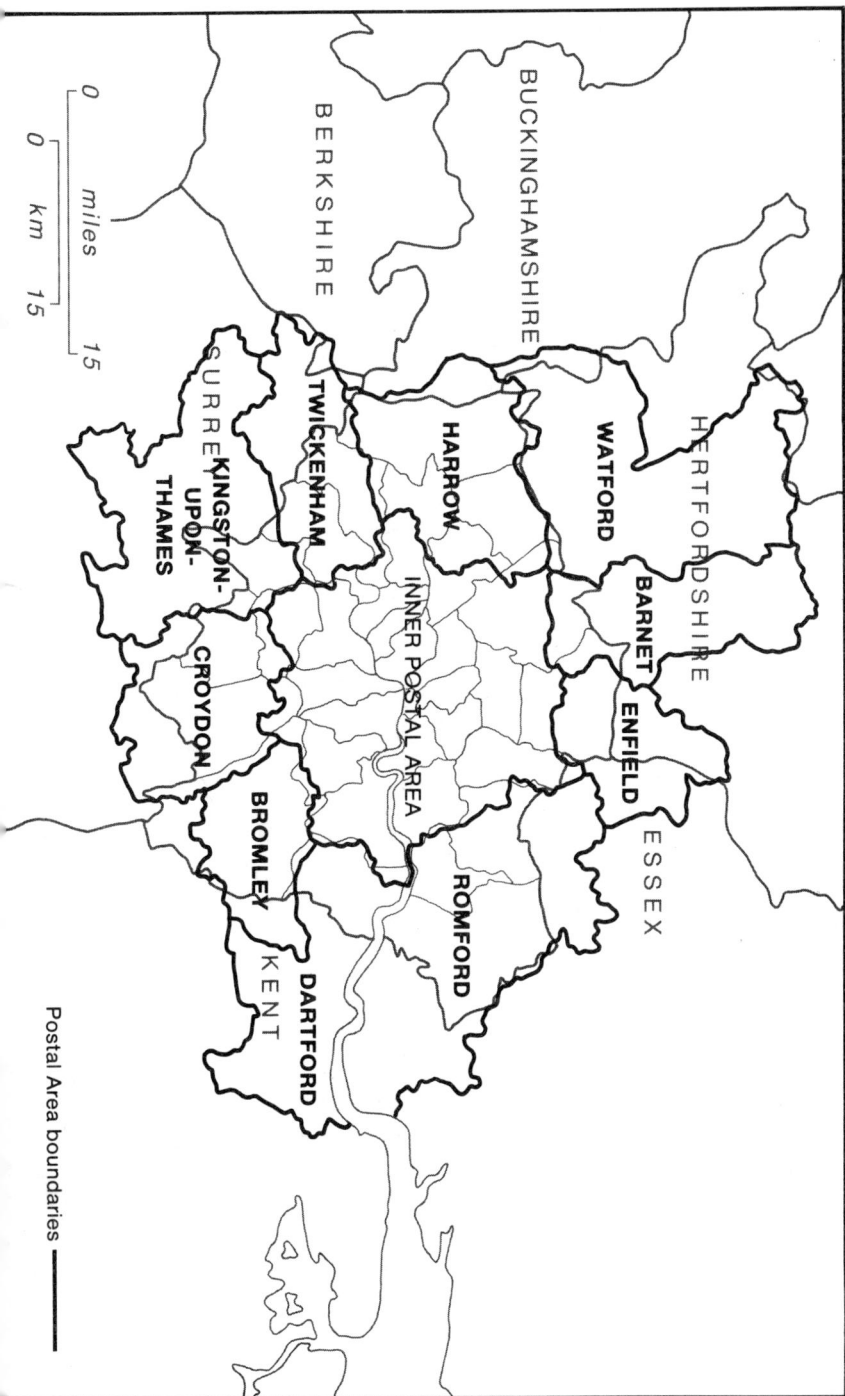

Map 18a The London postal region

Postal Area boundaries ————

BERKSHIRE

BUCKINGHAMSHIRE

HERTFORDSHIRE

ESSEX

KENT

SURREY

TWICKENHAM

HARROW

WATFORD

BARNET

ENFIELD

KINGSTON-UPON-THAMES

INNER POSTAL AREA

CROYDON

BROMLEY

ROMFORD

DARTFORD

miles

km

0

0

15

15

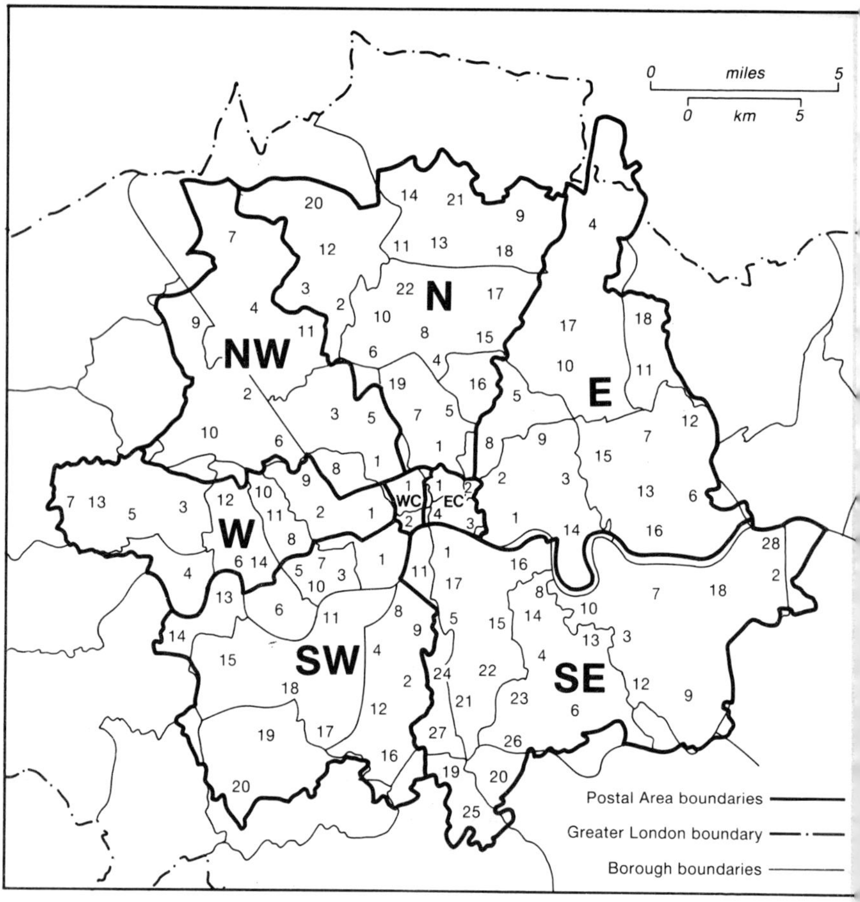
0 miles 5
0 km 5
NW
N
E
W
WC
EC
SW
SE
Postal Area boundaries
Greater London boundary
Borough boundaries

Map 18b The Inner Postal Area and Districts

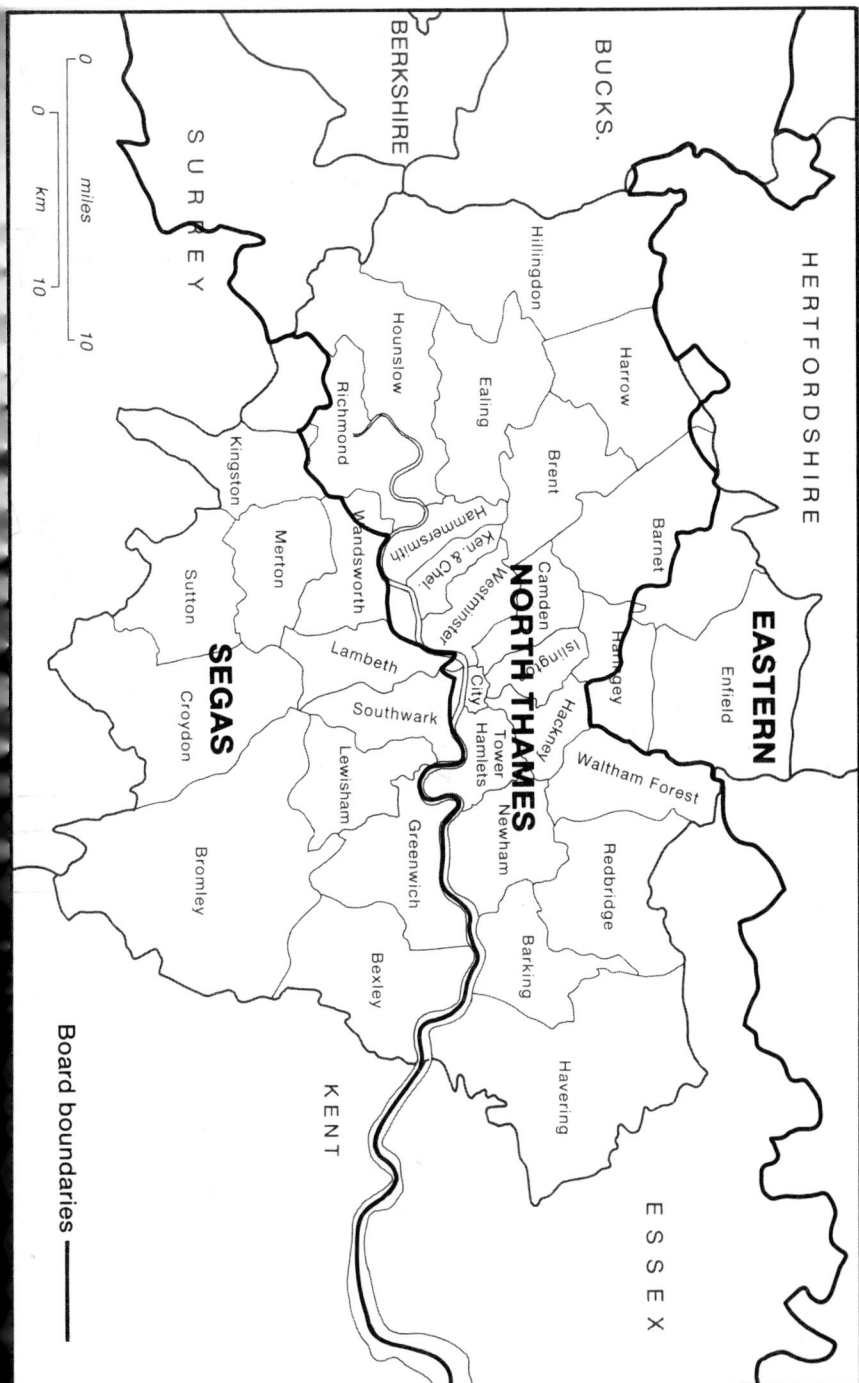

Map 19   British Gas Regional Boards

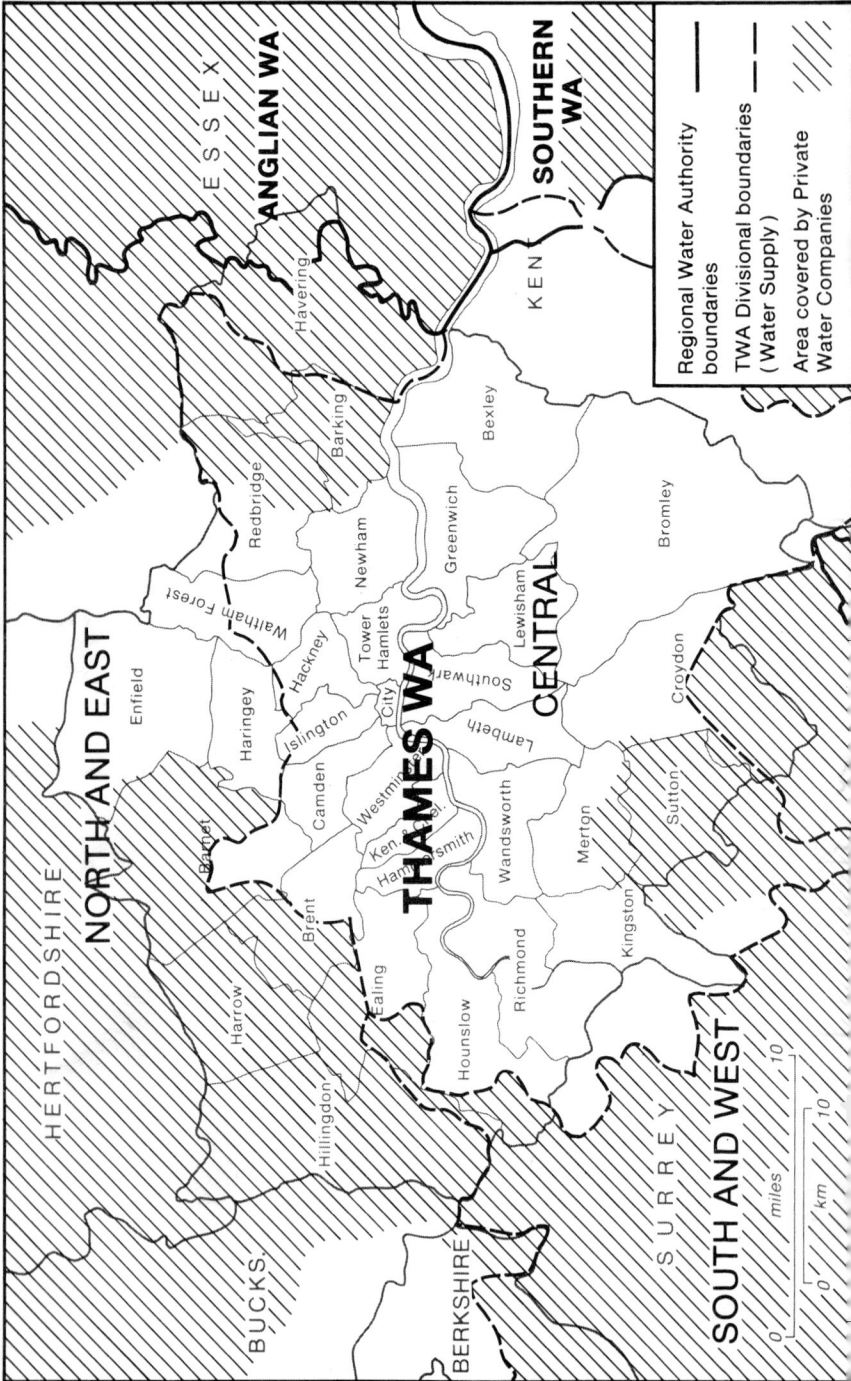

Map 20a   Regional Water and Land Drainage Authorities

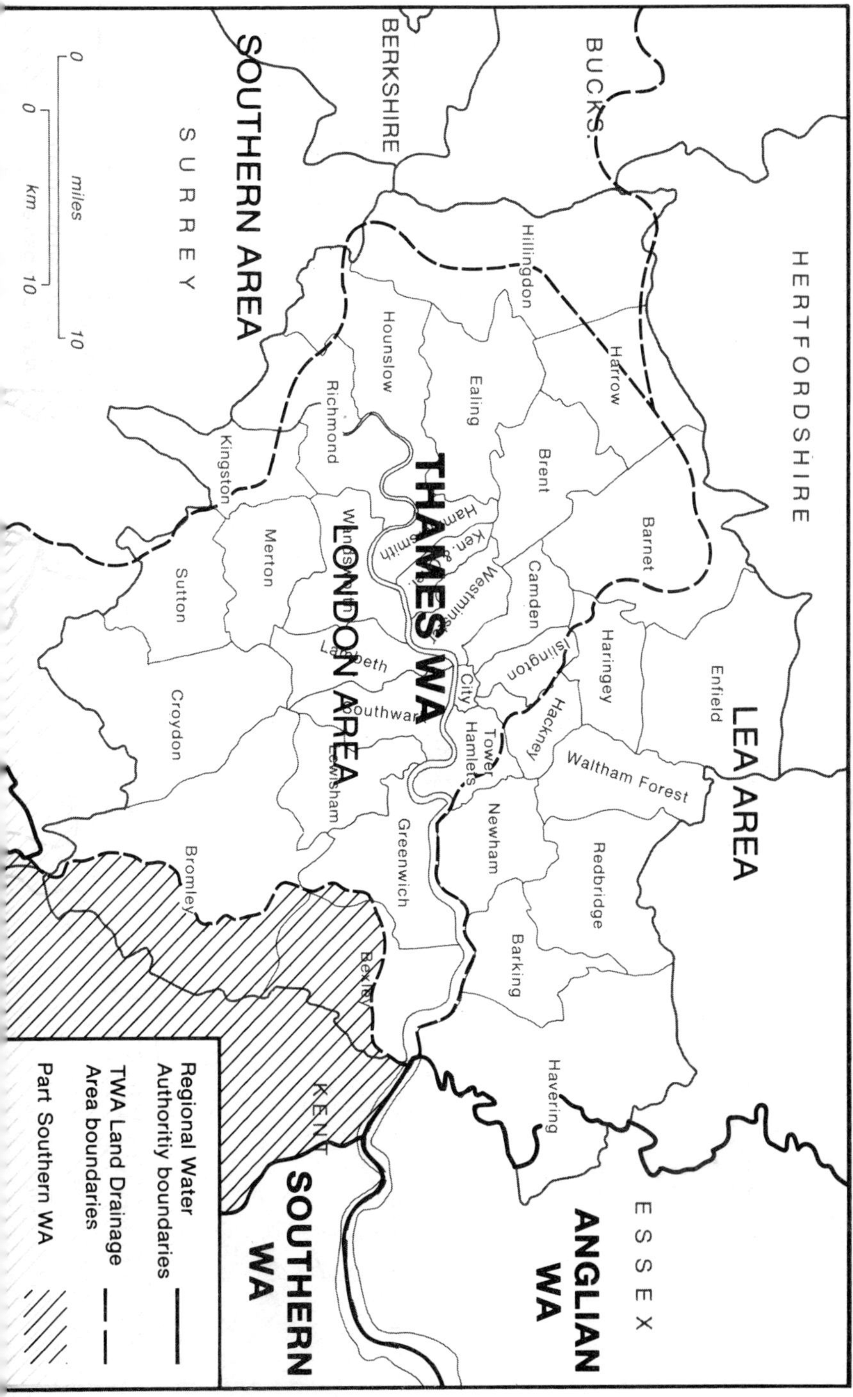

BUCKS.
BERKSHIRE
HERTFORDSHIRE
SOUTHERN AREA
SURREY
miles
km
0
10
Hillingdon
Harrow
Hounslow
Ealing
Brent
Barnet
Richmond
Kingston
THAMES WA
LONDON AREA
Ham'smith
Ken. &
Westminster
Camden
Haringey
Enfield
Islington
Merton
Sutton
Lambeth
City
Hackney
Croydon
Southwark
Tower Hamlets
Waltham Forest
LEA AREA
Lewisham
Newham
Redbridge
Greenwich
Bromley
Barking
Bexley
Havering
KENT
SOUTHERN WA
ESSEX
ANGLIAN WA
Regional Water Authority boundaries
TWA Land Drainage Area boundaries
Part Southern WA

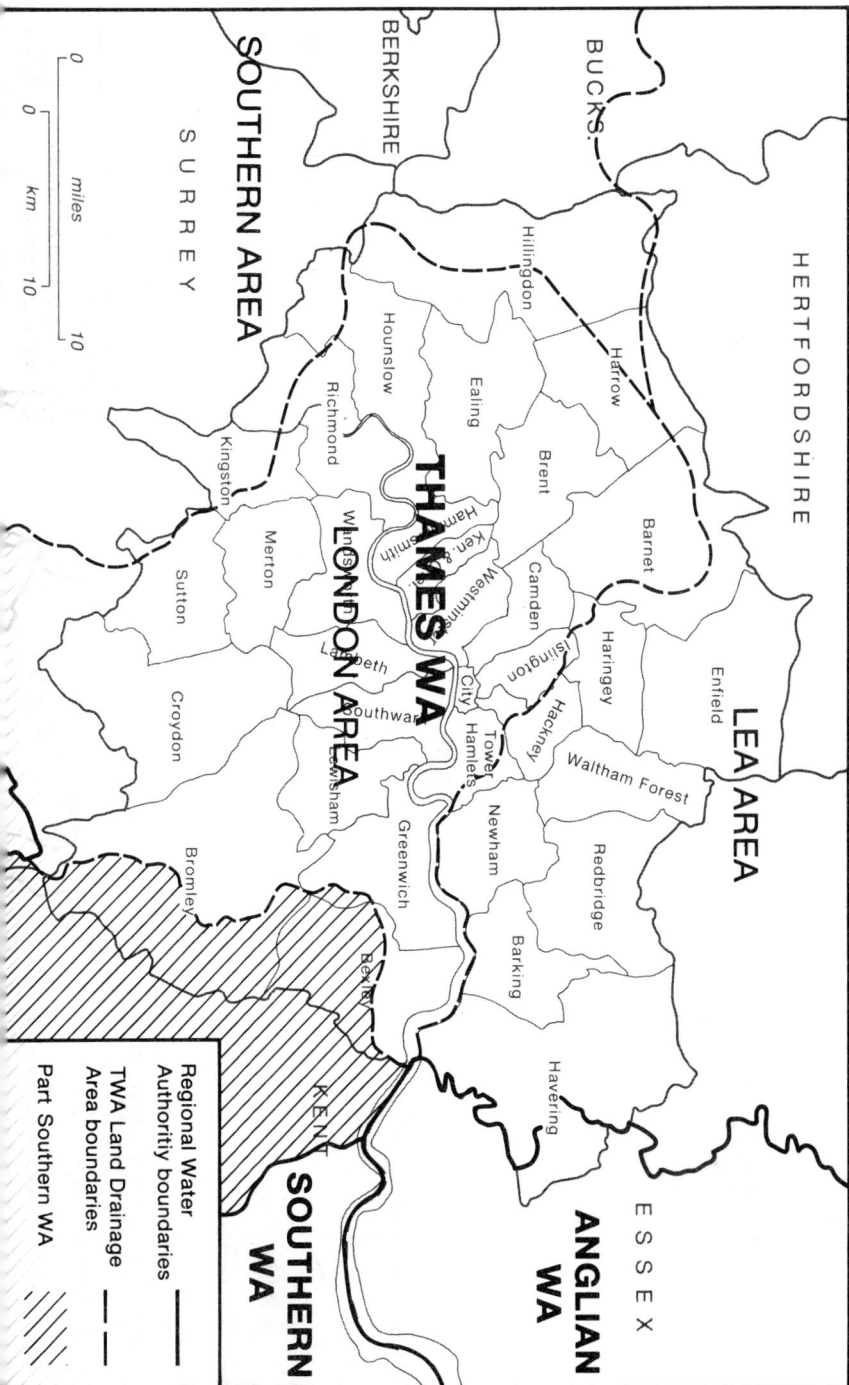

Map 20b Water supply by local companies regulated by TWA

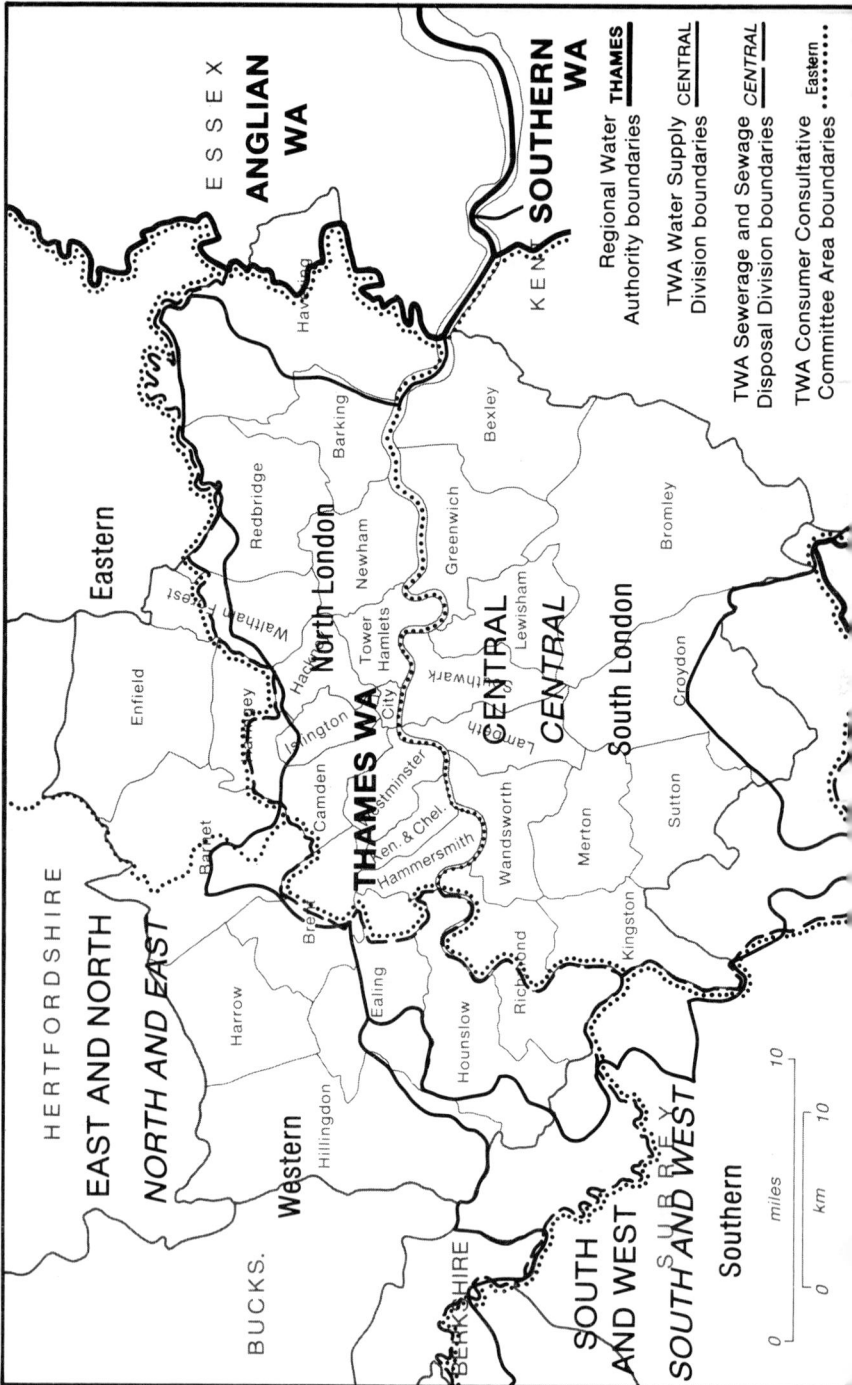

Map 20c Thames Water Authority: Divisions and Consumer
Consultative Committee Areas

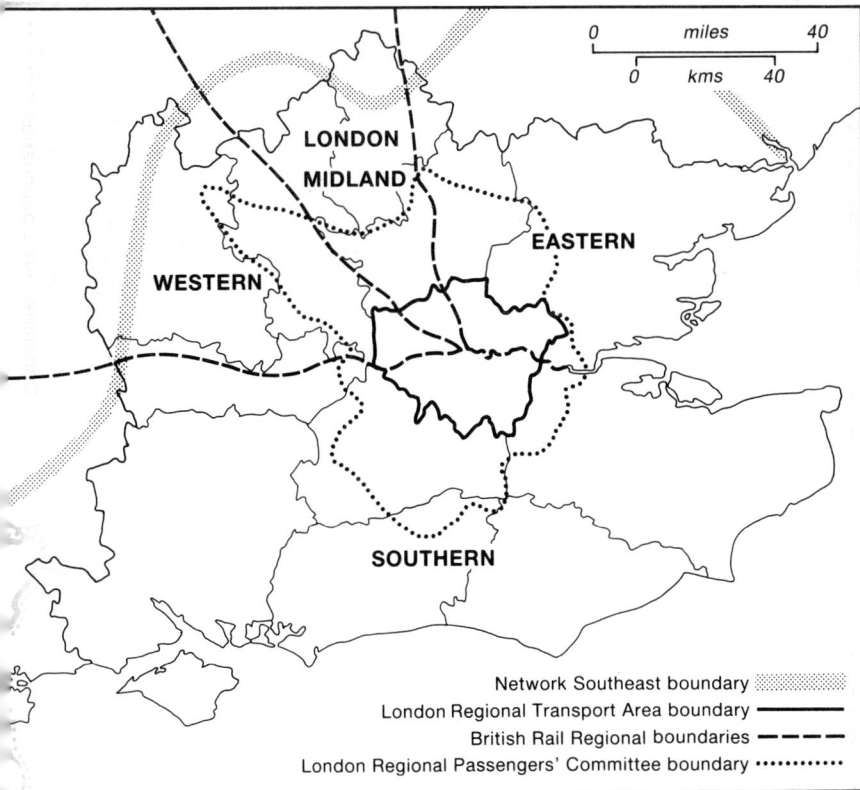

Map 21   Railway Administration

Network Southeast boundary ▓▓▓▓▓
London Regional Transport Area boundary ━━━━
British Rail Regional boundaries ━ ━ ━
London Regional Passengers' Committee boundary ••••••••••

LONDON
MIDLAND

EASTERN

WESTERN

SOUTHERN

0   miles   40
0   kms   40

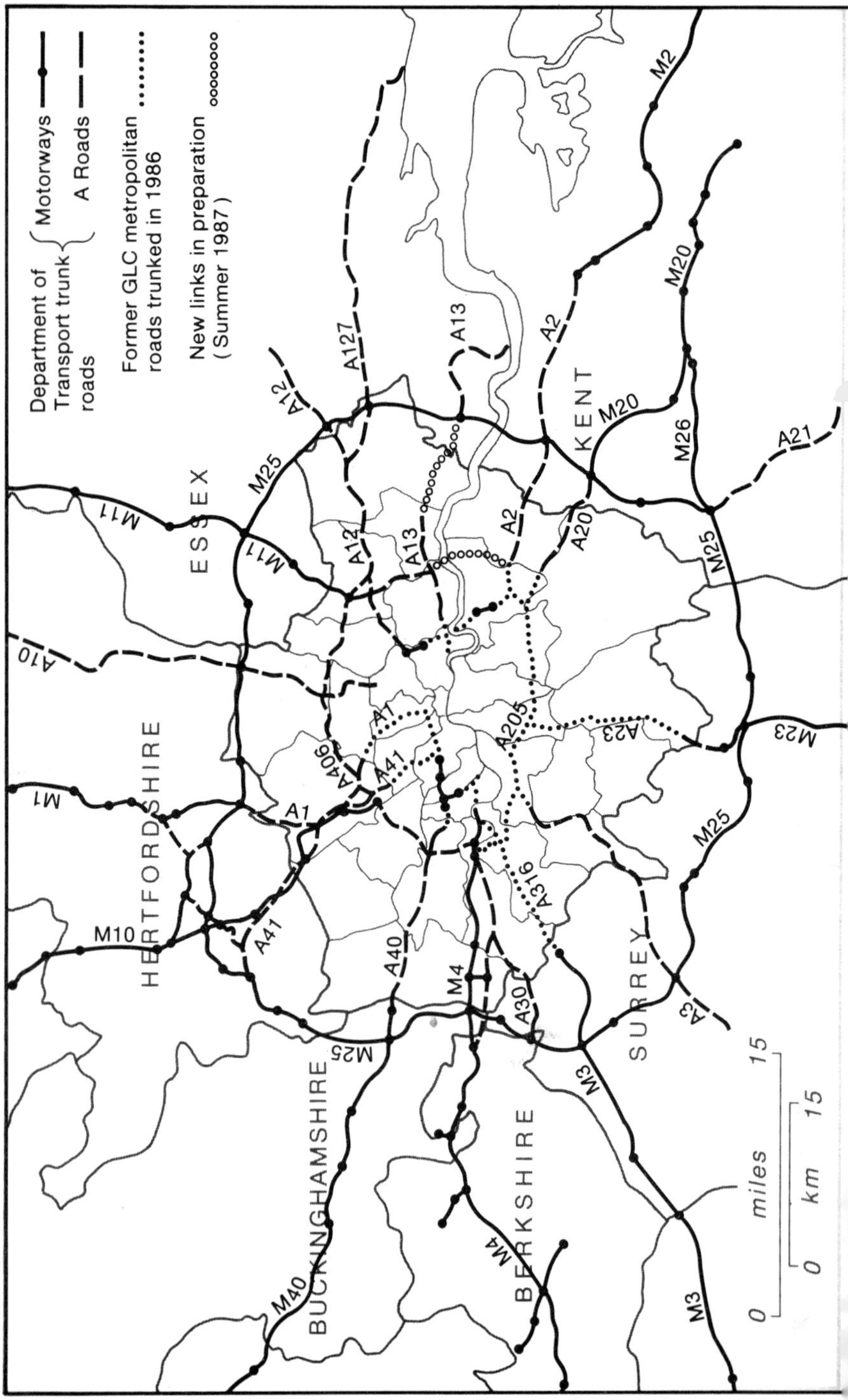

Map 22   The trunk road network

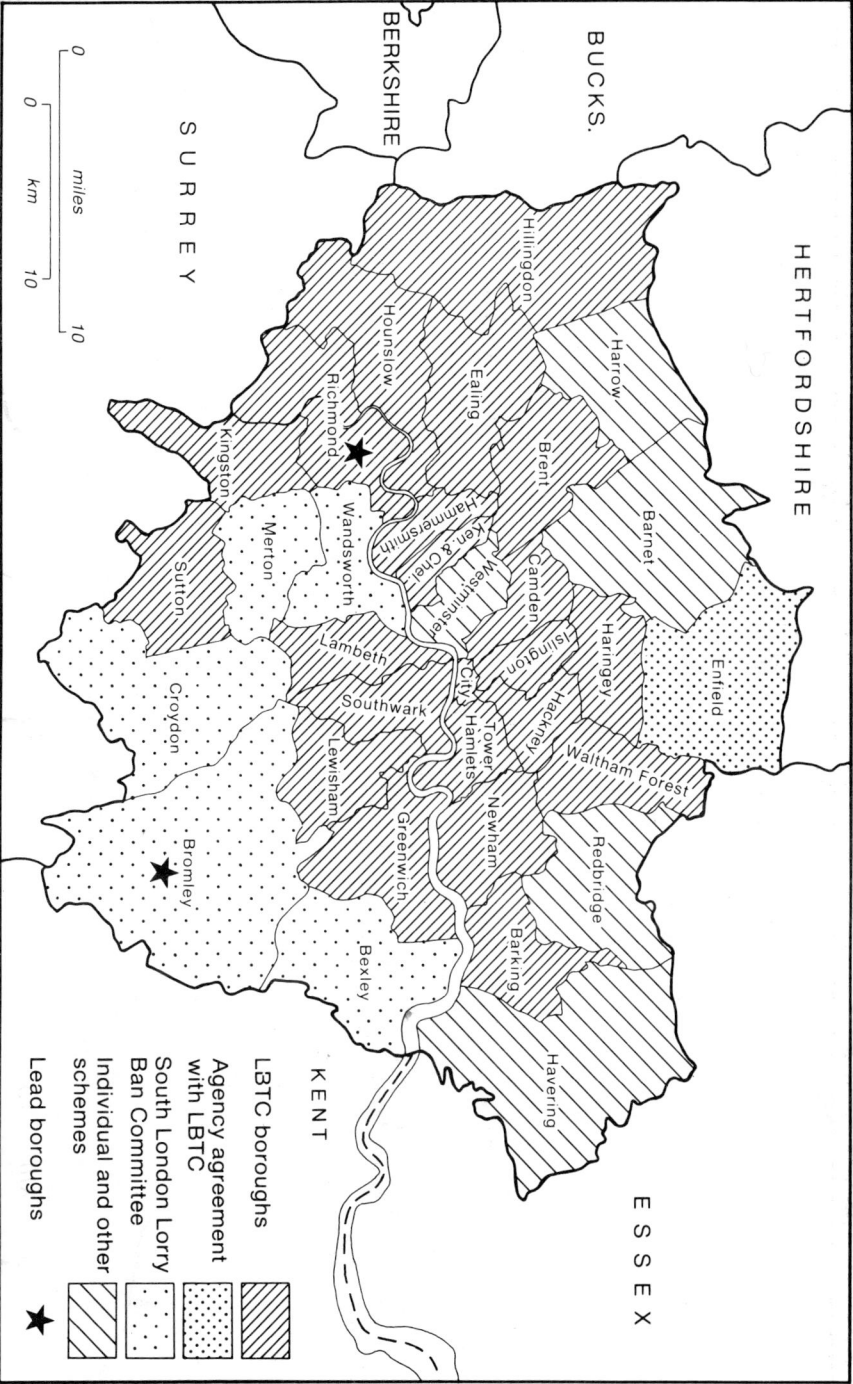

Map 23 Lorry bans

Legend:
- LBTC boroughs
- Agency agreement with LBTC
- South London Lorry Ban Committee
- Individual and other schemes
- ★ Lead boroughs

Boroughs shown: Hillingdon, Harrow, Barnet, Enfield, Hounslow, Ealing, Brent, Haringey, Waltham Forest, Redbridge, Havering, Richmond, Hammersmith, Ken. & Chel., Westminster, Camden, Islington, Hackney, Newham, Barking, Kingston, Wandsworth, City, Tower Hamlets, Merton, Lambeth, Southwark, Greenwich, Bexley, Sutton, Croydon, Lewisham, Bromley

Surrounding counties: BERKSHIRE, BUCKS., HERTFORDSHIRE, ESSEX, KENT, SURREY

INTRODUCTION

Two kinds of government business are carried on in London. One centres on the Palace of Westminster and Whitehall and is the stuff of high politics. The other runs the capital city itself, providing drains and sewers, schools and council estates, roads and libraries, pavements and parks, policing and public health. The high business of government could not function without the supportive web of local public service provision, nor could those other financial, commercial and cultural functions which jostle for floorspace in central London and make it one of the world's great cities.

Traditionally, the distinction between high politics and low corresponded with a division of functions between central and local government. That never fully applied in London, where central government has always run the police service and sometimes the trains and buses too. But until the very recent past, the majority of local public services were indeed provided by locally elected councils and services administered across the area of London as a whole fell to a council appointed by the electorate of London at large, the Greater London Council. That basically simple pattern was shattered by the Local Government Act of 1985, and replaced in the following year by a new and still evolving system for the provision of local public services which it is the purpose of this book to describe.

The debate over the abolition of the Greater London Council was long and bitter with as much issue made of the style of the reorganisation, and its partisan aspect, as of the deeper questions of local government design. The improvised and at times frankly gimcrack nature of the proposed new structures encouraged some opponents to predict the worst. Abolition would bring London 'grinding to a halt'. The immensely complicated supportive network of services which enables 6.8 million people to live and 3.5 million to work within 610 square miles would somehow 'break down'.

Pessimism was encouraged by the timing of the reorganisation, which happened to coincide with an intensely dynamic period in the history of one of the world's oldest and largest cities. Population decline, which has affected London since the Second World War (and much earlier in some of the inner boroughs) appears to have slowed down or stopped (see Map 2). The economy of the capital, like much of the rest of Britain, has altered rapidly in recent years, with massive growth in the service sector within an overall decline in employment. London is now at the centre of a region which is widely seen as having enjoyed far greater economic prosperity than the rest of the country, despite having some of the worst social and employment blackspots in Britain (see Map 3). Massive demands for land in some parts of the capital and in the surrounding area have been accompanied by soaring property prices. The geographical structure is being shaken up by long-term developments like the orbital motorway, the London Docklands redevelopment and Heathrow Airport Terminal Four, and in the private sector, the Big Bang and tourism growth.

London was going through a similar period of geographical upheaval during its last government reorganisation in the middle sixties. But that reform was at least carried out against a relatively stable political and institutional background. The recent changes, by contrast, must be seen as part of a generalised crisis in the role and financing of legal government and the public services. The four National Health Service regions which cover Greater London and the surrounding counties have had their resources cut back in order to redistribute services to the provinces. The expenditure screw has been tightening on local authorities in London as elsewhere. Capital investment, particularly in housing, has declined precipitously. Current spending has also fallen generally, though less so in a number of Labour-controlled inner boroughs where constant or rising current spending was sustained until 1987 by soaring rates and creative accountancy.

The turbulence of local government finance reflects political conflicts which have tended to take a more extreme form in London local government than elsewhere in the country. In the past ten years or so, individual boroughs have moved well to the left and right of the political spectrum. Right-wing authorities like Wandsworth and Westminster have sought to cut their spending and reduce employment by the council. Wandsworth in particular has privatised services. To the left, authorities like Lambeth and Haringey have sought actively to increase their services and employment, while seeking to redirect spending towards the needy and minority groups. Penalised by loss of grant, and since 1985, threatened by statutory ratecapping, left-wing councils have been locked since 1979 in an unprecedented financial struggle with the Conservative government, and after many years of ingenious manoeuvring, were in several cases, according to the Audit Commission in January 1987, near to financial breakdown.

'Breakdown' was, as we commented earlier, predicted by several Jeremiahs during the long Parliamentary struggle over GLC abolition. Dramatic predictions of this sort are often made on the eve of structural reorganisations and rarely come true. Administrative routines have an immense resilience that allows the majority of public services to limp on in some form through even the most cataclysmic upheavals, and besides, where a genuine failure of public services occurs the effects make themselves felt on the larger public, if at all, only at a time lag and in indirect forms such as increasing vandalism and violence, explicable in terms of criminality or some mysterious 'inner city' syndrome.

There were other specific reasons why the abolition of the GLC has proved less than cataclysmic. It so happened that the first Rate Support Grant settlement following GLC abolition in 1986 diverted over £200m of central money into London. London ratepayers made the agreeable discovery within weeks of the disappearance of the London-wide authority that their annual rate bills had shrunk by as much as £1,000. It lubricated the transition.

What is more, the reorganisation of London government, originally promoted on money-saving grounds, has in practice been carried out without any comprehensive pursuit of retrenchment. Direct expenditure on most services has been held constant, including the GLC's famous (to some infamous) programmes of grant-aid to the voluntary sector. The government has produced no soundly backed evidence for savings or costs arising from abolition. As predicted by the Greater London Group in *The Future of London Government* (1985), central government seems to have been happy to countenance the possibility of rising unit costs for services for the achievement of its larger political aim.

On the other hand, abolition did in some ways have a bracing effect on local government in London. It gave the 32 boroughs a new sense of their importance as the sole intermediary level between the individual citizen and the state. They inherited services from the GLC which gave them greater financial power than before, with some having substantial additions to their staff and functions. Many began to put fresh effort into presenting themselves to the public, reviving their images with new notepaper and logos and new street signs displaying the borough symbol and motto. The City Corporation has erected especially grand signboards painted glossy black and topped by classical moulding with the City crest and silver lettering in high relief. Trifling adornments like this have helped to create the sense of G L C abolition as a new beginning and not just a bad ending.

This book is a guide to the new government of London. The present arrangements are the product partly of statutory design and partly of spontaneous improvisation on the part of the London boroughs. Exceedingly complicated in themselves, they differ significantly from the structures of local government found anywhere else in Britain. The former services and staff of the G L C have been dispersed into an elaborate polycentric structure based on a wide variety of organisational forms.

Some services were picked up by quangos specially created for the purpose, such as the London Residuary Body. Others went to older appointed bodies such as the Thames Water Authority and English Heritage. Others again were reallocated to new London-wide local government bodies. The London Fire and Civil Defence Authority was the most important of these, with an annual budget of over £150m per year. Similar authorities were set up to regulate hazardous waste in the capital and for town-planning and grant-giving purposes. All these boards and committees had memberships made up from councillors nominated by each of the London boroughs.

Smaller groups of boroughs have also got together on a voluntary basis to set up other joint committees for functions like research and intelligence and housing policy, providing continuation of services which had previously been run by the G L C, or where they felt a new need to collaborate.

Lastly, central government has transferred a significant slice of powers and resources away from local government to itself. Direct intervention, promised as a panacea for the inner urban areas in Mrs Thatcher's third term, has already been practised on a major scale in inner London since 1981 through the agency of the London Docklands Development Corporation and the Manpower Services Commission. As a direct result of G L C abolition the centre's day-to-day involvement in direct management of the capital has increased markedly.

By 1988, these elaborate new arrangements are starting to settle down. Though abolition of the Inner London Education Authority and privatisation of some further borough services are a certainty, the basic structure of public services described in this Handbook is likely to hold good in London for some years to come.

The arrangement of the Handbook is simple. We begin with central government, arguably now the principal actor on the London government scene. Central government in Britain has traditionally not involved itself in the minutiae of direct rule and is not organised to do so. Chapter 1 shows how Whitehall has assimilated the new burden of London government that fell to it as a result of GLC abolition. We next describe, in Chapters 2 to 4, the elaborate system of major and minor quangos which have taken responsibility for providing certain services on a London-wide basis, as well as various local government bodies, voluntary and statutory, which operate across borough boundaries. Chapter 5 shows how the basic units of London government, the 32 London boroughs and the City, have been affected by the upheavals of the past two years, setting out their present range of functions and trends in staffing and spending.

The remainder of the Handbook addresses such specific issues as the question 'who speaks for London' (Chapter 6), who pays for London government (Chapter 7), and what Londoners feel, according to survey evidence, about their city and its government (Chapter 8). Chapter 9 puts the Local Government Act of 1985 into a larger context by showing where it fits into the great debate about metropolitan areas and how they should be governed. The last section of the book is a directory of the organisations which now run services in London. We have tried to provide the fullest possible details of their location, representative status, expenditure, staff and accessibility, and maps of the various organisational structures of services in London.

The pattern of government described in this Handbook is undeniably complicated. Over 60 separate bodies are described below, and almost 30 different ways of dividing up the Greater London area for administrative purposes are revealed in the maps. Getting to grips with the immense complexity of the new arrangements has been a challenge for us in writing the book as it is for all the people and organisations who depend on the local government system for everyday services. We hope that this Handbook will be a straightforward guide to them and a useful introduction for the outside observer; also, that it may play a small part in assisting the politicians, civil servants, councillors, board members, officers and other staffs who run our new machinery of London government, to do so responsively and efficiently.

Reference

Greater London Group (1985), *The Future of London Government*, by Clegg, T., Couch, R., Dunleavy, P. and Harding, A. Greater London Paper No 16. London: London School of Economics.

CHAPTER 1

Central Government and London

Introduction

The focus of this chapter is on the role played in the governing of London by central government departments headed by ministers answerable to Parliament. Local authorities all over the country are subject to Parliament; as statutory bodies they have only the powers granted by Parliament, and if they act beyond those powers the courts can annul these acts as *ultra vires*. Ministers too are granted powers by Parliament, and are also subject to the rule of *ultra vires*. Some of the legislation confers on ministers powers to control local authorities in various ways; such Acts constrain local authorities wherever they are located. Some Acts refer only to London local authorities, which, traditionally, have been more limited by central government than local authorities in the provinces. For instance, the Home Secretary has been the police authority in London, excluding the City of London, since 1829, so that his Home Office has been the body responsible for policing London, not an elected local authority.

The latest and most important statute dealing with London government is the Local Government Act 1985 which abolished the Greater London Council and distributed its functions among a variety of bodies. The Government in commending this legislation claimed that the result would be a major decentralisation of functions, mainly to the elected borough councils. Central government would acquire only a few new functions, chiefly of a strategic kind or to resolve disputes between boroughs or to ensure that the purposes of the legislation were achieved. Opponents of the Bill alleged that it increased centralisation, with Whitehall departments obtaining a vast amount of extra powers over London, estimated as from 40 to 123 in total, to initiate, to guide, to control, to direct, to monitor, to approve, to be consulted, and in default to execute. Five government departments took on these new powers:

Environment, Transport, Education and Science, the Home Office, and the Office of Arts and Libraries. The Opposition asserted that the true successor of the GLC was Marsham Street, the home of the Departments of the Environment and Transport, which acquired the largest share of the extra powers. When the Government stated that its objective was to decentralise, the then Labour MP for a London East End constituency, Ian Mikardo, said: 'The Secretary of State sounded like King Herod appointing himself president of the National Society for the Prevention of Cruelty to Children'.

Although the 1985 Act does increase the powers of ministers over London, in the period since abolition in April 1986, ministers and their civil servants have not used the powers to intervene in the running of London's affairs in the manner feared by the Bill's opponents. First, ministers and civil servants have not wanted to be held responsible for governing the metropolis with all its problems. Second, they wanted to show that the Act was a genuine measure of decentralisation, primarily to the boroughs, and have, therefore, been reluctant to involve themselves in London matters. Third, the very fact that ministers had a formidable battery of reserve powers may have encouraged the boroughs to avoid action that would trigger ministerial intervention. However, the powers are still written in statutory form and could be activated whenever ministers desired. In the future, when something occurs that meets the displeasure of ministers, they could rely on the Act as the legal foundation for intervention. A different government, a different minister, facing what they regarded as some crisis in London, would be able to act because they would find in the Act that they had the legal power to do so. Even if that power had never before been used, it could be used in the new circumstances. So, it is important to examine not just how legislation has been used but what the legislation allows and empowers ministers to do, and that is a great deal.

Not only have ministers and civil servants sought to distance themselves from London's government, except in a few cases like education, they have also sought during the passage of legislation to disperse functions from the GLC to the boroughs, or if that proved impossible, to joint arrangements between the boroughs on a single-service basis. They wished to avoid at all costs a single body with a group of services, since it might be seen as the GLC in exile, soon to arise like a phoenix as a revived GLC. The centre actively promoted the fragmentation of London's government. This objective was intensified by the ambitions of the service departments in Whitehall to promote the interests of their own particular functions, without regard for the health of local government in the capital. Although powers are granted to ministers, in practice it can hardly be expected that they will be able to take the decisions personally. Much will fall to their officials. Thus, the increase in ministers' powers has enhanced the powers of the civil service. The abolition of the GLC has substituted one bureaucracy for another (albeit smaller) one. A centralised bureaucracy has replaced a regional one. The upper tier of London government is Whitehall.

The Department of the Environment

In the Local Government Directorate there is one division, headed by a Grade 5 official, concerned with the implementation of the 1985 Act and policy on and liaison with the residuary bodies. It handles financial and general issues, and other property and staffing matters. There is a separate Greater London Regional Office of 128 staff, headed by a Director. In it are four divisions. One is for Greater London Housing, one deals with the London Docklands Development Corporation, and one with Urban Affairs, including the Urban Programme, City Action Teams, land initiatives and liaison with the voluntary grants scheme mentioned above. The fourth deals with land and planning, including the main statutory functions under the Planning Acts and related legislation, appeals and the preparation of 'strategic guidance'. The Property Services Agency, for which the Secretary of State is responsible, also has a London Regional Office. Its staff number 3,700. It should not be forgotten that almost all aspects of the Secretary of State's responsibilities affect Greater London to some degree.

Land-use planning

The Secretary of State is the strategic planning authority for London in land use. He is advised by the London Planning Advisory Committee, comprising one representative from each borough and the City, on matters of common interest relating to the planning and development of London. While the boroughs are to prepare the more detailed unitary development plans, they have to have regard to any strategic guidance he may give them and such other matters as he may direct them to take into account. He sets the planning process in motion and decides when the plan comes into operation. He may call in a development plan for his approval and modify it or reject it. Where he thinks a borough is not preparing an appropriate plan he may make his own plan and charge the expenses to the authority.

Ministers justified these powers by the need for the centre to take an overview of an area wider than that of the G L C, extending out to the M25 and the rest of the South East, and covering such matters as waste disposal, derelict land and mineral planning, and any topics that affected more than one borough, or where there were differences between boroughs. The minister could be involved by boroughs opposed to the plans of other boroughs that affected them adversely. The strategic guidance was to be an initial framework, not a substitute for borough plans, and the reserve powers were to bring in the minister when there were disputes between boroughs, and between them and a body like the Historic Buildings and Monuments Commission over conservation areas. Ministers saw their role as strategic and appellate.

In July 1986 the minister took the first formal steps towards issuing strategic guidance when he invited the London Planning Advisory Committee to give him advice on a number of items that might be in his strategic guidance, including the distribution of housing, commercial and industrial development, transport and land use, green belt and open land, minerals, and urban design. L P A C argued that the minister had not followed the proper procedure and in February 1987 his letter was supplemented with additional details after which phased studies of five key topics by groups of borough planning officers were set in motion. Some boroughs protested at this partial rather than strategic approach.

Waste regulation and disposal

The Secretary of State was granted by the 1985 Act what the opposition regarded as unprecedented powers to decide on the type of organisation to be responsible for waste regulation and disposal if he were dissatisfied with the arrangements for joint provision made by the boroughs, and he was to have special regard to the need for satisfactory arrangements for hazardous waste. Eventually he agreed to a scheme of nine authorities, consisting of one overall body responsible for waste regulation (the London Waste Regulation Authority), four statutory joint authorities, three voluntary groupings of boroughs and a joint scheme between the borough of Bexley and the county of Kent (see Map 15). He may dissolve any of them at any time or rearrange the distribution of their functions. So he, and his department, have to maintain a continuing watch over the way they carry out their duties. The minister stressed that he would intervene only if the boroughs failed to agree on satisfactory voluntary arrangements.

Grants to voluntary organisations

The Secretary of State has the power to set a ceiling for the total sum to be spent by the London Boroughs Grants Scheme. This provision was to protect councils which did not approve the total of grants but would be bound to pay towards them because of the approval of two-thirds of the boroughs. In 1987 the boroughs were unable to reach an agreed decision on the total of grants. As a result of this impasse, described more fully in Chapter 3, the minister sent a letter in March that indicated he was prepared to issue an order imposing a budget limit of £28.5m, just above that of the Conservative boroughs' proposal and below that advocated by the Alliance and Labour boroughs. To exercise this power the minister has to have an overall picture of the distribution of grants to voluntary organisations.

London Residuary Body

The Secretary of State is responsible for this body whose chairman and members he appoints, and to which he can issue directions. He is answerable to Parliament for its activities, or failures to act: questions are put to him as to why he has or has not issued a particular direction. His approach has been to say that day-to-day operations are a matter for the Body, but he has replied in some detail about the work of the Body, which suggests that he supervises its activities closely. He issued a formal direction in July 1986 about the form of the Body's accounts and annual report. The power to issue directions involves the minister in being held accountable for the distribution of a number of functions of the GLC which had to be allocated by the Body in the period after abolition. Since some of the service allocations have been controversial, like Hampstead Heath (see Chapter 5), Thamesmead Town, the Seaside and Country Homes or the London Research Centre, the minister and his department cannot fail to be closely involved in the work of the London Residuary Body. The Secretary of State's directive setting out the terms on which the Thamesmead Town was transferred to new control was a major example of his power over the LRB. The minister can allocate the functions where he likes through a direction to the LRB, and he can direct it to distribute capital monies from the GLC, and any receipts generated from sales of GLC assets, amongst the boroughs. The Department can be said to second-guess the LRB, but it prefers to conduct a dialogue with it rather than issue directions.

Information

The Secretary of State is required to make regulations requiring the boroughs to give him information about their staff numbers and the purposes for which they are employed. Despite calling for quarterly returns until June 1987 and annual returns for 1988 and 1989, the minister has stated that no record is kept centrally of the recruitment by successor or other public bodies of former GLC employees. Nevertheless, within his department, staff statistics are examined, thus bringing it into close contact with the detailed operations and management arrangements of the boroughs.

Boundaries of local authorities

The Secretary of State issued guidelines to steer the Local Government Boundary Commission in December 1986 about its review of the boundaries of London's boroughs, and between them and adjoining counties. They foreshadow only minor adjustments to take account of historical anomalies and recent changes in the pattern of development. The minister has guided the Commission to avoid radical change.

Finance

Under the Rates Act 1984 the Secretary of State set for 1988/89 a limit on the rates of (that is to say he 'ratecapped') 10 boroughs: Camden, Ealing, Greenwich, Hackney, Haringey, Lambeth, Lewisham, Southwark, Tower Hamlets and Waltham Forest. Other boroughs have been ratecapped in earlier years, as was the GLC before abolition. The Inner London Education Authority and the London Fire and Civil Defence Authority are also ratecapped under the 1985 Act for the first three years of their lives. The minister has the power to ratecap other boroughs if their spending and rates are more than he judges appropriate. He is responsible for the Rate Support Grant and for capital allocations to the authorities, and he decides the details of the London Rate Equalisation Scheme. Thus the Department is particularly involved in the spending and taxing decisions of London's local government, especially because of the large number of ratecapped councils in the capital. (See Chapter 6 for a fuller description of finance.)

Housing nominations

Under the 1985 Act the Secretary of State inherited some powers to nominate council tenants to housing under various GLC schemes for housing mobility – the Greater London Mobility Scheme, based on former GLC housing now held by the boroughs; the Seaside and Country Dwellings for retired people; and nominations to Thamesmead, the large GLC development on the Erith marshes. Although hoping that the boroughs would voluntarily develop new joint arrangements for housing mobility, the Secretary of State obtained the power to enforce a scheme himself, if necessary. In the event, the boroughs set up the

London Area Mobility Scheme as a voluntary joint committee (see p. 62). The Secretary of State has devolved to LAMS his nomination rights under the Greater London Mobility Scheme and the Seaside and Country Dwellings, but not the right to nominate tenants to Thamesmead Town. Currently the DOE pays the bulk of the administrative costs of LAMS.

Local valuation panels
The Secretary of State has the power to direct boroughs to make schemes.

Parliamentary pressure
The Department came to exercise an oversight over London government to some extent in response to persistent questioning in the House of Commons from MPs like Tony Banks of Newham NW, who regularly put down questions, often on detailed aspects, that pushed ministers and their civil servants to examine the minutiae of London government.

The minister has been less than forthcoming about the effect on the Department of the Environment of the abolition of the GLC. In reply to a Parliamentary Question asking for a list of the additional functions undertaken by the Department as a result of the abolition of the GLC, with the cost and total numbers of staff, he stated that the main specific responsibilities are the laying before Parliament of a report on the transfer of functions related to the protection of the countryside and the initial preparation of strategic guidance, involving only six staff at a cost of £55,000. Other work has been generated for existing officials, most notably dealing with the disposal of Thamesmead. It will probably be impossible to estimate the full cost to the Department (in terms of employees' time and other expenditure) of GLC abolition and subsequent changes.

Department of Transport

After the Department of the Environment, the department most involved with the governing of London is the Department of Transport. Its role is more direct and detailed. It is responsible for some of the most important governmental activities affecting London. Its ethos is more interventionist than that of the Department of the Environment, which continues to be partly influenced by its concern to promote a sound system of local government. The Department of Transport is more oriented to particular services, seeking to advance mobility in London, even if it comes into conflict with local government. Its functional imperative drives it into a sometimes tense relationship with the DOE.

Some observers have seen the Department of Transport as consistently pursuing over many years a policy to build extensive roads in London, both radials and a series of rings through Inner and Outer London. In the 1950s it advocated the setting up of the GLC to construct these roads, but when the GLC became too divided and eventually opposed to that policy, the Department turned to champion its abolition and the reallocation of road-building responsibilities to itself, so that it could embark on a massive programme of road building. With the abolition of the GLC the Department of Transport has acquired significant functions, giving it the potential to cut through the opposition from London boroughs to roads.

Roads and traffic management

Before abolition of the GLC the Secretary of State was responsible for 143 miles of trunk roads in London, their planning, development and maintenance. The Act of 1985 gives him direct responsibility for about 7 per cent of former GLC roads, 65 miles out of 895: those which play an important role in London-wide movement (see Map 22). Most of the GLC roads were transferred to the boroughs. On 300 miles of them, those which the minister designates as of strategic importance, the main distributor roads in London, his consent is needed before the boroughs can introduce measures that alter the capacity of the roads and affect through traffic, even such matters as cycle schemes and pedestrian crossings. This power was needed to ensure that a borough did not act in ways that adversely affect traffic or parking in another borough, or where one borough objected to another's proposal because of assumed adverse effects on its area. It was a safeguard in the interests of a wider community than one borough.

The minister has power by order to bring roads under his direct responsibility as trunk roads, on which his consent is required for traffic management schemes. He can issue guidance on traffic management to the boroughs, and act himself if they are in default, charging them for expenditure he incurs. Opponents of the 1985 Act used this increase in departmental powers as evidence that with the abolition of the GLC the consequence was greater centralisation. They raised the spectre of the Department acquiring powers to institute schemes of massive road building. The minister denied this accusation, pointing out that no big road schemes were planned, that changing the status of a road did not imply road works, and that studies and assessments of traffic black spots were all that were under way. In 1986 four such studies were published and further inquiries were set in motion. The Department is also responsible for the Thames bridges of Twickenham, Kew and Chiswick, and the Woolwich Ferry which is run by Greenwich as the Department's agent.

The operation of the computerised system of traffic lights in London, the Traffic Control System Unit, was intended by the Government to be a responsibility jointly of the boroughs, and, failing agreement between them, of the Metropolitan Police. But since the boroughs could not agree, and the Met refused to take it on, the Unit has been managed by the L R B, and then the City, as an agent of the Department of Transport. The Department of Transport has taken over some staff from the G L C Research and Intelligence Service who reviewed traffic conditions, and a few from the Road Assessment Unit who studied skid resistance of roads, and were subsequently privatised. It also took over staff from the G L C Road Safety Unit, which collected and analysed accident data, to ensure no hiatus in the service.

Public transport

By the London Regional Transport Act 1984 the Secretary of State is the sponsoring minister for London Regional Transport, able to issue it with directions, and as he is also responsible similarly for oversight of British Rail he seeks to co-ordinate their services.

He has both a strategic and more detailed role in controlling transport of all kinds in London. Other than for very local roads the real transport, traffic and roads authority for London is the Secretary of State.

The great scale of the Department's powers over London transport, roads and traffic management is indicated by the organisation of its staff who have to keep a close watch over the detailed activities of L R T and the boroughs, and can through the minister act directly themselves on important issues affecting movement in London.

Within the Railways Directorate is a division dealing with financial strategy and investment for the subsidised passenger railway system in London and the South East. There is a separate Directorate for Public Transport, London and Metropolitan Area, in which a number of divisions are deeply active in the government of London. The Public Transport London Division handles public transport policy in London; sponsorship of London Regional Transport; the structure of L R T, its corporate planning, finance and investment, contracting out and privatisation; all matters concerning L R T's subsidiary businesses; bus licensing in London; liaison between L R T and British Rail; L R T consumer matters; provision for the disabled; transport interchange; policing; and the Docklands Light Railway.

There are divisions for Traffic and Greater London Roads. The Traffic Policy division covers (for London and elsewhere) traffic regulation, parking control and enforcement, the orange badge scheme for disabled drivers, cycling, pedestrianisation and residential areas, transport aspects of tourism and inner areas policy. The Traffic Advisory Unit is concerned with technical advice on traffic management, including cycling and pedestrians. The Greater London Resources Division deals with Greater London highways and traffic policy, including the administration of designated road notification procedures; co-ordination of financial and resource allocation policies for London highways and the Woolwich Ferry; and lorry management policies.

Two divisions form the regional office for Greater London Roads and Traffic. One deals with traffic planning and control, trunk road improvement schemes, and highway maintenance and other highway and traffic matters in seventeen outer boroughs up to the M25. The other deals with such matters in the remaining London boroughs, and road appraisals and assessment studies. The Greater London Regional Office contains in all 170 staff, mainly involved in work on the construction and maintenance of trunk roads, Transport Supplementary Grant for the boroughs' local roads, the Woolwich Ferry, the traffic signal system, and traffic management on the designated road network.

Other divisions are responsible for economic advice on LRT and block grant and the grant related expenditure assessments, and for statistics about London traffic, such as speed surveys, and generally on urban transport.

Department of Education and Science

The Department has no division specifically responsible for London, but within its Schools Branch it has a division one of whose responsibilities is 'Reconstitution of ILEA'. This area will grow in importance now the Government has decided to abolish ILEA. But the ILEA, and the Outer London boroughs which are the education authorities in the rest of London, are closely watched over by the Department, especially as ministers are very interested in the provision of education in individual authorities. This political concern has stimulated increased involvement by the Department in London education, as when the Secretary of State called upon Her Majesty's Inspectors of Schools to make a special report on particular authorities, such as Brent in 1987.

The Secretary of State has extensive powers over ILEA, so much so that an opponent of the Bill described it as 'cabin'd, cribb'd, confin'd and capp'd by the Government'. He can direct it about the matters he regards as its main policy objectives on which it has to consult the boroughs, and he can decide on the form of consultation if there is no agreement between the ILEA and a borough. A power was taken in the 1985 Act to review before 1991 the exercise by ILEA of its functions.

Opposition to the Act maintained that these powers amounted to putting the ILEA under permanent review by the DES, which could at the end of the period dismember and abolish it. The minister justified these powers as necessary for the protection of the pupils of London. The review was needed in case the Government's hopes for the ILEA improving its standards were not realised and a totally different approach was required. He denied that the ILEA would be under continuous review or that the Government had decided to abolish the ILEA and were putting off the evil day. The review was needed to reassure the many groups worried about the performance of the ILEA. In fact the Conservatives' 1987 election manifesto committed the party to allow individual Inner London boroughs to get out of ILEA. This policy was implemented in a Bill published during late 1987, further analysed below in Chapter 3. In the light of this opt-out policy and the subsequent decision to abolish ILEA outright, the Government announced that the power to review ILEA by 1991 would be repealed.

The Home Office

Police

The Home Secretary is the police authority for London, excluding the City, responsible for the Metropolitan Police. Its Commissioner is in charge of operational matters, but since the Brixton riots and the Scarman Report, the Home Office has taken a more active interest in the Metropolitan force, including the exertion of more strict financial control, insisting it must stay within cash limits, and demanding some evidence of improvements in efficiency before allowing increases in force establishments.

The Home Office has no department specifically and only responsible for the London area. Seven civil servants within the Police Department watch over the Met, and the outcomes are very much a matter of personal negotiation depending on the personalities of the Home Secretary, the Commissioner and these officials. The Home Secretary appoints the Commissioner, and can issue him with directions about the administration and staffing of the force, and he has to give his approval to the Commissioner's proposals for the management of the Met. He appoints

the Receiver of Police, who is the finance officer, to whom he gives
directions about police fund receipts, and he issues guidance to the
Commissioner about consultation arrangements. He approves an annual
strategy report from the Commissioner. The Home Office has regular
discussions with the Commissioner in which views on matters of policing
policy are made clear. It is deeply involved in the policing of London.

Fire and civil defence

The Home Secretary has powers over the London Fire and Civil
Defence Authority to alter the numbers of members of the joint authority
and to reallocate responsibility for fire and civil defence to a borough or
group of boroughs, indeed to dismantle it. For three years after abolition
of the G L C he exercises control over the budget and staffing of the joint
authority. He is thus brought deep inside the authority, probing its
detailed activities, for instance approving its scheme for staff management to ensure its functions are provided economically, efficiently and
effectively. Opposition to the 1985 Act claimed that the minister had
control of who is employed, how they are employed, what they do, and
how they spend the money which is also controlled by the minister.
Ministers justified these controls for the first three years after abolition
as necessary to avoid the expansion of manpower and spending that had
occurred following reorganisation of local government in 1963 and
1972. Controls over the joint authority were also justified to ensure that
national standards of fire cover were maintained; no fire stations would
be closed nor fire appliances withdrawn without the minister's approval.

Coroners

The Secretary of State has to approve appointments by the boroughs of
coroners, to ensure no areas are neglected, and he has the power to
designate by order the boroughs that comprise a coroner's district and
their financial contributions to the service.

Probation

The Secretary of State has administrative oversight of the Probation
Committees, laying down ground rules for consultation with the
boroughs, and ensuring that the committees are representative.

Office of Arts and Libraries

Before abolition the Prime Minister, the City of London and the G L C
each appointed six members to the board of governors of the Museum

of London. The Prime Minister and City now appoint nine each, and divide the funding equally between them. The minister, in this case the Minister for the Arts, has to receive an annual report from the Arts Council about the former GLC responsibilities it acquired on abolition, specifically on how it has discharged its responsibilities towards them. This power refers to the Royal Festival Hall, the Queen Elizabeth Hall, the Purcell Room, the National Theatre, the National Film Theatre, and the Hayward Gallery, that is the complex of cultural buildings on the South Bank. An official of the Department attends meetings of the South Bank Board of the Arts Council at a cost to public funds in 1986/87 of £310. Museums of national importance may by order of the Minister be vested in trustee bodies appointed by the Minister.

Other Departments

Department of Health and Social Security

Greater London does not have a distinct regional office in the structure of the Department. For links with the NHS two branches within the Regional Liaison Division deal with London: Branch 2 is responsible for liaison with the National Health Service Authorities in North East Thames and in North West Thames and in East Anglia, while Branch 3 deals with liaison for South East Thames and South West Thames together with the North West and Merseyside. Branch 2 also handles both 'pan-London issues' and the special health authorities which are responsible for the London teaching hospitals. Officials responsible for pan-London issues initiate quarterly meetings of officers from the four Thames regions to consider problems specific to health authorities within London. This pan-London responsibility is the specifically London-orientated part of the DHSS. It is possible that DHSS structures will be reformed in the near future.

For carrying out his responsibilities towards personal social services, the Secretary of State is supported by the London Regional Office of the Social Services Inspectorate which deals mainly with the London boroughs. It comprises 14 professional staff and 9 administrative and secretarial staff.

His responsibilities for social security are carried out through the local offices of two London regions, which employ 9,890 full-time equivalent staff. One, for London North, is based at Wembley; the other, for London South, is based at Sutton (see Map 9).

Department of Employment

The Department was not affected by the Act of 1985. It continues to perform extensive governmental functions in London. London is one of the ten regions in the structure of the Manpower Services Commission of the Department, with regional directors for vocational education and training, responsible for around 700 staff. Greater London is a region for the Advisory Conciliation and Arbitration Service, with its own regional director and about 100 staff.

The Department now has a London and South East Region (split into three divisions which cover parts of London – see Map 12), which is responsible for the Employment group of services, including job-centres and benefit offices. Other services of the Department are managed centrally although there are local or sub-regional offices in London for redundancy payments, the Wages Inspectorate, the Employment Agency, Licensing, and the Careers Service Inspectorate.

The Departments of Employment and of Health and Social Security have the most staff performing functions in London. Their offices contain the largest bureaucratic presence of departments in London.

Department of Trade and Industry

The Department has no unit exclusively for Greater London although its functions concern trade and industry located in Greater London. Greater London is part of the South East Regional Office, whose remit extends widely over the Home Counties. It deals with technology transfer; support for innovation; liaison with industry, research and academic institutions; regional policy; economic and industrial intelligence; inward investment; and the London City Action Team.

Ministry of Agriculture, Fisheries and Food

This too has no staff specifically responsible for the Greater London area. Work affecting Greater London is dealt with by the appropriate specialist units such as the animal and plant health, horticulture, flood defence and land sales divisions, and by the South Eastern and Eastern regional offices.

Customs and Excise

Four 'collections' of Customs and Excise, out of 21 nationally, each under a Collector, deal with Greater London: London Airports, London City and South, London North and West, and London Port.

Inland Revenue
The Inland Revenue has for London four regional (income tax) offices out of 15 nationally: North, East, South and West.

Miscellaneous
The Passport Office has a London Regional Office, and the Central Office of Information has an office for London and the South Eastern Region.

Conclusion

The 1985 Act conferred on the minister wide powers by order to bring the Act into force, and to ensure that successor bodies discharged their new responsibilities economically, efficiently and effectively. By regulation the Minister could insist on the submission to him for approval of schemes covering the number of persons employed for particular purposes, the authority's arrangements for obtaining its services, supplies or facilities, and its organisation and management arrangements. Through orders he would be able to unscramble and redistribute functions to different combinations of the boroughs organised in a variety of ways. Controls and approval powers abounded. Opposition was especially vociferous against the power of the Secretary of State to make at any time by order any such incidental, consequential, transitional or supplementary provision as appeared to him necessary or expedient to give effect to the Act. 'Breathtaking' and 'unprecedented' were epithets used.

Ministers explained that such provisions appeared in legislation on local government reorganisation in 1963 and 1972 and would not be used to alter the system radically, only to bring into force the provisions of the Act. The courts would not allow a minister to range beyond what was incidental and consequential, and there was no intention to take the joint authorities out of local authority control. The manpower and budget controls for the initial three years after abolition were to curb empire building, the endemic disease, argued the minister, of local government. Taken with the existing central government powers over London government, the 1985 Act greatly extended Whitehall's influence and control. The powers of the Department of the Environment over land use and of the Department of Transport over traffic and roads involve these two departments in a great deal of second-guessing of boroughs, duplicating work they have already carried out, while the Environment Department's power of ratecapping makes that department effectively responsible for taxing (and indirectly expenditure) decisions of the ratecapped authorities, and to some extent of those authorities not ratecapped, since it must be assumed that the minister approves of their spending and taxing. Whitehall can be regarded as responsible for overall control of about 70 per cent of local spending in London, through its ratecapping powers over the boroughs, ILEA and London Fire and Civil Defence Authority, and through its control over the budgets of the Metropolitan Police and London Regional Transport. In London responsibility for the last two functions is, unlike in the provinces, not in any way a matter for local authorities, and thus questions about their operations have to be directed to ministers, because they are responsible.

Opponents of the Bill from all parties, including Conservatives, condemned it as centralising. Their language was often vivid. They said that the Bill conferred on ministers detailed, unparalleled and draconian powers to control day-to-day operations of London's government. The proposals smacked of totalitarianism, it was argued. It embodied the principle that Whitehall knows best. Former Prime Minister, Edward Heath, argued that the Bill 'would put an extraordinary accretion of powers into the hands of the Secretary of State' and he feared what another party in power would make of them. A former Conservative local government minister, Geoffrey Rippon, argued that the Secretary of State's powers were 'intolerably far-reaching and unacceptable'. The Government was said to want to tell the people what is good for them and what is not. But ministers insisted that the Bill was a measure of decentralisation. Ministers' powers were either to achieve the objectives of the legislation or essential to promote an overall strategic policy for London that could not be attained by the boroughs individually or jointly. The powers were in many cases reserve or default, to be used only if the boroughs failed to act or threatened to act in ways that adversely affected their neighbours.

The Act confers considerable powers on central government to govern London. They are there to be used by ministers. The present Government may have been reluctant to resort to them, but this restraint does not set a binding precedent for future ministers, who may welcome such large powers to enforce their will on London. Statutory powers should not be judged by whether ministers use them, but by how they might be used. Their potential is what counts.

Ministers and their departments are pressured to involve themselves in London's local matters when political forces stimulate them to intervene and local issues assume what ministers regard as national significance, as with the state of education in the I L E A and some London boroughs like Brent and Haringey. In the light of commitments in the Conservatives' 1987 manifesto, it appears that the centre will become more interventionist over housing in London now that problems of repair, management, resources and mobility have reached a crisis point. Intervention could also be expected in ethnic issues if social order is disrupted, or in traffic if the roads clog up. In such times of apparent crisis ministers turn to whatever powers they can find to solve the problems. They may even find that they have to rebuild local government in London, if the present tangle of arrangements fails to deliver accept-able services, and if the boroughs deteriorate because of difficulties in obtaining appropriate staff, intensified politicisation, financial collapse and breakdown of services. An alternative scenario sees ministers not strengthening local government but taking more to the centre, putting services into the hands of their civil servants who to them seem to possess Rolls Royce minds, rather than into the hands of local government officials who are felt to have motorcyclists' minds. There then might emerge a Department of London under a Minister for London. At least responsibility for London would be clearly located somewhere if such reforms took place. We return to these issues in Chapter 7.

At the moment the Government has further plans to change the current arrangements for the governing of London boroughs as well as abolishing the I L E A. The centre is not well organised to produce any plans. Each department is left to its own devices, consulting and co-ordinating with others where it, and they, see fit. There has been no central assessment or analysis of the results of the abolition of the G L C and how the new system is faring. The centre is itself fragmented in its dealings with London. Government's approach to London is piecemeal and temporary. Ad hocery rules.

Sources

This chapter is based on information from legislation, House of Commons' debates, parliamentary answers to questions, *The Civil Service Yearbook*, official press notices, leaflets and booklets, and conversations with officials.

CHAPTER 2

Centrally Appointed Bodies

Introduction

More than any other part of Britain, London's local services are in the hands of agencies appointed by central government. Public transport and police services are county council services in England and Wales (regions in Scotland), while in London, the government or an appointed agency are responsible for such provision. In addition, the abolition of the Greater London Council had the effect of passing a large number of residual services to the London Residuary Body, also a government-appointed organisation, which has joined London Regional Transport and the Metropolitan Police as a major provider of public services within Greater London. These three bodies spend about £2.5 billion a year, which compares with about £6.5 billion spent by the boroughs.

The origins and rationales of the three London-wide government agencies are significantly different. Transport services in London originally grew as private provision before being combined into a public corporation, and then, in turn, being made a local government responsibility at the end of the 1960s only to revert in 1984 to a board appointed by the government. London's police services, from their origins in the nineteenth century, have been directly controlled by the Home Secretary. LRB is a brand new London-wide appointed institution. Created in 1985, it took over a range of services from the GLC which it was not possible for the Government to pass on either to boroughs or to other bodies. As explained above, LRT and LRB are each controlled by boards appointed by the Government, while the Metropolitan Police is under the direct control of the Home Secretary.

Apart from these London-wide central government bodies, there are a number of other appointed bodies which provide local services within the Greater London area, notably the four Regional Health Authorities whose territories meet in central London, and the London division of the

24

Manpower Services Commission. Other national appointed bodies with London divisions are English Heritage and the Sports Council. The Arts Council does not have a London division, although there is a Greater London Arts body, and following the abolition of the G L C, responsibility for the facilities on the South Bank passed to the South Bank Board whose members are appointed by the Arts Council.

The South Bank Board is similar to the London Docklands Development Corporation in that it is an appointed body with responsibilities for services which are similar to those run by local authorities, but with a limited geographical coverage within London. L D D C is a high-powered, short-term quango, which will be wound up once the redevelopment of London's docklands has been completed.

Finally, the centrally appointed bodies operating within London (and also through the rest of the country) include several institutions with a strong London interest, as well as traditional public (and increasingly private) monopolies such as Thames Water, the Post Office, the London Electricity Board, and British Rail (particularly Network South East, which covers London and its surrounding area).

Centrally appointed bodies play a large and growing part in the provision of public services within Greater London. Many of them are either new or recently reformed, and there can be little doubt that they are often less accessible to the public than locally appointed bodies. We have found little evidence of efforts within the sponsoring departments of the appointed bodies to co-ordinate their approaches to London. Despite the fact that the resources to pay for most of the bodies concerned came either from national taxation or are effectively controlled by the Government, the Government takes little notice of the extent of its indirect powers over the capital. One of the few examples of cross-department co-operation is the City Action Teams (one of which is in London) which involve co-ordination of efforts by the Manpower Services Commission and the Departments of Trade and Industry, Environment, Transport and the Home Office. While there are inevitably a range of informal· and ad hoc links between centrally appointed bodies in London and the traditional forms of local government, there are few formal ones. The Department of Transport has some London-wide involvement with boroughs through the Greater London Advisory and Consultative Committee and the London Advisory Panel on Transport Schemes for the Mobility Handicapped, but its relationships are otherwise on a borough-by-borough basis. The Department of the Environment has a legally defined relationship with the London Planning Advisory Committee. L P A C acts as a focal point for other links between local government and central agencies (e.g. the Department of Transport). The Home Office is effectively forced to have links with local government London-wide because it is the sponsoring department for both the London Fire and Civil Defence Authority and for the Metropolitan Police.

Of course, the boroughs, ILEA and LFCDA as elected London local authorities can represent themselves in a relatively co-ordinated way through the London Boroughs Association and the Association of London Authorities. The fact that there are two (broadly party political) representative associations for London boroughs must, however, reduce the power of either body to speak effectively to central government and its appointed bodies.

Central Computer Service

CCS is a large and diversified computer service which handles payroll management, data processing, data protection, software development, systems installation, training and technical support, and kindred services.

CCS originated as the GLC computing service. As such, it worked for the GLC and for a wide range of public and voluntary sector clients, charging out its services on a full-cost basis. Since abolition the CCS, like several other former GLC services (for example, Seaside and Country Homes), has been moved temporarily under the control of the London Residuary Body which runs it on the same full-cost basis as before. Its clients have included ILEA (the largest user), the boroughs, Magistrates Court Committees, the Thames Water Authority, the London Area Mobility Scheme, the Historic Buildings and Monuments Commission, the London Research Centre, and over 200 other organisations in addition to the LRB itself.

LRB had to find a way of passing CCS on to either another public authority or to the private sector. Agreement was reached in 1988 that CCS would become part of the Hoskyns group.

For the moment, the Central Computer Service continues to work in County Hall and employs some 340 staff. It has no net expenditure as all its activities are charged to users on a full-cost basis. Meetings of LRB, its controlling body, are not open to the public. LRB's operations are subject to scrutiny by the Parliamentary Ombudsman, though not the Local Government Ombudsman.

City Action Team

The Department of Employment and M S C, along with the Departments of Trade and Industry, Environment, Transport and the Home Office are jointly involved in the Government's City Action Team (C A T) initiative. The London C A T was set up in 1985. Though physically based at the London Regional Office of the Manpower Services Commission in Grays Inn Road, the C A T is co-ordinated by the Employment Service of the Department of Employment. Its aim is to target government support in Inner London and to encourage private and voluntary sector investment with respect to specific local problems. It had a budget of £1m in 1986/87.

Specifically, C A T has programmes of three kinds: (1) schemes to promote local enterprises through workshop development, new technology and customer/supplier links; (2) schemes intended to address mismatches in the London labour market; and (3) various programmes of environmental improvement linked to employment in the tourist industry. So far, the London C A T has focused on Hackney, Islington and Lambeth, though projects in other parts of inner London may be supported in future.

Dial-a-Ride Scheme

The scheme was initiated in 1980 by the Greater London Council in consultation with voluntary organisations representing the disabled. Since G L C abolition it has been run by London Regional Transport, which receives from the Department of Transport an earmarked grant for this purpose, amounting in 1987/88 to approximately £6m.

The money goes to support 29 separate Dial-a-Ride services, their catchment areas mostly corresponding to borough boundaries. Together, there is a fleet of just under 120 specially converted vehicles, which can be booked over the phone and will carry disabled people or groups at fares broadly comparable to an equivalent trip by bus.

Greater London Arts

An appointed body, with members taken from local authorities, advisory panels and funding bodies (such as the Arts Council), G L A exists to promote the arts in the London region. It is one of a number of regional arts associations which together cover the whole of England. About three-quarters of the funding which G L A now undertakes was previously the responsibility of the GLC. This has meant that GLA's funding priorities remain heavily influenced by the GLC's allocation of resources, though efforts are being made to change the pattern of distribution.

GLA employs 41 staff, and spent £8.5m in 1987/88. Its offices are based at the Angel, Islington. Meetings of the GLA executive are open to the public, and an annual report is published.

Historic Buildings and Monuments Commission for England (HBMC), London Division

The Commission, known for most purposes as English Heritage, was set up under the National Heritage Act 1983. Appointed by central government, its main duties are to secure the preservation of ancient monuments and historic buildings; promote the preservation and enhancement of conservation areas; and promote the public's enjoyment and understanding of historic buildings and monuments. HMBC, as well as being a principal source of grant-aid for preservation and rescue archaeology in England, has direct responsibility for the care of some 400 government-owned properties.

At abolition in April 1986, the GLC's Historic Buildings Division based in Chesham House, Warwick Street, was taken over by HBMC to become its London Division. As such, it constitutes the only regional department of English Heritage, which is otherwise organised along specialist lines. A new sub-committee of the Commission, known as the London Advisory Committee (LAC), was established to replace the former GLC Historic Buildings Sub-Committee. Its membership, appointed by the Secretary of State, includes three former members of the GLC sub-committee and its Chairman, Robert Vigars, is a former Chairman of the Greater London Council. The LAC meets monthly and is the only sub-committee of English Heritage to do so in public.

English Heritage has acquired from the GLC an important power it does not possess elsewhere: that of directing local planning authorities' decisions on applications for listed building consent. All London applications – 3,000 in 1986/87 – are now referred to English Heritage, bringing it into direct policy relationship with the London boroughs and the London Docklands Development Corporation. The Commission's 'London Grants' scheme continues a former GLC scheme of grants for the repair of buildings or places of historical or architectural interest in Greater London. The London Division's historic building expenditure in 1987/88 of approximately £1.6m is almost wholly funded from government grant-in-aid to HMBC.

The Commission's London Division also took over from the G L C the responsibility for archaeology in Greater London. Under the provisions of the Museum of London Act 1986 it provides an annual grant-in-aid of about £0.5m to the Museum of London as core funding for the Greater London Archaeological Service. It also distributes grants in the order of £1m to fund specific projects, the great majority of them carried out by the Greater London Archaeological Service.

Thirdly, H B M C's London Division now runs the three historic houses acquired in earlier times on behalf of the people of London by the London County Council: Kenwood (on Hampstead Heath), Rangers (by Greenwich Park) and Marble Hill House (Twickenham).

The Home Loans Portfolio

The G L C, in common with other housing authorities, gave mortgages to individuals to buy homes. Repayments for these mortgages now produce an income for the London Residuary Body, which currently administers the Home Loans Portfolio. After deduction of any repayments of debt attributable to the houses concerned and the running costs, L R B passes on any cash benefit to London boroughs by way of a lower levy.

L R B wished to place the responsibility for the Home Loans Portfolio, as for all other services, with other institutions as part of winding itself up. As there is no net cost to the boroughs concerned (indeed, there may be net 'profit' for distribution among other boroughs) the Portfolio was not an onerous or unpopular responsibility. Richmond assumed responsibility. (Home Loans Portfolio should now, more accurately, be within London-wide Local Government Bodies.)

London Council for Sport and Recreation

Regional councils for sport and recreation were first established as fully autonomous bodies in 1976. A separate council for London was formed in 1985 following a review by the Department of the Environment. Its membership and terms of reference, as set out in a Department of the Environment circular in 1976, include representatives from each London borough, the Inner London Education Authority, the Lee Valley Regional Park Authority, and the governing bodies of sporting organisations and other statutory bodies with interests in sport and recreation. The chairman, one of the vice-chairmen and five members of the Council, are nominated by the Minister of Sport (who is a junior Environment minister). The Council is serviced by staff of the Sports Council.

The Council has five objectives:

1. To promote better understanding of the importance of sport and recreation to the well-being of society;
2. To encourage greater participation in sport and recreation by the population as a whole and, in particular, those groups where participation is presently low;
3. To ensure that appropriate facilities are available to permit this participation;
4. To afford opportunities for the development of excellence among those with the necessary talents;
5. To assure the recognition of London as a national and international centre for sport.

LRSC employs no staff directly, all its administrative and other costs being borne by the Sports Council. The Council is based at the Crystal Palace Sports Centre. Some funding of projects (over £1m in total) was taken from the GLC.

London Docklands Development Corporation

LDDC was created by Parliament in 1981 under powers established by the Local Government, Planning and Land Act 1980. Its eleven Board members, chairman and deputy chairman are appointed by the Secretary of State for the Environment and are accountable through him to Parliament.

Very wide powers are vested in the Corporation with the object of securing the economic regeneration of its designated area, which is broadly drawn to encompass London's former upstream docks and the immediately adjacent districts. Most of the land owned within its boundary by the three borough councils in Docklands (Southwark, Tower Hamlets and Newham) has been vested in the LDDC by order of the Secretary of State, together with extensive land-holdings of British Gas and the Port of London Authority. Over 1,500 acres of land and 425 of water have so far been acquired by or vested in the Corporation, which proceeds to make extensive direct investments in reclamation, site services, transport and environmental schemes before selling on for housing, industrial and commercial development. A total of 676 acres had already been disposed of by the autumn of 1987. The Corporation also encourages and supports business and residential development in Docklands by a variety of means, notably publicity and training, and it offers support grants for educational, social and recreational projects.

The Corporation's management structure is distinctive in three respects. First, L D D C does not have a single headquarters building. It has six modest premises located throughout the Docklands area, linked by internal fax mailing systems, a telex and electronic file transfer system, and various computer networks. Second, the Corporation is run on the 'matrix management' philosophy, with no hierarchical separation of staff and line functions. The six Chief Officers with corporation-wide responsibilities work alongside the four Area Directors responsible for planning and projects. Some staff have dual responsibilities and report to both an area and a functional director. Third, L D D C has a highly flexible personnel policy. Its core staff of 100 (including Board members) are supplemented by almost as large a group on fixed-term contracts, and extensive use is also made of consultants and temporary staff.

L D D C receives from Government an annual grant-in-aid of some £50m. Having helped to create a Docklands property boom through its pro-business stance, it has been able to supplement its grant by a fast-growing surplus earned on land development, which amounted to £37m in 1986/87. The Corporation attaches great importance to attracting private investment into the London Docklands. According to its own estimates, net public expenditure of £275m in the area between 1981 and 1987 brought in private investment of £2,242m. The resulting high leverage ratio of 9:1 is regarded by L D D C as a key measure of its success.

Meetings of the L D D C Board are held in private, although the public are permitted access to the meetings of the Planning Sub-committee.

London Regional Passengers' Committee

The L R P C is a statutory body created under Section 40 of the London Regional Transport Act 1984 to represent the interests of public transport passengers in the London area and make recommendations about the services and facilities provided by the two major transport operators, London Regional Transport (for buses and Underground), and British Rail (for suburban rail). It is unique in representing both bus and rail passengers, replacing the previous London Transport Passengers' Committee (appointed by the G L C) and the Transport Users' Consultative Committee (T U C C) for London. But the L R P C continues to be represented along with seven other regional T U C Cs on the Central Transport Consultative Committee, the national passenger body for B R services. It is responsible for all services within the area whose boundaries stretch beyond the L R T network, from Slough to Upminster, and from Horsham to Hitchin (Map 21).

There are currently 25 Committee members, out of a legal maximum of 30, appointed by the Secretary of State for Transport on the basis of nominations from local authorities, business organisations, trade unions, and groups representing commuters, pensioners, the disabled and children. It also has a staff of seven, plus two liaison officers for LRT and BR.

The Committee can consider a wide range of matters affecting public transport services, and can respond to suggestions and complaints from both individual passengers and transport interest groups and local authorities. LRPC is required to hold an inquiry and report on objections concerning any proposal by LRT or BR involving closure of a passenger rail station, but is not permitted to comment on the setting of fare levels, or, in the case of BR, decisions to reduce overall levels of service. It can, however, make suggestions on changes in the frequency and timing of services, travel conditions, safety matters, the needs of specific categories of passengers (disabled, children, women, etc.), the provision of information, ticketing and staff conduct. The Committee also inherited the GLC's duties in relation to performance monitoring, examining periodic reports prepared by the transport operators themselves on crowding, punctuality, cancellations, cleaning, ticket queues, etc. The Committee is organised into four sub-committees regarding various aspects of passenger transport: (1) service provision, (2) information and marketing, (3) facilities and (4) performance monitoring. Meetings of the full Committee are open to the public, while minutes to sub-committees are available for public inspection.

With the removal of control over public transport by an elected London-wide council the LRPC has become important as one of the means of access to policy-makers available to commuters and local residents in the capital. The Committee has become engaged with a number of important strategic issues, including two major inquiries into station closures in Central London (Broad Street and Marylebone), the state of intersuburban services in Greater London, the effects of traffic congestion on bus services and the creation of the Docklands Light Railway. More recently, it has begun to voice its concern about the effects of the expansion of one person operation (OPO) and the possible deregulation of bus services in London.

London Regional Transport

Background

London Regional Transport was set up in 1984 to take over from the GLC the running of all bus and tube services in the capital. LRT's general duties, as set out in section 2 of the London Regional Transport Act 1984, are:

(1) in accordance with the principles from time to time approved by the Secretary of State and in conjunction with the Railways Board, to provide or secure the provision of public passenger services.

(2) In carrying out that duty London Regional Transport shall have due regard to –

(a) the transport needs for the time being of Greater London; and

(b) efficiency, economy and safety of operation.

The section goes on to require LRT and the Railways Board to co-ordinate their services in the capital.

The Act empowers the Secretary of State to determine financial objectives from time to time. His first determination was that, among other things, LRT should reduce costs by at least 2.5 per cent a year in real terms, that revenue support should be reduced to £95m in 1987/88 (from £192m in 1984/85) and that LRT should maintain a broadly stable relationship betwen fares, prices generally and the fares on the British Rail London Commuter services.

There were two other important new requirements in the 1984 Act. One was that there should be established separate, wholly-owned bus and underground subsidiaries and separate companies for other parts of the organisation. These are to provide for the clear identification of costs and performance and clear responsibility for them, and for the involvement of private capital where appropriate. The second new requirement is that LRT and its subsidiaries should invite open tenders for some of its activities and that outside tenders should be accepted unless it could be demonstrated that LRT employees could do the job more cheaply or more effectively themselves.

Prior to 1933 London's public transport services were operated, in competition, by several companies responsible to private shareholders. The bus companies were profitable but the railways experienced chronic financial difficulties. From 1933 until the end of the 1960s all the major operating concerns were administered as a single nationalised industry. In 1969 the London Transport Executive was created as an operating enterprise responsible to the locally elected Greater London Council under an arrangement closely analogous to the passenger transport executives and passenger transport authorities set up in 1968 in the other major metropolitan areas. The Department of Transport has retained responsibility for the British Railways Board as a separate nationalised industry since nationalisation in 1947.

Significant amounts of revenue subsidy became necessary for London Transport for the first time in the mid 1970s to finance deficits. During the early 1980s increasing revenue subsidy became a deliberate feature of GLC policy in order to reduce fares and preserve levels of service in the face of rapidly increasing costs. This culminated in a House of Lords decision that the policy was in contravention of the powers granted to the GLC by the 1969 Act.

Under the London Regional Transport Act 1984 the organisation reverted to that of a traditional nationalised industry, responsible to the Secretary of State for Transport and through him to Parliament.

Control and consultation

London Regional Transport is controlled by a twelve-person Board, which comprises the Chairman and Chief Executive, the Member for Finance, the Chairman and Managing Director of London Buses Limited, the Chairman and Managing Director of London Underground Limited, and eight non-executive, part-time members. The Board meets every four weeks. Detailed matters are dealt with in the weekly meetings of the Executive Committee which comprises the directors of various LRT functions in addition to the executive board members. There are several other specialist committees and boards such as London Transport International Services Limited, Docklands Light Railway Limited, the Budget and Investment Review Group, the Finance Policy Committee, the Property Board, the Audit Committee, the Central Business Committee, the Design Committee, and the Business Boards for Advertising, Catering, the Museum and Builders.

By the end of its first year (and every three years thereafter) LRT was required to publish a Statement of Strategy covering the policies and plans of LRT and its subsidiaries. This it did after consultation with more than 350 organisations and persons with a known interest in public transport, the statutory consultees – the British Railways Board, the local authorities and the London Regional Passengers' Committee – and after seeking the views of individual passengers through the distribution of 50,000 copies of a consultation document. The responses are summarised in the Statement of Strategy.

LRT routinely publishes a quantity of material, ranging from its own

Annual Report and Accounts and those of its subsidiaries, through the Annual Business Plan to miscellaneous reports such as the recent studies on coach stations and bus lanes, press notices and publicity material. It consults with British Rail and local authorities on detailed service changes and it has a continuous dialogue with the independent London Regional Passengers' Committee whose members are appointed by the Secretary of State. There is, of course, day-to-day communication with the Department of Transport and, as with any nationalised industry, L R T, the Department of Transport and the Treasury operate a system of corporate planning (over three years) and external financing limits.

Finance

L R T draws down grant from the Department of Transport to cover the gap between general revenues and operating expenditures, within agreed limits. Grant is also received in respect of specific capital expenditures which have been approved by the Board and the Department of Transport. The total intake of funds in any one year must lie within the External Financing Limited (E F L) for that year. The Secretary of State may recover up to a maximum of two-thirds of the total grant by a levy on the London boroughs. Various special arrangements are made for financing transport for the elderly and infirm such as the 29 Dial-A-Ride services for the disabled and the Taxicard scheme of discount cab rides for the disabled (see pp. 87–88); as for the free travel concession to pensioners resident in London, the boroughs reimburse L R T according to an agreed formula which is designed to put it in the same net revenue position as they would have been had the concession not existed. L R T treat the income on a par with other commercial income.

The 1985/86 Report and Accounts show that the Secretary of State's objective of reduced financial support for revenue purposes was virtually achieved a year early. This was partly through beating the targets on unit cost reduction but more particularly because of an unanticipated buoyancy of receipts which has been particularly marked on the Underground. Service levels have been generally preserved and general fare increases have kept pace with inflation. However, the fares structure has been altered to favour the Travelcard and other forms of pre-paid travel at the expense of ordinary tickets. There has been a rapid increase in the use of period passes and some 60 per cent of bus trips and 80 per cent of Underground trips use these in the morning peak. This has the advantages of considerably reducing the delays and other costs associated with ticket issuing. The average fare paid per passenger mile has been falling as extra trips are made by card holders at no extra fare. The cards appear to have generated extra revenue in total. However, a significant dis-advantage has become apparent as load factors increase and crowding becomes a problem. The Underground is having to undertake signifi-cant new investment expenditure in order to provide sufficient capacity to carry its new traffic. Another difficulty raised by cards which allow unlimited travel on the services of more than one operator concerns the loss of routine information about travel patterns and the allocation of the revenues. This is already a point of controversy between London Buses and London Underground and it is likely to become an issue between British Rail and L R T as usage of their joint Capital Card increases.

For 1985/86 traffic and other income totalled £673m and costs of operations £935m. Capital expenditure on London Buses was £40m and on London Underground, £135m. The major items of investment were new buses, the station modernisation programme and the Docklands Light Railway which had cost a total of £77m when opened in July 1987.

London Buses employed 24,670 staff in March 1986, London Underground 21,600, Bus Engineering 1,420 and the centre and corp-orate activities 4,230: a total of 51,920 staff declining in 1987 to 47,300.

Current and future developments

The bus engineering function has been made into a separate subsidiary company, selling services to London Buses (and some outside com-panies) on a commercial basis. London Buses are free to give their work to other outside contractors providing they match price and quality. Bus Engineering Limited have reorganised their factory at Chiswick, and closed the other one at Aldenham. London Buses have themselves changed their maintenance practices, with a higher proportion of work being done at the garages and less periodic rebuilding of vehicles.

L R T is putting an increasing proportion of the bus routes out to competitive tender (about 10 per cent to date). L R T specifies the service details and tenderers compete for three year contracts to operate them. Revenues are remitted in full to L R T. Approximately half of the tenders have been won by London Buses at a substantially reduced cost compared to their other services, in some cases by means of setting up small specialist operating enterprises. The remaining tenders have been won by other public sector bus companies or private operators. London Buses have increased the proportion of one person operation to 70 per cent assisted by the increased use of travel cards.

There are dormant provisions in the Transport Act 1985 to extend the deregulation of bus services to the L R T area. There is a possibility that a future government will enact these provisions – or something similar – with the result that London Buses would face the prospect of free entry competition on its services. This would have fundamental implications for the structure of London Buses and for its relationship with LRT, with London Underground and with other operators.

As agent to the Secretary of State for Transport LRT has completed a study of options for the construction of a new long distance coach terminal for London. The preferred site is on the old goods depot at Paddington and LRT have prepared a planning application for a facility which is becoming increasingly necessary as coach travel grows rapidly and swamps the capacity at the present coach station at Victoria and the surrounding streets.

London Underground has been able to transfer most of its vehicle maintenance from its factory at Acton into the depots, an important factor being the reduced requirements of more modern rolling stock. Acton is being reorganised and reduced in scale to concentrate on the more major maintenance items. Trains are being converted to one person operation. A programme of station modernisation continues including replacement of many lifts and escalators. The installation of the Underground Ticketing System – a major new investment – has begun. This will reduce the requirements for staffed ticket barriers and reduce opportunities for fraud. A new initiative is to be taken to improve passenger security against crime. The Underground's two power stations are to be closed and replaced by power drawn from the National Grid. New trains and signalling are being purchased in order to respond to increasing passenger demand, in addition to the normal renewal process. Docklands Light Railway is a separate subsidiary. There are plans to extend the Docklands railway east to the Bank or Monument and west to Beckton. In both cases the investments would be largely financed through a charge on the consequential land development values.

LRT now relies very heavily on both small and large computer and telecommunications systems. They are used in a conventional way in accounts, payrolls, personnel, production management and stock control. Their use is also growing very rapidly in train and bus control and in electronic signalling, where they are responsible for a major technical change. The Docklands Light Railway is driverless. Another important innovation has been in providing real time information to passengers with the widespread introduction of indicators on the Underground. Experiments have shown that it is also technically possible to do something similar for bus passengers, but the scale of investment here has yet to be decided.

London Residuary Body

The London Residuary Body (LRB) is a corporate body which was established on 12 August 1985 in accordance with Part VII of the Local Government Act 1985. Its basic function is to manage the GLC's loan debt together with administration of that part of the superannuation fund not apportioned among other authorities and any outstanding legal rights and liabilities (sections 58–63 of the 1985 Act). As such it was required to undertake a fairly non-contentious managerial task, albeit in a highly charged political atmosphere. However, because of the complexity of the abolition process, the speed with which it was undertaken, and the political climate in which it was to be implemented, a broad range of former GLC responsibilities which were not transferred to other bodies have become the responsibility of LRB. As a result, LRB has assumed a highly contentious role.

The status of LRB is not straightforward. Its members (between 5 and 10) are appointed by the Secretary of State and in exercising its functions it is required to comply with any directions given to it by him. Also under Schedule 13 LRB is required to produce an annual report which must be sent to the Secretary of State and laid before Parliament and it falls within the jurisdiction of the Parliamentary Commissioner for Administration. But LRB is not a Crown body and for many purposes it is treated as a local authority. Furthermore, LRB is open to scrutiny by the Local Commission for Administration in relation to conduct concerning former GLC responsibilities. Thus, it is in part open to scrutiny by the Parliamentary Commissioner and in part to the Local Commissioner. As such it is unusual. Despite putting LRB under the scrutiny of the two Commissioners, the Secretary of State took the curious step of using the extremely broad reserve powers in section 101 of the 1985 Act to exclude it from the provisions of the Local Government (Access to Information) Act 1985. This has the effect of ensuring that LRB has complete freedom to regulate its own proceedings. LRB's unusual status may be explained by the fact that its basic function is to act as the Secretary of State's agent in overseeing the transference of the residual functions of a major local authority and the winding up of its affairs.

LRB's basic function, therefore, is to create the conditions for its own abolition; it is under a statutory duty 'to use its best endeavours to secure that its work is completed as soon as practicable' and must by 1990 submit to the Secretary of State a scheme for the winding up of its affairs (section 67). Its main responsibilities are to make redundancy and compensation payments to former GLC staff; to manage certain services previously run by the GLC pending their transfer to another body; to dispose of the assets of the GLC; to pay pensions to former GLC staff; and to service the GLC's loan debt and to deal with other legal liabilities. These functions will be examined in turn.

Redundancy and compensation payments

LRB inherited around 4,000 of the GLC's 21,000 staff, about half of whom work in areas which they expect will be transferred to the boroughs; the other half are core staff. Consequently, the numbers of former GLC employees who receive compensation and redundancy payments from LRB under the arrangements in section 59 of the 1985 Act is dependent on the arrangements currently in hand for the transfer of services and assets.

Transfer of services

LRB aims to have all services transferred either to the boroughs or successor authorities by the end of 1988. A range of services have been transferred since 1986. Take, for example, research. The Research and Intelligence Unit of the GLC collected information on all developments affecting London. This research service was used not only by the GLC but by all the London boroughs and many other public bodies. During 1986/87 agreements were concluded under which responsibility for this service was assumed, from 1 April 1987, by the boroughs with Islington as lead borough. The new arrangement, under the title London Research Centre, contains two separate schemes, one (under section 88 of the Local Government Act 1985) funded by all London boroughs and another (under section 101 of the Local Government Act 1972) funded by 16 boroughs.

However, it is unclear at the present time what will happen to a number of services. No permanent arrangements have been made, for example, in relation to the London Scientific Services. This branch is a centre of excellence with responsibility for promoting health and safety provisions, testing of materials, monitoring of environmental pollution and the like. It is possible that a lead borough could take over responsibility for the service or that the staff themselves run it on a charging basis. In 1986/87 its expenditure was recovered from the boroughs on a population basis but in 1987/88 expenditure has been met on the basis of priced service contracts and specific job charges.

The Traffic Control Systems Unit was another specialised agency which LRB inherited from the GLC. The LRB maintained responsibility for this work under a two year contract with the Department of Transport, with the Department meeting the full cost of the work. This contract ended on 31 March 1988, and the responsibility has now been transferred once again, as explained below.

Finally, the Central Computer Services. The GLC had established an extensive data network connecting all council departments and the ILEA, with direct links to many other bodies. As explained above, CCS passed into the hands of a private company in the summer of 1988.

Asset sales

Under the 1985 Act (Schedule 13, paragraph 7) LRB must in general dispose of land at the best consideration that can reasonably be obtained. Given that it is also required to act speedily there is a potential conflict between these two duties since LRB was left with a total of around 9,000 properties to dispose of. These properties include industrial, commercial and housing properties as well as GLC parks. Many of these were vested in successor bodies on 1 April 1986 and therefore LRB's function has been to carry through the process of property transfer. Other properties are to be marketed and sold.

LRB has sold the GLC's industrial properties to a single purchaser, Inner City Enterprises (ICE). This portfolio consists of some 140 properties including sites, workshops and groundlease estates which, in a confidential report commissioned by LRB, is believed to be valued at between £30m and £50m. The sale to ICE proved contentious. First, the Labour controlled boroughs felt that they should have been given the right of first refusal of the properties. Second, these boroughs complained and threatened court action over the lack of consultation by LRB over the proposed disposal. Third, it was felt that ICE has no track record as a developer. ICE was set up in 1983 by a group of financial institutions following their trip to Liverpool with Michael Heseltine in the wake of the Toxteth riots. Its function had been to aid inner city regeneration by assembling and funding development packages. Its experience was therefore with funding rather than development and management. Given the strong hints in *Streamlining the Cities* that the GLC's industrial properties would be transferred to a single agency it was possible that LRB was simply following the Government's wishes on this sale.

The controversy surrounding the sale of commercial property has focused on the central office accommodation at County Hall. Since 1 April 1987 LRB has charged market rents for all users of central office accommodation and has served notice, effective from 31 March 1988, terminating ILEA's present rights to occupy County Hall; this notice was unsuccessfully challenged in the courts. Currently LRB is marketing

County Hall and in furtherance of this objective applied for planning permission for change of use to, among other things, a hotel. A public local inquiry in relation to this application was held in April 1987. The inquiry concluded that County Hall should continue to be used for local government purposes. The Secretary of State rejected this conclusion.

By the time of its abolition the G L C had ceased to be a major housing authority since most of its stock had been transferred to the boroughs during the late 1970s and early 1980s. In terms of housing property, then, the principal issues concerned Thamesmead Town and the G L C's Seaside and Country Homes. The alternatives for Thamesmead were to transfer responsibility either to the London boroughs in which it lies or to Thamesmead Town Ltd. As explained below (pp. 52–3) a referendum was held and residents opted for the latter arrangement. The main difficulties which arose from this proposal concerned finance: whether finance could be obtained to complete the township and whether Thamesmead Town could afford to pay the market price for the development. L R B concluded that Thamesmead Town's offer was not the best consideration that could reasonably be obtained but the Government, presumably because the proposal is consistent with its policy of transfer of the public sector housing stock to housing trusts, issued a section 65 direction requiring the transfer to take place. Camden council sought judicial review of this direction.

The G L C also owned over 3,000 dwellings in 19 counties to enable London council tenants of retirement age to move to the seaside or country thereby releasing accommodation in London. The G L C gave 50 per cent of the nomination rights to London boroughs and held 50 per cent for mobility schemes. Ownership of these properties is expected to be transferred, as explained below, to a housing association during 1988. The homes will remain available for letting by London boroughs under the London Area Mobility Scheme of which Camden L B C is the lead borough, so there will be no housing loss to London.

Finally, on the issue of the disposal of assets there is the matter of the 5,500 acres of G L C owned parks and open spaces (and 11,000 acres of green belt land). The parks have been transferred to the boroughs, and in the case of the half-developed Burgess and Mile End Parks will impose a major financial burden on Southwark and Tower Hamlets. L R B has experienced greatest difficulty over the transfer of the 790 acres of Hampstead Heath, as explained in Chapter 5 below.

Superannuation fund

By the end of 1988 LRB intends to have transferred all services to lead
boroughs or successor authorities and to have disposed of all properties.
This will leave LRB primarily responsible for the GLC superannuation
fund. At the time of abolition this fund, in addition to providing for
22,400 existing pensioners, 4,650 former contributors and 13,700 GLC
employees, administered the pension obligations of 12,800 ILEA employees and 9,000 employees from over 100 other bodies. The fund will
be apportioned as regards staff transfers to the boroughs but this still
leaves a substantial fund with which to deal. The most efficient arrangement would clearly be to retain the fund on an ongoing basis but
currently no final decision has been made as to whether this might be
achieved by setting up a joint committee of boroughs or by effectively
privatising the fund.

Loan debt

The GLC's debt may be divided into housing debt (£1.7bn) and the rest
(£600m). Responsibility for servicing it is transferred with the asset to
which the debt relates so LRB's role has been that of managing the debt
pending the establishment of arrangements for its full transfer. However, since local authority borrowing is through a consolidated loans fund
it requires considerable administrative effort to apportion debt to assets.
During 1987/88 real loans relating to the housing transferred debt were
parcelled up and reattributed to the boroughs. Furthermore, it is also
expected that the boroughs will approve a scheme for taking over the
residue debt.

Final accounts

Finally, LRB has legal responsibility for the preparation of the final
accounts of the GLC (section 63). This exercise proved controversial
because of the GLC's forward funding decisions during 1985/86. In a
1986 court judgement the House of Lords struck down certain forward
funding decisions of the GLC in favour of the new Inner London Interim
Education Authority and a number of voluntary organisations. As a
result, this money was vested in LRB by virtue of section 62 of the 1985
Act. The bulk of it was subsequently distributed to the boroughs on a
population basis.

   Following the success of that action LRB itself brought an application
for judicial review of the GLC's decision to enter into contracts with
Satman Developments Ltd one minute and 40 seconds before the
Department's general consent to enter into contracts was withdrawn and
four days before abolition. The contracts, worth £78m, concerned the

renovation of old GLC housing stock which had been transferred to the boroughs. In *R.* v. *Greater London Council, ex parte London Residuary Body* (1986) (unreported), however, LRB failed in its application. Nevertheless, final GLC accounts were eventually closed and audited.

Winding up

LRB was well on course to be wound up by March 1991; however, the proposal to abolish the ILEA inserted into the Education Reform Bill, 1987, led the government to propose that LRB's life be extended in order that it may wind up ILEA's affairs.

London Scientific Services

London Scientific Services is an agency service of the London Residuary Body. It provides scientific expertise and advice to local authorities, particularly the London boroughs, and to other public bodies such as the London Fire and Civil Defence Authority and other successors to the GLC. Its specialisms include air pollution, building maintenance, materials testing and chemical analyses.

LSS employs 120 staff of whom 20 are administrative. Expenditure – £3.6m 1987/88 – is financed on a commercial basis from the sale of services to clients. The future of LSS is uncertain, as LRB intended to find an alternative arrangement for running LSS by April 1988. Lead borough control, a form of scientific foundation or privatisation seemed the most likely options as of December 1987.

Manpower Services Commission

The MSC is an agency established in 1976 to run public employment and training services. The Commission is not a government department, though its staff are civil servants. Its main headquarters are in Sheffield, and there is a London Regional Office in Gray's Inn Road.

The Commission has ten members who are appointed by the Secretary of State for Employment following consultations with employers, employees, local authorities and education interests. Commissioners are advised on local matters by 55 Area Manpower Boards. London has four such Boards. MSC appoints the chairmen and members are nominees from the Confederation of British Industry, the Trades Union Congress, the education service and from other interested bodies. The Boards scrutinise employment and training schemes and have recently become involved in the recognition of schemes for Approved Training Organisation status.

In October 1987, Employment and Enterprise services left M S C control and were placed directly under the Department of Employment. M S C is now concerned only with training and is likely to be renamed accordingly the Training Commission. The staff of M S C's London region was depleted from 2,400 to 700 as a consequence of the 1987 reorganisation. The geography of the public employment and training services has also become somewhat complicated, as may be seen in Maps 12 and 13. The Employment Service of the Department of Employment has a London and South East Region, split into three divisions, two containing parts of London (the Eastern and Southern divisions). M S C, on the other hand, retains a separate London Region, one of nine in Great Britain, which corresponds to the local government area of Greater London. Within it are six area offices, each of which has an area manager. Inner London is split into two areas (north and south of the Thames) while outer London divides into quadrants. The Area Manpower Boards are organised differently again, with only four areas, each covering roughly one and a half training areas.

The training services provided by M S C fall into three broad categories. First, there are two major operations for the under-19s, the Youth Training Scheme and the Technical and Vocational Education Initiative. Secondly, its training schemes for adults include the Community Programme, the New Job Training Scheme and various courses of business training for small firms and the self-employed. Third, M S C makes grants to employers for retraining of existing workers. Each area office has a budget and arranges its expenditure to suit local circumstances. Consequently there is some variation in the training mix offered by the six London M S C areas.

The Metropolitan Police

Functions

The Metropolitan Police, generally known as the Met, has primary responsibility for the maintenance of law and order throughout the Metropolitan Police District, a large doughnut-shaped area, extending beyond Greater London but excluding the City (Map 10). The Metropolitan Police District includes and slightly exceeds the territory of the old G L C. The Met defines its functions as preventative, responsive and reactive. It aims to prevent crime and disorder by street patrolling, gathering intelligence and public relations. It responds with immediate action when a crime is committed, a disorder occurs or an emergency arises. It reacts after crime and disorder to investigate causes and to arrest the offenders.

Most of the functions of the Met are similar to those of the 43 police forces in England and Wales. But unlike other police forces, the Met has special responsibility for the protection of royalty and diplomats, for aspects of national security (Special Branch) and for providing services to and co-ordination between other police forces in England and Wales.

Organisation

The Met is also different from other police forces in Britain since it is not responsible to a local police committee but to the Home Secretary, the sole police authority for the Metropolitan Police district. The Home Secretary's main role in this respect is to control the budget and appoint the Commissioner who is the head of the force. Almost all the main decisions on overall strategy and force policy are made by the Commissioner in association with a policy committee that includes the Commissioner, the Deputy Commissioner, the four Assistant Commissioners, the Receiver and the Deputy Receiver. Each Assistant Commissioner is responsible for a department. The first of these departments deals with personnel and training whilst the second is responsible for all management services including research, information and complaints. The Territorial Operations Department oversees and co-ordinates the work of the police stations, and is also responsible for the mounted police, police dogs, the Thames Division, the territorial support group and traffic wardens. Lastly, a Specialist Department is responsible for royalty and diplomatic protection, Special Branch, the National Identification Bureau, the Forensic Science Laboratory and the specialist crime squads.

The Receiver and the Deputy Receiver are Crown officers appointed to run the Met's finances. The Met employs 27,368 police officers and 13,384 civilian personnel. The figures for total employment by the Met in 1987/88 are shown in the Directory. Thirty-eight per cent of its staff work at headquarters. A reorganisation in 1986 subdivided its territory into eight areas and 75 divisions. At the head of each area is a Deputy Assistant Commissioner and under him at the head of each division a chief superintendent. Thus operational control is in the hands of police officers with its summit in the Met's headquarters at New Scotland Yard.

The Met and the Community

Although the reorganisation into eight areas coincided in time with the abolition of the GLC, there is little evidence of significant links between the two changes. The Police reorganisation did potentially facilitate co-operation and liaison with the boroughs in so far as the Areas now correspond with local government boundaries. Area 8 is the same as a single borough, the City of Westminster, while the others coincide with groups of boroughs. During the last two decades, in London as elsewhere, there has been a growing debate about the relations between the police and local communities. The Met's position has been that community liaison and public relations in general are essential for effective policing though it is essential that operational control should remain in the hands of police officers. Certain local councils, notably the now-defunct G L C and the Labour controlled boroughs, have sought to make the Metropolitan Police accountable to elected local authorities, a demand rejected by successive Commissioners and Home Secretaries. Following the Brixton riots in 1981, the Scarman Report, and the 1985 Tottenham riots, both the Metropolitan Police and several local councils have made efforts to·establish closer cooperation by means of liaison committees. The members of these committees include police representatives, M Ps, M E Ps, representatives of local councils, representatives of community groups and until 1986 representatives of the G L C. In addition to those consultative committees, ten Labour boroughs have non-executive police committees.

Finance

The Receiver negotiates the annual budget with the Home Secretary. Fifty-one per cent of income to finance the budget comes from a specific government grant, while the remaining 49 per cent is financed by rates and block grant. The Receiver simply informs each borough of the police precept, the amount which must be added to the rates and passed on to the Met. The local authorities have no power to dispute or modify the Receiver's decision. The police precept is one of several precepts and levies made upon London's ratepayers by non-elected appointed bodies. At 15.40p in the £ for 1987/88, the police precept is higher than that for 1986/87 (14.20p in £).

In 1987/88, the Met's budget was £1,083 compared with £1,003m in 1986/87. In 1986/87, police pay represented £538m, civilian pay £126m and pensions £112m. Other major categories of expenditure included: supplies £70m, communication £26m, transport £22m.

One of the reasons why the budget of the Metropolitan Police has increased at a time of strict control on other local expenditure is the major national increase in police salaries agreed in 1979 and subsequent indexation of salaries with living cost. In 1985 the average total earnings of a constable were £16,100 and an inspector £22,600. Salaries are only part of the explanation of the rising cost of the Metropolitan Police. Police numbers have also risen – the Met is the only police force in England and Wales which has grown substantially during recent years. Acquisition of expensive new technology including computers and sophisticated riot equipment has also added to costs.

Museum of London

The Museum was established under the Museum of London Acts of 1965 and 1986 to combine under a single roof the two major London collections of the London Museum, founded at Kensington Palace in 1911, and the City Corporation's Guildhall Museum, established in 1826. It has been housed since 1976 in London Wall and employs over 400 staff. The Museum attracts around half a million visitors each year. Only a portion of its extensive collection can be displayed at London Wall. Plans are afoot to open a new Museum in the Docklands, on a site to be determined.

Before abolition of the Greater London Council, the City of London, the Prime Minister and the G L C each appointed six members to the Museum's governing body, and contributed equal shares to its costs. Since abolition, the City and the Government's Office of Arts and Libraries have appointed nine members each to the Board, and they split the net cost, which was just over £4.5m in 1986/87.

In addition, under the Museum of London Act 1986 the Museum receives from English Heritage a block grant for the core costs of the Greater London Archaeological Service. It maintains a computerised sites and monuments record for all of London and a full-time archaeological staff who cover excavations in all except the five boroughs to the east of the River Lea, where the service is provided by the Passmore Edwards Museum. The total English Heritage grant in 1986/87 was £1.3m, the balance of archaeological costs being met from developers' grants.

Total Museum of London expenditure in 1986/87 was £8.3m.

Port of London Authority

The Port of London Authority, established in 1909, exists under the provisions of the Port of London Act 1968. Its Board has ten non-executive members who are appointed by the Secretary of State for Transport, and four executive members. Sir Brian Kellet is Chairman,

and Mr J. N. Black, Chief Executive of the Authority, is Deputy
Chairman of the Board.

The Authority is organised into three Divisions.

1. The Tilbury Division runs the major dock complex at Tilbury, where
   almost all the dock activity of the Port of London has been concentrated since 1981.
2. The River Division, based in offices at Gravesend, Tilbury and
   Richmond, runs navigation and river conservancy on the tidal
   Thames from Teddington to the sea. It operates the Thames Barrier
   on an agency basis for the Thames Water Authority. It also handles
   the marketing of the port as a whole, through the separate London
   Port Promotion Association (L P P A) which has its premises at Tilbury
   Docks.
3. The Property Division deals with all P L A land surplus as a result of
   the closure to shipping since 1981 of all the enclosed docks upstream
   of Tilbury. The greater part of the vast, and potentially remunerative,
   property holdings west of the River Lea has been compulsorily
   acquired by the London Docklands Development Corporation, leaving the P L A with only residual holdings by St Katharine's and in
   Poplar. Of the Royal Docks, to the east of Lea, the Royal Victoria
   Dock has already been vested in L D D C and the Royal Albert Dock
   will follow in due course, with financial compensation currently under
   negotiation. The only land which the Authority will retain in the long
   term is the London City Airport, which has been developed on its
   freehold. The Property Division has become an increasingly important contributor to the financial health of the Authority.

The public has no right of access to the papers or meetings of the P L A.
Its Annual Report and Accounts are available for a fee.

Regional Health Authorities

Four Regional Health Authorities provide health services in the Greater
London area. The North West Thames Region covers the boroughs in
the north-west quadrant of the capital and the non-metropolitan counties immediately outside the Greater London boundary. Three other
regional health authorities cover the North East, South West and South
East quadrants of London plus their neighbouring non-metropolitan
areas. Members of the Regional Health Authorities and the District
Health Authorities into which each region is divided are appointed by the
Secretary of State for Social Services. All health authorities are account-

Table 2.1   NHS Staff and expenditure

	Expenditure (£bn)		Staff
	Current*	Capital	
NE Thames	1.666	0.066	68,832
NW Thames	0.979	0.066	54,829
SE Thames	1.057	0.055	61,626
SW Thames	0.812	0.053	45,635

Source: CIPFA, 1987.

able to the Secretary of State. There is no direct local authority involvement in health authorities, although some local councillors are members of health authorities. There are also some joint health authority – local authority initiatives, such as the 'Care in the Community' programme, whereby local authorities receive extra resources to allow the transfer of social services clients from NHS institutions to local authority facilities. The four Thames health regions employ 231,000 people, though a significant proportion of these work in non-metropolitan county areas outside Greater London. The regions spent about £4.25bn in 1985/86. A breakdown of staff and expenditure is provided in Table 2.1.

Meetings of regional and district health authorities are not open to the public. The operations of health authorities are open to scrutiny by the Parliamentary Ombudsman.

The London Ambulance Service, which operates ambulance services within the Greater London area (see Map 14), is administered by the South West Thames Region on behalf of all the Thames regions.

The Royal Parks

The Royal Parks are the personal possession of the Sovereign although the public may use them freely. Their origins are diverse. Some are the relics of royal hunting preserves and were closely associated with a royal home and served as one of its principal amenities. In some cases the royal home still exists as at St James's and Kensington Palaces. The Secretary of State for the Environment is responsible for the management of the Royal Parks under the Crown Lands Act 1851 and subsequent legislation. Ownership remains with the Sovereign and the Secretary of State has no powers to sell or lease land or buildings without specific legislative authority.

The Royal Parks comprise:

Bushy Park	440 hectares	Hyde Park	139 hectares
The Green Park	21 hectares	Kensington Gardens	116 hectares
Greenwich Park	79 hectares	The Regent's Park	162 hectares
Hampton Court		Richmond Park	955 hectares
Gardens and		St James's Park	35 hectares
Home Park	267 hectares	Primrose Hill	23 hectares

The day-to-day management of the Parks (with the exception of Hampton Court Gardens and Home Park which have their own administrator) is the responsibility of the Bailiff of the Royal Parks, who is appointed by the Secretary of State with the approval of H M The Queen. The Bailiff is also responsible for the maintenance of some other open spaces in London, for example Parliament Square and Brompton Cemetery, and the grounds of some of the other public buildings such as the Tower of London.

The Bailiff of the Royal Parks Office has overall responsibility for policy, management and finance of the Parks. It co-ordinates works, purchases machinery, furniture and equipment, deals with contracts and licences to outside bodies, considers requests for use of the Parks for organised events and ceremonies, and maintains overall financial control. The day–to–day running of each Park is carried out by the individual Park Superintendent. Each has an industrial workforce, and is assisted by one or more assistant superintendents, as well as a small group of administrative staff.

The Royal Parks Constabulary (R P C) is a non-Home Office police force responsible for the policing of the Royal Parks (except Hyde Park which is policed by the Metropolitan Police) and is part of the Department of the Environment. Its Chief Officer is the Superintendent who is responsible through the Bailiff to the Secretary of State for the Environment. The R P C was formed in 1974, following the Parks Regulation (Amendment) Act of that year. Prior to that, the officers were known as park-keepers, although they had all the powers and privileges of a constable.

Seaside and Country Homes

The agency, as its name suggests, is responsible for what were previously the G L C's country and seaside houses, some 3,500 properties in all. Administration of the stock originally passed to the London Residuary Body which sold the service to the North British Housing Association in 1988.

Seaside and Country Homes are now managed by the North British Housing Association. Costs in 1987/88 were about £2m, and these were at that time included in L R B's budget. In future, the ex- G L C homes will continue to be made available to council tenants from Greater London. Nominations for houses will be made via the London Area Mobility Scheme.

South Bank Board

The South Bank Board is landlord for the entire complex of cultural buildings on the South Bank of the River Thames beside Waterloo Station. These include the Royal Festival Hall, the Queen Elizabeth Hall, the Purcell Room, the Hayward Gallery, the National Theatre and the National Film Theatre, together with the open space between the Theatre and County Hall. With the exception of the National Theatre and the National Film Theatre, the Board manages the entire complex and the open space.

The Centre evolved from the building of the Royal Festival Hall by the London County Council on derelict land, construction that was completed in time for the Festival of Britain in 1951. The Queen Elizabeth Hall and Purcell Room date from 1967 with the Hayward Gallery opening the following year.

The South Bank Board is appointed by the Arts Minister. Its responsibilities date from April 1986 when it assumed the role previously taken by the G L C. It employs over 200 staff, and its administration is located in the Royal Festival Hall. Expenditure in 1986/87 was £11.7m of which £8.7m are funded by the Arts Council. Meetings of the Board are not open to the public, though there is public access to papers and reports.

Thames Water Authority

T W A is the regional water authority which covers the Greater London area. Its region embraces all the Thames Valley and parts of Essex, Hertfordshire, Kent, Surrey and Buckinghamshire. At present, T W A along with other water authorities in England and Wales, is a government-appointed body, though the Government has long-term plans to privatise it.

The Authority is one of the largest water undertakings in the world, with overall responsibility for the total water cycle throughout the 5,000 square miles of the Thames river basin. Its services encompass water conservation, water supply, sewerage treatment and disposal, pollution control, flood control, land drainage, fisheries, river navigation, river-based recreation, and wildlife conservation. It regulates the independent water companies (Essex, Lee Valley, Colne Valley, Rickmansworth, Sutton, North Surrey and East Surrey) which continue to supply much of suburban London's water. It also has a growing overseas consultancy business.

At GLC abolition the Authority took from it responsibility for eight of the London piers as well as for the Thames Barrier, the associated tidal and flood defences along the banks of the river and at the mouths of its tributaries, and land drainage for all of London except the catchment areas of the Rivers Cray and Darenth in LBs Bromley and Bexley which fall within the Southern Water Authority for land drainage purposes.

The Authority is divided into three divisions, as shown on Map 20(a). The boundaries between divisions are drawn rather differently for purposes of water supply on the one hand and sewerage and sewage disposal on the other. Most of London falls within the Central Division for both purposes.

The Chairman of the TWA is Roy Watts, and there are 15 other board members. Some element of local involvement is brought about through Consumer Consultative Committees, of which London has two (North and South). CCC members are taken from local authorities, business interests and water companies, and include one Board member.

Total TWA staff in 1986/87 was about 9,000 and overall turnover was £550m. Resources are raised from water rates, and charges from smaller items such as licences for fishing. As with most other appointed bodies, TWA Board meetings are not open to the public, though an annual report is published. The Authority's headquarters are in Reading, Berkshire.

Thamesmead Town

Thamesmead Town is a non-distributing private company limited by guarantee, but without share capital. Thamesmead had been planned by the GLC as a strategic housing development for London. The Council's architects had originally planned that a small town serving the needs of 60,000 people should be built on the 1,700 acres of the Erith marshes, much of the land having been formerly used for several centuries by the Royal Arsenal at Woolwich. Rising costs coupled with policy changes meant that the GLC were forced to revise their plans and as a result, when fully developed, Thamesmead will be a balanced community serving a population of 40,000.

When the Government proposed to abolish the GLC a decision had to be reached about the future of Thamesmead, which lies partly in Greenwich and partly in Bexley. Residents were consulted by means of a referendum held in October 1985 which presented them with three options: to come under the control of (1) Greenwich, or (2) of Greenwich and Bexley, or (3) to transfer to a community-based company. Residents opted for the formation of the company now known as Thamesmead Town. Immediately after GLC abolition in April 1986 Thamesmead passed into the control of the London Residuary Body.

As the transfer from LRB to the new company could not be achieved at once, the LRB appointed the Company as their agents. Thamesmead Town effectively ran Thamesmead from that time until 27 July 1987 when a transfer of business took place. The Board of Thamesmead Town is chaired by Clive Thornton (previously with the Abbey National Building Society) and includes nine members elected by the residents. Total staff is about 350, including administrative and maintenance workers. It is intended to complete the development of the extensive Thamesmead site using funds from the private sector supplemented by some proceeds from asset sales.

The Theatres Trust

The Trust was created by Act of Parliament in 1976 as the result of a private member's bill in the House of Commons. It exists 'for the better protection of theatres for the benefit of the nation', commenting on planning applications affecting theatres throughout the country and making various small grants towards their maintenance, restoration or purchase by local trusts.

In 1986 the GLC decided to transfer to the Theatres Trust the freeholds of the Garrick Theatre, the Lyceum and that part of the Lyric Theatre which it owned. Under the terms of the abolition legislation this required the consent of the Secretary of State for the Environment, which was finally given for the transfer of the Garrick and Lyric only, the question of the Lyceum being left for the London Residuary Body to decide. It is hoped that the Lyceum freehold will eventually be transferred to the Trust, and that after 40 dark years the 2,000-seat theatre will once again become live, perhaps as a home for dance.

Under the terms of the Theatres Trust Act 1976 the 15 Trustees are appointed by the Minister for the Arts. Apart from a small contribution (£11,000) by the Minister to the Trust's running costs, its income is derived from donations and subscriptions, and (as from March 1986) from ground rents from the Garrick and Lyric Theatres.

Traffic Control System Unit

The TCSU, previously located within the GLC, is responsible for managing and maintaining London's 2,660 traffic signals, crucial to effective traffic management in the capital. Its functions include ensuring the smooth running of the computer-regulated Urban Traffic Control (UTC) system covering most of Central and Inner London (and operated on a day-to-day basis by the Metropolitan Police), the installation and modification of traffic signals required for new traffic management schemes, and research and development work to modernise existing traffic control systems within the capital. After considering various alternatives, including both transferring control to a joint borough committee and privatisation, the Department of Transport itself took over responsibility for the Unit upon GLC abolition, to be run by the London Residuary Body under an agency agreement lasting until the end of March 1988.

The TCSU's budget comprised just over £12.0m in 1987/88 and £12.4m in 1988/89, and is funded jointly by the various highway authorities in Greater London, with the DTp providing £2.3m this year (1988/89) for its trunk roads, the London boroughs £7.3m for borough roads, and an additional £2.8m being apportioned between the two. At present the Unit has a total staff complement of 96. In addition, extensive use is made of contractors and consultants.

Each year the TCSU prepares a programme of work in consultation with the LBs, and then seeks final approval from the DTp. However, the choice of schemes and priority awarded to them lies entirely with the Highway Authorities which, for most of London's roads, are the individual boroughs.

The TCSU has maintained its high standards of reliability since abolition, with 98 per cent of traffic signals functioning at any given moment, and the UTC computer available 99.5 per cent of the time. A new fault control system is being introduced, whereby signal malfunctions are reported automatically to the central computer, allowing significant savings in terms of the time and money spent dealing with some 24,000 faults that occur each year. The TCSU also claims that during 1987/88 it had saved 18 per cent on costs over previous years through renegotiating maintenance contracts with the private firms which do the actual work of repairing signal faults.

The Urban Traffic Control computers remain at New Scotland Yard. However, the replacement system is being installed at Kings Buildings and it is planned that the entire system will have been transferred there by 1990.

The Secretary of State for Transport has decided to retain his present traffic control functions and ownership of the traffic control equipment in view of the absence of proposals for satisfactory joint arrangements from all the London local authorities. The Corporation of the City of London agreed to take over the management of TCSU and provide a similar agency service, for a five-year period, from 1 April 1988.

Trust for London

The Trust for London is a funding arrangement for voluntary groups in Greater London set up by the Secretary of State for the Environment by an Order made under section 49 of the Local Government Act 1985. This idea originated during the debate over GLC abolition in response to widespread concern about the effects of a possible shortfall in funding for voluntary organisations following the GLC's disappearance. The Government proposed to create a supplementary resource for the voluntary sector, using the annual income from a £10m endowment earmarked from the proceeds of sales of GLC land assets, in addition to provision by the London Borough Grants Scheme and transitional funding via individual boroughs. The Trust is administered by the Grants Committee of the City Parochial Foundation, which acts as Trustee. It received its initial endowment from the London Residuary Body in March 1987, and is expected in future to distribute about £500,000 to various voluntary groups each year.

Reference

CIPFA (1987). *Health Service Trends, the CIPFA Data Base*. London: Chartered Institute of Public Finance and Accountancy.

CHAPTER 3

London-Wide
Local Government Bodies

Introduction

At the abolition of the GLC a number of local government controlled authorities and committees were created to provide services for the whole of the Greater London area. Express provision was made for several of them in the Local Government Act 1985 which, for the first time in British constitutional history, made extensive use of the idea of indirectly elected joint boards responsible for providing particular services throughout a metropolitan area. By this device the Act sought to reconcile large-area services with a small-area structure of local government. Board membership was to be compulsory for all local authorities within the service area. Being a legal entity in its own right, with its own staff and bank account, the board was supposed to be more effective at getting things done than weaker forms of co-operation such as joint committees. But being made up of nominees from local councils, it is felt to offer local accountability, at least more so than the quangos discussed in the previous chapter.

In the case of London, Parliament created four joint bodies for major GLC functions unsuitable for devolution to the individual boroughs or for transfer to Whitehall. Two other major local London-wide bodies discussed in this chapter continue voluntary efforts which had started prior to the removal of the GLC.

By far the largest of the new local bodies is the London Fire and Civil Defence Authority which runs the London Fire Brigade and the London-wide civil defence effort. With expenditure exceeding £150m per annum, the LFCDA is a major authority by any standards. A second, much smaller new authority was set up to regulate waste within the capital. Like LFCDA, the London Waste Regulation Authority continued to provide what had previously been a GLC service. Both the LWRA and LFCDA have memberships made up of one councillor from every individual borough council, and each authority has its own discrete administration. LFCDA charges a precept on all London ratepayers, while LWRA is financed by a population-based levy on each borough.

Three new statutory London-wide committees were set up by the Government. The London Planning Advisory Committee exists to advise the Government about matters of concern to more than one borough. The London Boroughs Grants Committee has a large budget (£28.5m in 1987/88) to fund voluntary organisations which benefit two or more boroughs. The London Area Mobility Scheme is responsible for household mobility between public sector dwellings, continuing schemes which were previously operated by the GLC and by the boroughs. Like LWRA, LFCDA, LPAC, LBGC and LAMS have memberships made up of one councillor from each borough. Unlike LWRA and LFCDA, the three joint committees rely on 'lead' boroughs to provide day-to-day administration. Both LPAC and LBGC are financed by a population-based levy on each borough. LAMS receives funding from the DOE as well as from a levy on the boroughs. Another, small, London-wide committee was set up after abolition to retain the research function previously undertaken by the GLC's Research and Intelligence division. This Committee controls part of the London Research Centre.

In addition to the five new London-wide authorities/committees, we describe various other London-wide local government bodies some of which existed prior to GLC abolition. The London Boroughs' Children's Regional Planning Committee is a joint committee which advises the boroughs on policy concerning children. The London Research Centre, which was previously the GLC's research and intelligence unit, is now run by a joint committee of the boroughs, at least for part of its work. The London Recycling Forum, the London Rate Equalisation Scheme and SERPLAN are all joint arrangements which existed during the GLC era but have acquired new significance since its abolition.

There are, therefore, a number of London-wide local government bodies, despite the abolition of the GLC. Taken with the metropolitan quangos discussed in Chapter 2, the institutions considered in this chapter made it clear that the removal of an elected London-wide authority in no way abolished the city-wide administration of what are generally considered local authority-type services.

The continued existence of London-wide authorities within local government was something of a defeat for the Government and a minor triumph for the Opposition. During the passage of the Local Government Act 1985 several attempts were made to extend the use of such

London-wide authorities. The London Planning Advisory Committee, the London Waste Regulation Authority and the London Boroughs Grants Committee were each set up in their present form as a result of amendments to the original Bill. Labour, the Alliance and a number of peers in all parties wished to maintain London-wide provision in a number of areas, and were successful in some.

The total power and expenditure for the extra bodies is relatively small. L B G C, the largest, spends less than £30m a year (under 3 per cent of the G L C's budget). Yet for an Opposition facing a Government with a large majority, even the symbolic effect of stronger London-wide successor authorities was something of a success. In short, the pattern of London-wide local government after 1986 represented a compromise between the Conservative Party, which wanted to minimise it, and the opposition (along with many interest groups), which wanted to keep as much of 'Greater London' provision as possible.

The Concessionary Fares Scheme

Under sections 50–53 of the London Regional Transport Act 1984 the boroughs have powers to set up concessionary fare schemes on a collective, London-wide basis for pensioners and the disabled. The G L C previously funded this scheme for pensioners, at a cost of £69.2m in 1985/86, permitting 970,000 pass-holders free travel on the buses and tubes and a half-price concession on British Rail services within Greater London on weekdays at off-peak hours and weekends. The London Regional Transport Act 1984 provides for borough funding of this scheme after G L C abolition by means of either their own voluntary scheme or a statutory 'Reserve Powers' scheme set up by London Regional Transport.

The voluntary scheme, which has been put into effect in each year, involves the boroughs entering into joint arrangements for travel concessions with L R T, British Rail or other operators. It requires their unanimous agreement concerning all conditions and terms, and is subject to an annual review. The boroughs employ a travel concessions officer within the London Advisory Panel on Transport Schemes for the Mobility Handicapped to help manage the scheme and monitor developments. They have so far been able to maintain the same level of benefits as in the G L C scheme, at a cost of £78m in 1986/87 and £87m in 1987/88, apportioned among the boroughs on the basis of population. Those eligible for passes under this London-wide scheme, however, are defined relatively narrowly as pensioners (men 65+, women 60+), the blind, and the 'mobility handicapped' (i.e. with impaired ability to walk); whereas the Transport Act 1985 allows the deaf or dumb, the mentally handicapped, certain other categories of disabled people, and travel companions to be included within similar schemes created by local authorities outside the capital.

The 'Reserve Powers' scheme was added to the Act after pressure from pensioners' bodies and the Opposition in Parliament, who feared that the boroughs might let the scheme lapse altogether. This statutory scheme will be implemented by LRT in the event that the boroughs do fail to reach any agreement, although even in this case they must continue to fund the scheme. In contrast to the current arrangements, however, this fallback option only provides free travel on LRT services from 9.30 a.m., and does not allow for reductions on BR. These conditions may be further altered by the decision of LRT alone. It also remains to be seen whether either scheme can survive once the bus services in London are deregulated, as independent operators may refuse to participate. Already, LRT has allowed the existing level of provision to be eroded by refusing to allow use of the present passes on some of its new 'commercial' bus routes.

Greater London Employers' Secretariat for Local Authority Services

The Secretariat (GLES) is a voluntary joint arrangement of 32 London boroughs, plus the London Fire and Civil Defence Authority, the Inner London Education Authority, the London Residuary Body and a range of voluntary and housing bodies. Boroughs are full members, while other organisations are associate members. The Secretariat exists to provide advice to members on the pay and conditions of their employees.

GLES has two major working committees: the Greater London Whitley Council and the Greater London Joint Council. These councils are responsible for administrative and manual workers respectively, and meet about four times each year. A number of further committees and sub-committees exist for specific purposes.

The Secretariat is financed by a flat-rate levy on each borough (£17,000 in 1987/88) plus a subscription from the associate members which reflects the size of their workforce. Additional income is derived from the Local Government Training Board towards the cost of GLES' training provision. Expenditure by GLES covers training, advice on pay and conditions and a subscription to national negotiating organisations such as the Local Authorities' Conditions of Service Advisory Bureau. GLES is based at Victoria.

Greater London Record Office and History Library

The Record Office and Library are run and funded by the City of London on behalf of London as a whole. They originated in County Hall. The archive holds the records of the GLC, LCC, Middlesex County Council and all their historic predecessors, and the library was formerly the reference collection for members of the Council. Both are major collections in their own right, the archive extending over almost 100,000 linear feet of shelving, and the book collection amounting to as many volumes. Additionally, the Record Office holds unparalleled collections of half a million photographs and prints of London, indexed by street, as well as engineering and architectural drawings of great historic and technical interest.

The library and photographic collections are open for reference by the general public. Research access to the archive is dependent upon the nature, content and date of the material in question.

In 1982 the Greater London Council, in order to relieve the pressure of space on its archive in the basement of County Hall, acquired premises in Northampton Road, EC1. At abolition, this became the principal address of the Head Archivist and the 42 staff, though a significant portion of the holdings remain at County Hall and are presently the subject of negotiation with the London Residuary Body.

The Greater London Record Office and History Library has no management committee or advisory panel but is directly accountable to the Town Clerk of the Corporation of London.

The budget for 1987/88 is £1.76m, and the City Corporation's contribution to the London Rate Equalisation Scheme is reduced to take account of this expenditure. In effect, the cost of the Record Office and History Library is borne by all London boroughs.

London Advisory and Consultative Committee

This Committee is a non-statutory body set up after GLC abolition to provide a London-wide forum to allow exchanges of views between the Government and the London boroughs on policies for highways and traffic management in the capital. It is composed of one representative from each borough, and is chaired by the junior minister responsible for roads and traffic. The Committee has so far met only twice, with little visible impact on Government thinking in this area. In future, however, it may provide a useful channel for boroughs to defend their interests in a more forceful way than through individual representations to the D Tp or lobbying by the ALA or LBA, provided all 33 authorities find areas of common ground and present a united stance. It is proposed to meet annually.

London Advisory Panel on Transport Schemes for the Mobility Handicapped

LAP is a London-wide voluntary body set up by the London Co-ordinating Committee to provide advice to the London boroughs on matters relating to four types of travel schemes for the elderly and disabled in Greater London: the Concessionary Fares Scheme, Taxi-card, Dial-a-Ride and community transport services. The LAP has as yet no executive functions, but provides a means for the major agencies and interests involved in these schemes to exchange information, and to advise and co-ordinate the views of the boroughs on aspects of the schemes such as the level of charges, legal agreements, eligibility criteria and publicity. Membership is composed of 15 officer representatives drawn from the following bodies: the LBA and ALA, the London Directors of Social Services Association, the Department of Transport (as observer only), London Regional Transport, the London Regional Passengers' Committee, and four voluntary organisations (the Greater London Association for Disabled People, Age Concern (Greater London), the London Community Transport Association and the London Dial-a-Ride Users' Association). The National Advisory Unit for Community Transport, which is based at Cranfield Institute of Technology, is also represented. Five working parties have been set up, covering finance, legal arrangements, technical advice, research and ethnic minorities.

Hammersmith and Fulham acts as lead borough, providing for a Chair, Secretary and Administrative Assistant, and the administrative costs incurred by it are reimbursed by payments from the 33 boroughs on the basis of population. These amounted to £20,000 in 1986/87 and £45,000 in 1987/88 (the travel schemes themselves being funded direct-ly by the LBs and/or other agencies). The Secretary also acts as Travel Concessions Officer for Greater London, responding to inquiries from the public at large. Recently, a members' steering group, with three members appointed by the London Boroughs Association and three by the Association of London Authorities, has been set up to oversee the Panel.

London Area Mobility Scheme

The London Area Mobility Scheme is a voluntary joint arrangement set up under section 101 of the 1985 Act. It involves, with varying degrees of participation, all 33 boroughs, and is accountable to them. The purpose of the scheme is to facilitate the movement of applicants for and tenants within London's stock of social housing, both council and housing association owned.

L A M S administers a number of schemes which were previously run by the Greater London Council and by the boroughs, including the Greater London Mobility Scheme and the Inter Borough Nomination Scheme. Its numerically most important scheme is the London Mutual Exchange Bureau which handles between 2,000 and 3,000 lettings and moves across London each year. L A M S provides 900 lettings per year, on a quota basis, to the single homeless and refugees. It can nominate tenants to a significant proportion of the council stock and also has exclusive nomination rights to Seaside and Country Homes. Altogether L A M S places some 5,000 tenants each year.

The lead borough is Camden. Staff establishment is 55, though the actual number of employees is somewhat smaller. The Scheme has its own offices at Waterloo. Its revenue expenditure for 1987/88 was £1.8m and its capital budget (contributory to housing association schemes) £2.5m, the bulk of funding being provided by the Department of the Environment. A small proportion of funding was provided by the boroughs as a flat rate levy, and it is expected that in future the boroughs will provide an increasingly large share. Meetings of the controlling committee are open to the public, while its operations are subject to scrutiny by the local ombudsman.

London Boroughs'
Children's Regional Planning Committee

All 32 London boroughs and the City of London are involved in the Committee, which meets four times a year. The Chair is currently held by Cllr Sandy Marks of Islington. The Committee exists to support the boroughs in fulfilling their child care responsibilities, especially in relation to the planning and efficient use of shared specialist resources.

The Committee is supported by a Principal Advisor, six social workers

and four support staff based in Gray's Inn Road. The Unit peforms three
sorts of work:

1. regional planning of facilities and placements – the Committee
   maintains a directory of local authority residential resources from
   which it advises where children in care can be placed;
2. an inspection service for private children's homes (three boroughs do
   not participate in this aspect of the Committee's work);
3. administration of the Panel of Guardians Ad Litem and Reporting
   Officers. Only 24 of the 33 members participate in this, the remainder forming their own separate Panels of Guardians as shown in Map
   11.

Camden serves as lead borough on the Committee, providing administration and legal services.

  Total expenditure for 1987/88 was some £334,000. This is raised in a
complex fashion:

1. all boroughs pay equal contributions for the regional planning work,
   which accounts for two-thirds of total expenditure;
2. the 30 participating boroughs pay for the inspection service in
   proportion to the number of children placed in homes covered by the
   scheme at 31 March of each year;
3. the 24 participating boroughs pay equal shares towards the cost of the
   Panel of Guardians.

The London Boroughs Grants Scheme

Background

The experience of the London Boroughs Grants Scheme (L B G S) since
G L C abolition has been a rather troubled one, and it is one of the few
London-wide successor bodies in which open confrontation between
political forces in Greater London has emerged. This conflict reflects
the importance which the issue of grant funding for voluntary bodies has
taken on in the capital, and continues earlier controversies surrounding
G L C initiatives in this field under the last Labour administration at
County Hall. Similar controversies have arisen in Greater London Arts,
which also inherited G L C-funded organisations.

  G L C support for the voluntary sector grew enormously during the
period 1981/86. While in 1981/82 revenue grants of £5.4m were
distributed among some 700 groups, by 1985/86 funding had risen to
£82m for over 2,500 organisations in a wide variety of fields. This

Table 3.1   Sources of Post-GLC Replacement Funding
            (1986/87)

Source	£m	%
DOE transitional	12.19	14.6
Arts Council	9.39*	11.2
Sports Council	0.55	0.7
LRT	5.00**	6.0
BFI	0.57	0.7
CRE	0.56	0.7
Other central (Home Office, DHSS, DES)	0.4	—
Total central	28.30	33.9
LBGS	26.36***	31.6
GLC forward funding	1.96	2.3
Borough transitional	4.06	4.9
Borough main programmes	22.81	27.3
Total local	55.20	66.1
Total Replacement Funding	83.50	100.0

*   Excludes £9.25m funding for South Bank and contingencies.
**   Dial-a-Ride scheme funded by central government grant.
***   Excludes £0.64m in administrative costs.
Source: NCVO/LVSC (1987) *After Abolition*, Figs 2 and 3.

increase is mainly attributable to the deliberate policy adopted by the Labour majority in County Hall, but is also part of a general trend in recent years for all levels of government in Britain to rely more heavily upon the voluntary sector, in a context of public sector retrenchment and heightened social stresss. Both the overall level of financial support and the activities of some of the groups funded by the GLC in its final years, however, provoked Conservative criticism and hostility. This was particularly the case where support was given to bodies active in the fields of police monitoring, Third World and Irish Republican causes, or catering to the specific needs of ethnic minorities, women, gays and lesbians, which also drew much unfavourable attention from the media.

One major objective of Conservative supporters of GLC abolition was precisely that of eliminating the resource base of voluntary groups in the capital which they perceived as radical or pernicious. The burgeoning of voluntary organisations in London, however, and increasing public sector dependence on their manpower and skills as policy instruments, have given this sector considerable political importance. During the parliamentary debate over abolition legislation in 1984/85, the voluntary groups organised under the aegis of the National Council for Voluntary Organisations (NCVO) and the London Lobby Group were successful (with the help of a sympathetic House of Lords) in extracting a number of concessions from the Government concerning mechanisms to replace GLC funding after abolition. These had the effect of quadrupling the level of support put forward in the Government's original proposals.

The LBGS is only one of a number of funding sources set up to replace the GLC. The others include so-called *transitional funding* for local projects (in 1986/87 financed 75 per cent by the Department of the Environment, reduced to 50 per cent in 1987/88 and 1988/89 and to 25 per cent in 1989/90 before disappearing, with the London boroughs making up the rest), various centrally appointed quangos (the Arts Council, the Sports Council, the British Film Institute, the Commission for Racial Equality, London Regional Transport), forward funding provided by the GLC itself, and the main spending programmes of the London boroughs. The contribution of these sources to funding voluntary groups previously supported by the GLC in 1986/87 is shown in Table 3.1.

The total amount of revenue funding provided in 1986/87 represents 97 per cent of replacement requirements after taking inflation into account. In all, only 93 bodies out of over 2,500 previously supported by the GLC were denied funding. Many others, however, suffered cuts or long delays in obtaining grants. Funding for capital projects, which received £20m from the GLC in 1985/86, has been greatly reduced, as neither transitional funding nor the LBGS provide for capital grants. There has also been an important indirect impact of abolition on some groups through the withdrawal of GLC training courses and other support services, as well as the potential loss of former GLC-owned accommodation leased at 'peppercorn' rents.

There has been no significant reduction in the number of organisations funded in the period since 1987, while there is one new source of support, however, in the form of the Trust for London (see p. 55).

Membership and organisation

The London Boroughs Grant Scheme was established under the provisions laid out in section 48 of the Local Government Act 1985 following a decision by a majority of 20 of the borough representatives on the London Co-ordinating Committee in August 1985. All 32 boroughs and the Common Council of the City of London are constituent members, with Richmond-upon-Thames acting as the lead borough. The scheme was established for two years (i.e. up to 31 March 1988), with the provision that it could only be revoked thereafter by a majority of the councils. No individual council may opt out of the scheme.

The boroughs each nominate an elected member to the London Boroughs Grants Committee, which takes all policy and expenditure decisions, with the exception of determining the overall budget for the Scheme, as required by section 48 of the Act. This budget must be approved by a two-thirds majority of the councils themselves. The Committee usually meets monthly, and must meet at least twice a year in July, to decide overall policies, and in November to vote a recommendation on the budget. Committee members normally serve for a full year, but can be replaced by their councils with a month's notice. The Committee appoints its own chairman, vice-chairman and deputy chairman, and has a Steering Group (eleven members) to advise on policy matters, an Appointments Sub-committee (five members) on staffing, and an Appeals Sub-committee (five members) to reconsider individual funding decisions. There is also a Personnel Sub-committee (five members). Members are usually briefed before committee meetings by borough grants officers on the needs of their own areas, and attend party caucuses prior to the formal sessions. The political composition of the Committee has shifted over time as a result of borough elections and by-elections. By mid-1988 it had 13 Conservative members, 16 Labour, three SLD, one Independent and an SLD chair.

The role of the lead borough, Richmond, has been to establish and support, on behalf of the other councils, the Grants Unit which actually administers the scheme. Richmond employs all staff in the Unit, and provides it with personnel services, legal and financial advice, internal auditing, computer facilities, accommodation, purchasing of equipment and supplies, and press and public relations work. This arrangement has the advantage of reducing overheads and allowing running costs to be easily identified. Richmond is reimbursed for these costs by the other councils. The lead borough may renounce its role, with twelve months notice to the other members with effect from the end of the financial year in which notice is given, but its withdrawal would have the effect of terminating the scheme.

The Grants Unit is responsible for implementing the scheme and providing advice to the Committee on policy decisions and individual grants applications. When set up the Unit had a complement of 34 staff, including a director, 18 professional staff, and 15 in central administration and clerical work. Its staff has since grown to 42. The work is divided between an administrative division and four service divisions:

(1) housing, (2) social services, (3) employment and training, environment and transport, arts and recreation, and (4) community, ethnic minorities, co-ordinating, advice and administrative projects. The Unit also has a Race Advisor.

For an informed allocation of grant resources the Unit must monitor social needs in Greater London, as set out in section 48(10) of the Local Government Act 1985. In 1986/87, this service was contracted from the London Research Centre through a Social Review Team.

Finance

The Scheme has experienced continuing difficulties, as well as some adverse publicity, in fixing an annual overall budget. The London boroughs fund almost all of this budget through contributions in proportion to their share of Greater London's population. Some additional subsidies are received from the Urban Programme, D H S S joint funding arrangements, and the Regional Health Authorities (together about £0.45m in 1987/88). Problems have arisen from the need to secure consent for a given level of funding from two-thirds of the boroughs, when in practice the polarisation of the political parties on this issue has made consensus impossible. Concerning the budget for 1986/87, the Conservative majority on the Grants Committee rejected the Grant Unit Director's recommendation of £28.24m and advocated the lower figure of £24.64m. This was vetoed by the blocking minority of 12 Labour boroughs. Three more Committee meetings were required before a compromise budget of £27m was finally agreed by the necessary 22 councils at the end of January 1986. The budget included the following items:

Baseline provision	£21.96m
10% contingency reserve	2.20m
10% reserve for new developments	2.20m
Administrative costs of Unit	0.64m
	£27.00m

The delay in setting a budget created considerable uncertainty and difficulties among the voluntary bodies awaiting decisions on their grant allocations, in some cases well into the new financial year. The Grants

Unit made contingency funding available for up to three months, later extended to six, to organisations previously supported by the GLC, in order to prevent redundancies.

Agreement proved even more difficult over the 1987/88 budget, in the aftermath of the May 1986 elections. In effect, the Grants Committee had become a 'hung' council, but one in which even the combination of the votes of Alliance boroughs with either of the two larger parties would be insufficient to secure the passage of the budget. In the face of grant applications totalling £56.8m, the Director of the Grants Unit recommended an expenditure level of £31.5m, allowing for a real increase of £2.5m in grants over 1986/87 and a more realistic assessment of administrative costs. The Labour members argued in favour of raising the budget to £32.2m while the Conservatives put forward a lower alternative of £26.85m. Neither side was willing to accept a compromise (the Alliance proposed £30m), even after seven successive meetings, and by the beginning of March 1987 the deadline approached for many voluntary organisations and LBGC itself to issue redundancy notices. At the eleventh hour, the Secretary of State for the Environment intervened by setting a maximum expenditure ceiling for the Scheme of £28.5m, as he is empowered to do under section 48(5) of the Local Government Act 1985. Both sides in the dispute were thus forced to accept this imposed figure, establishing a precedent for central government control over the level of the Scheme's expenditure.

The 1988/89 budget of £28.5m was approved unanimously in November 1987.

Operation

Differences of political opinion have also emerged within the Grants Committee over the nature of individual projects to be funded by the Scheme. Problems here are less acute than in the case of the overall budget, as both the setting of eligibility criteria and approval of individual grant applications require only a simple majority vote of Committee members, without referral back to the borough councils.

The Local Government Act 1985 allowed considerable latitude to the Grants Committee to define eligibility criteria for funding applications. Section 48(11) only specified that eligible voluntary organisations carry out activities of direct or indirect benefit to more than one borough in Greater London. Other bodies of more local interest should therefore apply to the individual borough councils. More detailed criteria were drawn up by the London Co-ordinating Committee in July 1985 when the LGBS was constituted, on the basis of recommendations from a management consultant firm, Hay-MSL. These criteria allowed applications from voluntary organisations providing: (a) a service for the benefit of Greater London as a whole; (b) services which contribute to a London-wide strategy and priorities recognised by the Scheme; and (c) services of an innovative character of potential benefit to London as a whole. Initially, these criteria were interpreted in practice as requiring projects to cover at least four boroughs in order to become eligible for funding, but after a legal challenge from Greenwich, applications concerning only two or three boroughs are now considered. Even those groups whose activities were limited to a single borough could be eligible, if they contributed to a London-wide strategy or 'pattern of provision' in the following areas: (1) single homelessness; (2) drug and alcohol abuse; (3) women's aid refuges; and (4) community centres for ethnic minorities. Following the change of political balance on the committee after the May 1986 borough elections, legal and advice services were included as a fifth category.

Organisations promoting political causes, campaigning to change the Government's national policies or providing national services were to be excluded from the Scheme. Applications from educational bodies would also be refused, because the Inner London boroughs, as opposed to the Outer boroughs, were not local education authorities. In principle, funding can cover all types of spending, including capital expenditure. In practice, however, the Scheme does not have a capital allocation of its own, nor have the boroughs been willing to transfer any part of their allocations, so that up to now only a small number of one-off capital grants of up to £6,000 have been made available.

In 1986/87, 1,101 groups, 700 of which were previously funded by the GLC, submitted applications requesting a total of £89.9m. By the beginning of December 1986, 795 projects were approved by the Scheme, involving £25.37m expenditure. Of these grants, £24.16m was GLC replacement funding for 639 projects, and £1.21m went to new development by 156 groups. In the end, only 12 London-wide groups previously funded by the GLC were actually denied funding. Decisions to reject 16 other groups were reconsidered by the post-May 1986 Committee, and 3 other bodies (including such controversial organisations as the Gay London Police Monitoring Group and the Lesbian Policing Project) were rescued by the Appeals Panel of LBGS. Conservative members, especially those from Outer London, have been bitterly opposed to many of these grants. There is also a somewhat parochial tendency among the boroughs to insist that their own areas receive a proportionate share from the Scheme. At one point, LB Merton even

Table 3.2   Distribution of LBGS Funding by Division (1986/87)

Division	Funding (£m)		%	No. of groups		%
Community	6.90	R		153	R	
	0.39	ND		60	ND	
	7.29		28.7	213		26.8
Employment & Arts*	7.67	R		214	R	
	0.48	ND		49	ND	
	8.15		32.1	263		33.1
Housing	6.00	R		141	R	
	0.19	ND		21	ND	
	6.19		24.4	162		20.4
Social Services	3.60	R		104	R	
	0.56	ND		26	ND	
	4.16		16.4	130		15.1
	24.16	R		639	R	
	1.21	ND		156	ND	
Total	25.37		100.0	795		100.0

R =   Replacement funding.
ND = New development.
* Includes Arts (183 groups), Employment and Training (53), Sports and Leisure (26), Environment (15) and Transport (9).

Source: National Council for Voluntary Organisations/London Service Council (1986).

threatened to withhold part of its contribution to the LBGS, complaining that groups and priorities in Merton were being ignored by the Scheme.

In 1986/87, major recipients of LBGS funding were the black community (17.7 per cent), the homeless (12.8 per cent), umbrella organisations (10.1 per cent), women (9.8 per cent) and the arts (7.4 per cent). The distribution among the Scheme's four main service divisions is shown in Table 3.2

In order to carry out its work effectively, the Scheme has found it necessary to develop extensive links with other agencies. Discussions between officers from the Grants Unit and civil servants from the DOE and the Home Office are very frequent (weekly), and more occasionally with other ministries such as the DHSS and DES. Other contacts take place with bodies such as the Arts Council, Greater London Arts, LRB and the London Research Centre, involving officers and sometimes Committee members. These links ensure co-ordination of the various funding arrangements for the voluntary sector that now exist in Greater London, avoiding duplication of efforts and pooling resources to support certain projects. The Grants Unit and GLA, for example, set up joint packages to rescue community arts programmes and theatres following abolition. Close liaison also exists between the Grants Unit and relevant borough officials, who provide specialist advice and keep the Scheme informed of local policy priorities and needs.

The Scheme has also set up consultation procedures with the voluntary sector itself, which operate at both officer and member levels. The Voluntary Sector Forum, made up of 16 representatives elected by the bodies eligible for L B G S funding, meets regularly with the Director of the Grants Unit to discuss policy issues, and provides input into the work of the Social Review Team. The Scheme funds a part-time post within the London Voluntary Service Council in order to service the Forum. There are two formal meetings each year between the Forum and the Grants Committee's Steering Group and Forum representatives are invited to attend the Steering Group's own meetings. Individual voluntary organisations are consulted by the four main service divisions of the Grants Unit, and officers participate in two London-wide working parties on drug and alcohol abuse and on single homelessness (serviced by the Grants Unit itself). Finally, both the voluntary bodies and the general public have the right to observe full Committee meetings, and to have access to L B G S papers and accounts.

London Co-ordinating Committee

The London boroughs and the City of London were required by the Local Government Act 1985 to set up a joint committee before 1 September 1985 to make preparation for the abolition of the Greater London Council. The L C C was chaired by Sir Peter Bowness, leader of Croydon Borough Council. Similar committees were set up in the six metropolitan counties.

The L C C was given a number of legal duties which included preparations to transfer G L C services to individual boroughs; consideration of whether functions could with advantage be undertaken jointly, and whether joint committees should be set up for research and for voluntary organisations. L C C was also expected to co-operate with the London Residuary Body and other new authorities such as the London Fire and Civil Defence Authority and to obtain information from the G L C as necessary.

The Committee existed from August 1985 until April 1986 by which time all the necessary transfers from the G L C had been made. Onward transfers of responsibility from the L R B to other institutions are considered in Chapter 2.

The London Fire and Civil Defence Authority

The London Fire and Civil Defence Authority is a statutory joint authority established under section 27 of the Local Government Act 1985, with responsibility for a number of functions including firefighting, fire precaution and regulation, petroleum licensing and civil defence.

Background

The operation of the London Fire Brigade since 1965, when the GLC was set up, was not a subject of political controversy, and it has generally been seen as providing essential services for Londoners in an effective way. Overall policy for these services under the GLC was set by the Public Services and Fire Brigade Committee. The 114 fire stations in London were divided into eleven operational divisions, providing fire cover according to performance standards set by the Home Office. The Greater London area presents particular problems in this respect, with a dense population and large concentrations of flammable materials and hazardous chemicals. Of its territory 55 per cent falls within the two highest risk categories defined by the Home Office (compared to only 15 per cent in the other metropolitan counties). The Fire Brigade has been faced with an increasing demand for its services, rising from 55,516 calls answered in 1966 to 119,536 in 1984. Many of these calls involved 'special services' – life-saving or rescue operations which are unrelated to fire. From 1984, the Brigade took over salvage work, following the disbandment of the London Salvage Corps, previously funded by the insurance companies. The Brigade also carries out important fire prevention work by enforcing fire regulations in offices, factories and hotels and providing specialist advice concerning other buildings requiring registration or licensing, which entailed inspections of 23,000 plans and almost 100,000 sites in 1983/84, as well as mounting publicity campaigns on prevention measures aimed at the general public.

During the last Labour administration, the GLC made an effort to increase the resources at the disposal of the Fire Brigade. Earlier cuts in manpower were reversed, with the addition of seven fire appliances and 168 uniformed firefighters. At the end of 1984/85, the Fire Brigade employed 6,972 firefighters, supported by about 1,100 white-collar staff. An ambitious building programme begun in 1984 provided for starts on two new fire stations, as well as modernising one of the older stations each year. Other major schemes included a project for centralised mobilisation of rescue operations by computer costing over £7.5m, and a

£15m refurbishment of the Fire Training School in Southwark. These projects were not completely realised due to central government constraints on capital spending, which fell from £11m in 1983/84 to £4.5m budgeted in 1985/86. Estimated gross revenue expenditure on the fire service in 1985/86 was £147m.

The Fire Brigade relied heavily on expertise and services from other GLC departments, which provided almost 150 staff included within the Council's Fire Programme. The Scientific Services Branch in the Director-General's Department was of particular importance, as its Operational Fire and Safety Group offered a 24-hour support and advice service to the Fire Brigade on incidents involving chemicals and hazardous substances. GLC scientists also intervened in fire investigations to determine the causes of incidents. Other forms of assistance by the Branch to the Brigade included a computerised databank on hazardous chemicals, CIRUS; a central risks register on premises in Greater London known to contain special hazards; the Hazchem Code which is used to label equipment and premises and provides immediate guidance on emergency measures in case of fires and spillages; and testing Brigade equipment and fire prevention devices such as smoke detectors. The Brigade also made heavy use of the GLC's Central Computer Service (e.g. in its centralised mobilisation project), Supplies Department (purchase of uniforms and equipment), Technical Services (construction and refurbishment of fire stations), as well as the Council's financial, legal and personnel services. At the same time, the Brigade assisted other departments in their work, such as Architecture and Civic Design (enforcement of building controls and licensing requirements) and Housing (advice on access routes and fire safety in housing estates).

Civil defence under the GLC proved to be more controversial, following the GLC's declaration of a 'nuclear free zone' for Greater London in March 1982, and the reluctance of the Labour administration to comply with Home Office regulations defining its statutory duties in this field. The GLC did set up a Greater London War Risk Study (GLAWARS) and provided emergency planning for natural disasters and major industrial accidents. Emergency planning and nuclear policy work entailed revenue spending of £1.2m in 1985/86 (offset by a 75 per cent grant from the Home Office for civil defence), and employed 31 staff.

Membership and organisation

Following the passing of the Local Government Act 1985, the new London Fire and Civil Defence Authority was set up on an interim basis in the Autumn of 1985, and assumed the GLC's powers on 1 April 1986.

The Authority is composed of 33 members, appointed by the London boroughs and the City of London. In contrast to previous examples of joint boards in British local government, the 1985 Act contains measures designed to increase the accountability of members of the LFCDA and other joint authorities to their constituent local councils. Members of the LFCDA must be elected local councillors, and according to section 31 of the Act their appointments can be revoked at any time by the borough councils, with one month's notice to the Authority. Section 41 specifies that the borough councils are to make arrangements to enable councillors to question LFCDA members on the discharge of their functions on the borough's behalf. Critics of the new Authority, however, claim that members are too numerous to be effective, and that the principle of indirect election and accountability is both cumbersome and undemocratic. The Act does lay down that appointments should reflect the balance of parties within each borough (section 33), but as there is just one member per borough, they in fact represent only the largest party group in each council. The political composition of the LFCDA has shifted with changes in the ruling parties in the London boroughs following the May 1986 borough elections:

Pre-May 1986:   18 Conservative   13 Labour   1 Alliance   1 Independent

Post-May 1986:   14 Conservative   15 Labour   3 Alliance   1 Independent

While section 34 of the Act calls for election by the Authority of a chairman and vice-chairman, in practice the LFCDA operates in a similar fashion to other local authorities, with power in the hands of a Leader supported by a majority party group or coalition. Since LFCDA was established, both the Chairman (P. Jones, LB Bromley) and successive Leaders (1986/87: R. Neill, LB Havering; 1987/88: C. Tandy, LB Bexley) have all been Conservatives, with the support of Liberal members after May 1986.

Meetings of the LFCDA are held at six-week intervals. Much of the Authority's business is carried out in four committees: Policy and Resources (chaired by the Leader, with a Scrutiny Sub-committee and Civil Defence Sub-committee); Urgency (dealing with matters requiring decisions between full meetings); Personnel (with panels for senior staff appointments and grievances); and Disciplinary Appeals. Changes in this committee structure and other details of management require consent or may even be prescribed by the Home Secretary during the initial three-year period following abolition, under powers granted in section 85 of the 1985 Act. The work of the Authority is carried out by three main departments: Clerical and Finance, the Fire Brigade (headed by a Chief Fire Officer), and Civil Defence. Manpower levels must also be approved by the Home Office. At present the Authority employs 8,359 staff, with 1,200 in central administration and 7,159 in fieldwork, including 6,665 uniformed officers. The latter figure implies a reduction of almost 400 since abolition, but is less than original estimates produced by the GLC (up to 1,400). Civil defence work, on the other hand, has been bolstered by additional staff over former GLC levels, bringing the total to 41.

The Fire Brigade has been redeployed within five new areas coinciding with borough boundaries, rather than the previous 11 divisions under the GLC (Map 14). This arrangement has apparently stimulated the parochial interests of Authority members in the level of fire service provision in their own local areas. The idea of Area Sub-committees of members to oversee the Brigade's operations has so far been rejected. The Home Secretary does, however, retain reserve powers under section 42 of the 1985 Act to allow either individual boroughs or groupings to form separate fire authorities, breaking up the existing LFCDA.

The Authority is dependent on outside bodies such as the Central Computer Service and London Scientific Services for many of the support services which the GLC previously offered. The LFCDA has so far resisted the obvious solution of taking responsibility itself for these services, which are vital to the Fire Brigade. The ILEA acts as a purchasing agent and has provided medical back-up. Other services, such as legal counsel and printing, are now contracted from the private sector.

Finance

The LFCDA's gross revenue budget totalled £166.7m in 1986/87 (an increase of 5.1 per cent in real terms over GLC spending on the fire service and civil defence during the previous year) and £182.3m in 1987/88. About 80 per cent of spending is devoted to salaries and pensions (see Table 3.3). Net expenditure in 1986/87 was well in excess of the DOE's own comparable assessment of expenditure needs. The Authority's current income is derived mainly from precepts on local rates, which it is empowered to issue within Greater London by the Local Government Act 1985. Under section 68(6), however, during an initial three-year period these powers have been made subject to the Rates Act 1984 which allows the Secretary of State for the Environment to set maximum limits on precept levels ('ratecapping'). The Authority was thus forced to apply precepts of 7.7p in 1986/87 and 8.07p in

Table 3.3 LFCDA Gross Expenditure and Income (estimate) (1986/87 and 1987/88)

	1986/87 (£m)	1987/88 (£m)
Gross expenditure		
Fire staff	91.3	97.7
Other staff	18.8	19.4
Pensions	23.5	29.7
Running expenses	23.2	26.7
Debt charges	2.6	1.6
Pay/price increases	5.3	5.2
Contingencies	2.0	2.0
	166.7	182.3
Income		
Civil Defence Grant	1.0	1.3
Pensions contributions	9.0	9.7
Other	4.3	4.3
	14.3	15.3
Net expenditure	152.4	167.0
To be met by precept	152.4	163.0
Use of balances	—	4.0
Grant Related Expenditure (GRE)	(125.1)	135.9

Source: LFCDA

1987/88. These precepts are levied on all London ratepayers, which means that the LFCDA is financed in proportion to authorities' total rateable values. Because of the wide gap between planned expenditure and the Government's assessment of its need to spend – known as grant-related expenditure (GRE) – the LFCDA has failed to receive any block grant in either year. It has been given specific grants for civil defence, and obtains income from pensions contributions, petroleum licences and other minor sources.

Capital expenditure by the LFCDA is also limited by central government controls. The Secretary of State prescribed a capital allocation of only £4m in 1986/87, which was raised the following year to £7.9m. Continuing contractual commitments of £3.2m were inherited from the GLC for the Central Mobilisation Project and new and refurbished fire stations at Ilford and Tooting. Additional spending of £1.3m was planned in 1986/87 for new starts on fire stations at Barnet and Islington and for equipping the new Area Command structures, the excess over the allocation being absorbed by slippage and anticipated spending on the next year's budget. In 1987/88, £2.8m was to be spent on previous commitments, and £5.1m on new starts. Acquisition of new fire appliances and vehicles is financed by leasing, and has thus escaped capital spending restrictions.

Operation

The nature of the fire service and civil defence in Greater London has meant that it is crucial for the LFCDA to maintain continuing relationships with a number of outside bodies. The Authority is answerable to the Home Office for the level of fire cover and service provided by the Fire Brigade, and standards are enforced by the Fire Service Inspectorate. Plans regarding manpower limits and internal organisation must be discussed and approved by Home Office civil servants. Civil defence is also subject to extensive Home Office regulations, and entail frequent joint exercises with other bodies. Other matters, such as funding and expenditure limits, involve the DOE. Links with the ministries involve both informal contacts and formal meetings between the LFCDA board and ministers or civil servants.

Members and officers have also needed to co-operate with agencies within Greater London such as the Metropolitan Police (emergency operations), the LRB (computer and scientific services), the LRWA (storage and disposal of hazardous wastes), the Thames Water Authority (flood control), and the London boroughs (emergency planning). Enforcement of fire regulations on buildings, provision of advice on fire prevention, and publicity campaigns on safety in Greater London bring the LFCDA into contact with private bodies and the general public. Subject to some restrictions in the Local Government Act 1985 the general public in turn enjoys rights of access to the Authority's meetings and documents. Its activities come under the scrutiny of the Local Government Ombudsman.

London Planning Advisory Committee

Background

The word 'Planning' in LPAC's title refers narrowly to statutory responsibilities of local and central governments under the Town and Country Planning Acts to establish policies for, and administer control over, property development and land use. Planning in this sense is necessarily a 'strategic' or London-wide concern. The effects of any major development project, whether by public or private sector, will ripple through

London regardless of borough boundaries, and consistency and con‑ tinuity are needed in the handling even of small developments. So the day-to-day operation of Town and Country Planning Acts in London, as in any great metropolitan area, requires some form of planning authority to take a view of the area as a whole, and frame land use policies within it.

Since the abolition of the GLC, which was created primarily to fulfil this role, the strategic planning of London has been a matter for central government. In its original form, the 1985 Local Government Bill not only transferred the administration of London-wide planning from County Hall to Whitehall but left local elected representatives with no formal voice whatsoever in the making of policy beyond their own borough boundaries. General policy became an exclusive preserve of the minister, who was to be advised by an ad hoc commission of his own choosing.

The loss of a London-wide strategic planning authority proved to be one of the most controversial and hotly contested aspects of GLC abolition. The government was chiefly concerned to prevent the emerg‑ ence of any body which might assume the role of a successor authority to the GLC. The only concession that could be won, in a House of Lords amendment, was the substitution of LPAC, a statutory joint committee of London boroughs, in the consultative role in place of the proposed Commission. The inter-borough advisory committee consequently has a statutory right to existence. Each of the 33 local authorities contributes a member. Havering plays the role of 'lead borough', providing premises and administrative overheads.

Membership and organisation

Like all the new joint committees which play such an important role in London government today, LPAC has had a sensitive political balance since the local elections of May 1986, which produced 15 Labour members, 14 Conservative, 3 Alliance (the latter including Hillingdon, a hung borough) and 1 Independent. The Committee, which meets four times a year is chaired by an Alliance member representing Richmond – Sally Hamwee. Because the more important decisions, those involving money, require a two-thirds majority, both Labour and Conservative groups can exercise a potential veto.

Counterbalancing its highly politicised deliberations, the Advisory Committee is advised in turn by a panel made up of chief officers from the London boroughs. The panel, nominated by the various professional communities – contains six borough planners, three engineers or sur‑ veyors, two chief executives and one finance officer. The Committee has an establishment of 25, now headed by the Chief Planning Officer, John Popper, formerly Deputy Planning Officer with Islington.

Finance

L P A C is funded by all London local authorities, contributing on a per capita basis. The Committee cost £520,000 to operate in 1986/87 and had a budget of £589,000 in 1987/88 and £1m in 1988/89. Staff account for 50 per cent of its costs, rent, rates and overheads for 30 per cent, and the remaining 20 per cent of the L P A C's income is channelled straight through as London's contribution to S E R P L A N, the standing conference of South East local authorities on planning matters (see pp. 86–87).

Operation

L P A C has three principal agenda areas. Its main task and statutory *raison d'être* is to make representations to the Secretary of State on behalf of the London boroughs over the so-called Strategic Guidance, which is intended, under the 1985 Local Government Act, as a central government substitute for the Greater London Development Plan, providing a framework of general policy within which the boroughs can prepare Unitary Development Plans for their areas. Eventually, London should be covered by a patchwork quilt of such plans, each incorporating Strategic Guidance in an opening section.

There are no precedents for statutory policy guidance of this sort. Its scope and content are controversial since they will in effect define the policy boundaries for borough planning authorities. Some Labour boroughs are concerned to make use of planning powers to pursue redistributive social policies, and believe these should be incorporated into the Strategic Guidance just as the late G L C proposed to incorporate them as alterations to the Greater London Development Plan. Southwark, in a paper to L P A C, argued that guidance should be given on more than eighty topics, many relating to specific minorities. The general position of the present Government is that planning intervention should confine itself to a short list of policies for land use, based upon the physical and aesthetic aspects of development.

The outcome is an agreement with the D O E that L P A C will produce a first draft London Planning Advice, addressing nine issues. On *Housing*, the task is to decide what each borough's share should be of the 150,000 houses allocated to the London area, by agreement between the minister and S E R P L A N, over the coming decade. The other topics to be covered are *Open Space and the Green Environment, The Economy and Employment, The Physical Environment, Tourism, Shopping, Traffic and Transportation,*

Skylines and High Buildings, and *The Urban Structure*. The draft is due to be forwarded to the Secretary of State before the end of 1988 so that boroughs can set to work on their Unitary Development Plans the following year.

L P A C's second role is to advise from the point of view of London as a whole, on major development proposals before local planning committees. L P A C has set out criteria to distinguish major from minor developments, and has a voluntary system for the referral of developments above the threshold. Some authorities, such as the City of London, refuse to refer any applications to L P A C. The City of Westminister declines to participate in a formal consultation procedure but is prepared to *notify* L P A C of major applications. Docklands developments, despite their importance, are not referred to L P A C by the London Docklands Development Corporation though the Docklands boroughs may do so, and the L D D C has considered L P A C comments on some cases. The system has obvious weaknesses. Nevertheless, the majority of London boroughs do work within L P A C's guidelines, and the Committee passes comment on between five and ten major developments at each of its meetings.

Miscellaneous other matters come before L P A C. It has arranged an officer-level Thameside Working Party to ensure co-ordination between the riparian boroughs, the Thames Water Authority, the Port of London Authority and the London Docklands Development Corporation over waterfront development. It has contributed responses or put points of view on various legal or policy matters, for example submitting evidence on important development proposals such as new mega-stores in the home counties, or commenting on the report of the Nuffield Commission inquiry into the planning system (Nuffield Foundation, 1986). Paradoxically it seems to be easier for L P A C to frame a view on proposals outside London. On London planning issues members tend to split on geographical and party lines and the only basis of agreement may be to ask the Secretary of State to call in contentious applications (such as Canary Wharf) and subject them to a public inquiry.

Commentary

L P A C exemplifies quite clearly the general unsuitability of joint voluntary committees for policy-making or even policy advice. It can move only at the speed of its slowest member. It has been handicapped by the indifference both of authorities such as the City which regard strategy as an irrelevance, and by some Labour boroughs deeply committed to strategic intervention and hostile to co-option into a merely advisory role to government.

Besides, L P A C is only one among several actors in the planning field. Matters relating to historic buildings and conservation are the preserve of the London Advisory Committee of the Historic Buildings and Monuments Commission. The Department of Transport has its own Greater London Advisory and Consultative Committee, meeting about once a year on an ad hoc basis. The Department's increasingly strong presence in the capital through trunk road schemes, urban traffic control and traffic management may also lead in time to a further new voluntary joint committee of the London boroughs. The G L C's former research and intelligence unit, now the London Research Centre (L R C), though arguably an essential element of any strategic planning function, is also quite separate from L P A C, which has to buy in from L R C on a commercial basis much of the strategic information it needs.

Lastly, L P A C has undoubtedly been impeded by its location in the outer eastern suburb of Romford, an hour's travel time from central London and outside the 01-telephone area. Romford and Richmond (which provides the chair) are separated by 38 stops on the Underground. Allocating strategic planning to Havering as lead borough was the most effective way imaginable of downgrading its importance. Initial attempts to move the unit into Central London were blocked by Havering, which regards its lead borough role as a firm commitment until 1991 at least and has leased office accommodation and appointed staff on this basis. L P A C's peripheral location is a matter of some inconvenience for its officers, who necessarily liaise with the Departments of Environment and Transport, the L B A, A L A, S E R P L A N, L R C, and other centrally located agencies. It also has the effect of minimising the development of members' contacts with officers between meetings, which might strengthen its tenuous corporate identity and sense of purpose.

London Rate Equalisation Scheme

The London Rate Equalisation Scheme (L R E S) is essentially two mechanisms for redistributing part of the very large rateable resources of Central London to the rest of the capital. The operation of the Scheme is described in Chapter 7.

In addition to the use of L R E S to redistribute resources, it has been used since the abolition of the Greater London Council to finance a small number of bodies and institutions. As with the general operation of the Scheme, any funding of institutions must be approved by the Secretary of State.

Two boroughs, the City of London and the City of Westminster, received the Secretary of State's agreement to finance organisations via LRES. The City of London finances (at least part of) its contribution towards the Museum of London and the Greater London Record Office in this way, while Westminster contributes towards the London Festival Ballet and the English National Opera through LRES. The four contributions totalled just under £5m in 1986/87 and in 1987/88.

The method of funding these special arrangements is relatively simple. At the time when the finances of the GLC were being sorted out prior to the abolition of the authority, calculations had to be made about the operation of the block grant system and about LRES. In coming to a final decision about this financial reorganisation, which was intended to leave London and the rest of the country in the same position they would have been in if the GLC had not been abolished, the Government added on to the assumed expenditure of the Cities of London and Westminister the amounts which would be given to fund organisations via LRES.

By adding the contributions to the English National Opera and the other institutions to spending in this way, the block grant and LRES then operated together in such a way as to spread the cost of the contributions over the whole of London. In effect, the payments by the two Cities into the new LRES were slightly smaller than they otherwise would have had to be, while the receipts of the receiving authorities were correspondingly smaller than they might have been. In this way, the cost of the four contributions was spread over the whole of London.

Because contributions to and receipts from the new LRES were fixed in 1986/87 at a level which would remain the same in cash in the future, the arrangements for funding institutions through LRES were not altered in 1987/88 or 1988/89. The reform of local government finance in England and Wales in 1990 will remove the need for LRES.

London Recycling Forum

The Forum began in 1983 under the GLC as an informal gathering of local elected members and officers from most London boroughs to discuss current issues and ideas in the field of waste reclamation and recycling. It has since become open to attendance from environmental groups, voluntary organisations, representatives of the reclamation industry and visitors from local authorities outside London. There are usually four to five meetings each year, which are both hosted and

provided with secretarial services by the London Waste Regulation
Authority.

London Research Centre

The London Research Centre is comprised of two parts: the London
Research Programme and the London Supplementary Research Programme, with each programme being controlled by a separate committee. The Research Programme is controlled by the London Research
Committee, which is made up of one member from each borough and is
set up under section 88 of the 1985 Act. The Supplementary Research
Programme is controlled by the London Supplementary Research
Committee, which is made up of one member from each of the 17 participating boroughs and is set up under section 101 of the Local Government Act 1972.

The Research Programme runs the Research Library, population and
statistics and road safety research. The Supplementary Research Programme researches planning, transport, housing, economic activities
and other social and community services. Taken together, the two
programmes replicate parts of the work previously undertaken by the
GLC Research and Intelligence Department.

The lead borough for both parts of the Centre is Islington. In total 138
staff are employed, with about half in the Research Programme and half
in the Supplementary Research Programme. The Research Programme
spent £1.7m in 1987/88 and the Supplementary Research Programme
£1.2m, with funding being provided by the relevant boroughs within each
joint committee. At present, LRC is based at County Hall though it will
move to Kennington in late 1988. Both programmes undertake work for
which charges are made. Meetings of the controlling committees are
open to the public.

London Tourist Board

The London Tourist Board and Convention Bureau is a voluntary body,
controlled by a committee appointed by the London Boroughs Grants
Committee, the English Tourist Board, the British Tourist Authority,
and other members. It exists to promote London as a centre for tourism
and conferences. Its offices are located at Victoria.

LTB employs 70–80 staff (varying with the season), and spent £1.6m in
1986/87, of which £360,000 was on ex- GLC functions. Income is raised
from a subvention from the English Tourist Board, from the LBGS, from

membership fees and from earned income. The public do not have rights of access to meetings, though an annual report is published.

The London Waste Regulation Authority

The London Waste Regulation Authority (LWRA) is statutorily responsible for the regulation and control of the waste generated by both the public and private sectors of London. In addition it licenses the activities of and provides a co-ordination forum for the sixteen Waste Disposal Authorities (WDAs) who are now responsible for the actual disposal of the capital's waste, as explained in Chapter 4.

Background

Until its abolition the GLC was statutorily responsible for disposing of household and commercial waste, licensing all waste disposal operations and preparing a waste plan as required by the Control of Pollution Act 1974. During the debate about abolition it was clear that this unitary structure was unlikely to survive abolition of the GLC. Waste disposal was one of the services which the Government believed could be best performed by the boroughs. However the size and complexity of London's waste disposal function meant that a simple devolution of responsibility to the boroughs turned out to be neither politically nor practically possible.

The Government chose to establish a three-tier system for waste management. *Collection* is handled by the individual boroughs. *Disposal* is run through sixteen Waste Disposal Authorities. *Regulation and monitoring* is the statutory responsibility of the LWRA.

To make matters even more complicated the WDAs, as shown in Map 15, fall into two distinct categories. The twelve boroughs which co-operated with the Secretary of State before abolition of the GLC have been categorised as WDAs in their own right and are wholly responsible for the waste disposal operation within their borough boundaries. These borough WDAs have come together voluntarily into three groups in order to run certain major facilities taken over from the GLC. (Bexley has chosen to make a separate arrangement with Kent County Council.)

The remaining boroughs were compulsorily combined by the Secretary of State for the Environment into four statutory WDAs, legally on a par with the individual boroughs in the 'voluntary' category. These variations in organisation are compounded by differing attitudes towards co-operation and charging on the part of the various disposal authorities, some of whom happened to do better than others out of the carve-up of

GLC assets. The role of the regulatory authority is not an enviable one.

Membership and organisation

The 33 members of the LWRA are not elected directly but are appointed by the member authorities. The political composition of the Authority in 1988/89 is Conservative 14, Labour 15, Alliance 3 and Independent 1. The Conservatives take the Chair in 1988/89.

Meetings of the full Authority take place three times per year and are open to the public. Executive committee meetings take place approximately every six weeks and the public are also admitted to these.

Finance

Under the provisions of the 1985 Local Government Act, the LWRA raises revenues by a precept on the 33 London boroughs. Its budget for 1986/87 was £2,897,000 which rose to £3,130,000 for 1987/88. In part this increase is to pay for increased LRB charges, and to pay for LWRA's rental of County Hall offices and attendant services (security, cleaning, etc). Apart from the provision of services charge, there is a continuing debate within the Authority as to the appropriate scope of activities which it should undertake and its consequent staffing and financial requirements.

Operation

The LWRA currently employs 79 staff. They have also called on the services of the London Scientific Services but this assistance has been limited to a specific budget allocated annually. For financial, legal and personnel services, the LWRA draws on the London Fire and Civil Defence Authority. The organisation is hard-stretched. At the moment there are in the Greater London area more than 1,000 *known* producers of special waste, defined as containing substances from a specific list of chemical compounds at a concentration which could cause death or serious damage to human body tissue or with a flashpoint of 21°C or below. Because of under-staffing, not more than 50 per cent of these can be visited annually. In addition there are 200 licensed waste disposal sites which must be visited monthly as well as the need to monitor constantly the activities of around 300,000 non-household waste producers.

However, it is the practice of illegal dumping of waste, or flytipping, which is coming to dominate the concerns of LWRA and is exerting a particular strain on their resources. The Authority estimate that there are up to 1,000,000 tonnes of flytipped waste dumped in the London area. A 'hotline' for the public to report incidents has been established

(01-928 9988) but there is still the need for LWRA staff to deal with prosecutions.

The demands of regulatory work have obliged LWRA to limit its work in the fields of prevention and long-term planning. For example, waste recycling was a high profile activity of the former Pollution Control Division of the GLC but is now a borough matter. The boroughs' commitment to waste recycling is proving to be patchy. The LWRA are taking steps to encourage greater recycling by individual waste producers and the Authority acts as host to the London Recycling Forum, where as described below members and officers of the London boroughs can meet with environmental groups and representatives of the waste re-clamation and recycling industry.

Perhaps the greatest challenge facing the Authority over the longer term is the co-ordination of waste disposal. At the moment most of the capital's 15 million tonnes of waste is disposed of in landfill sites outside the London area. However, the number of available sites within a reasonable distance of London will decrease significantly in the next ten years. Because of the high cost of transporting waste over long distances, alternative disposal methods will have to be found. The LWRA would like to move towards a planned solution to the disposal of London's waste. Its aim is to co-operate with boroughs in the preparation of waste disposal plans, making use of a major computerised database maintained by the Authority, the Solid Waste Information System (SWIS).

SERPLAN (London and South East Regional Planning Conference)

SERPLAN is a voluntary body founded in 1962. It consists of 64 elected members of local authorities in the South East, on the following basis:

1. up to three members nominated by each of the 12 county councils;
2. up to sixteen members nominated jointly by the 32 London borough councils through the London Planning Advisory Committee;
3. twelve members representing the 98 district councils of the Conference area, one for each county area.

The Conference is not an executive body but an advisory organisation which monitors and comments on major transport and planning issues affecting the region and co-ordinates joint policies on matters of common interest, such as (for example) the problem of waste disposal, the impact of regional shopping centres, the maintenance of open land in the

Green Belt, the implications of the Channel Tunnel, or the allocation of building land for housing.

The Conference Chairman has traditionally been appointed from outside the membership so that he or she is not associated with a particular authority. The chair is currently held by The Revd Lord Sandford. There are full meetings of Conference at least twice a year. A Members Policy Group (21 members) and an Officers Advisory Panel look into policy issues, assisted by working groups and steering groups of local authority officers or the secondment of individual specialists. A small Secretariat of 15 full-time staff, based at SERPLAN's office in Central London, clerks the Conference, the Members' Policy Groups and officer groups and prepares reports. It may also do detailed work on policy issues.

Reports to Conference are publicly available and where appropriate are published with press notices. Conference meetings are not open to the public or press.

SERPLAN has an income in the order of £500,000, contributed by the county councils and the London boroughs on a population basis.

Taxicard Scheme

In March 1986, the London boroughs agreed to organise joint funding of the GLC's Taxicard scheme for the disabled, after the Government refused to step in to save it following the Council's demise. This scheme, begun in 1983 in Southwark and now London-wide in scope, allows cardholding members (only the blind or mobility handicapped are eligible) using one of 4,500 licensed radio-taxis to pay a flat fare of £1 for fares of up to £7 (increased from £6 in 1987/88). The boroughs subsidise the difference, at a total cost of £4.6m in 1986/87, each authority paying a share of the costs based on the number of members in their area. The scheme at present is administered by LRT, and monitored by the Travel Concessions Officer employed by the boroughs within the London Advisory Panel on Transport Schemes for the Mobility Handicapped. Proposals to change the scheme require unanimous approval among the boroughs. Several Tory boroughs were initially reluctant to join, and Hillingdon only agreed after the Conservatives lost control of its council in the borough elections of May 1986. Membership in the scheme since it was taken over has risen drastically, from 26,300 renewing their cards in April 1986 to about 50,000 at present, with an average subsidy of £127 per year for each cardholder. Because of the cost implications, there has been some resistance to making any improvements, with Bromley blocking a move to allow new cab companies to participate, and Barnet dropping out altogether in 1987/88, in favour of its own local scheme using minicabs. Following a review of the scheme, however, the remaining boroughs are due to agree on new conditions for a six-year period beginning in April 1988.

References

Greater London Council (1984). *The Greater London Development Plan As Proposed to be Altered by the Greater London Council*. London: Greater London Council.

L V S C / N C V O (1987). *After Abolition*. London: The London Voluntary Service Council and National Council for Voluntary Organisations.

Nuffield Foundation (1986), *Report to the Nuffield Foundation*. London: The Nuffield Foundation.

CHAPTER 4

Local Government Bodies for Parts of London

Introduction

G L C abolition had the effect of increasing the number of part-London local authorities. The Inner London Education Authority was the biggest example of a new authority established by law, but not the only one. Four new waste disposal authorities were also created for parts of the capital. I L E A had, of course, existed prior to 1986, but as a sub-committee of the G L C. Once the G L C had been abolished, a new arrangement was needed. For the first time the Authority was an individually constituted council in its own right after 1986, with directly elected members. I L E A provides education in the twelve inner boroughs and the City. The four statutory waste disposal authorities were set up after abolition to provide waste disposal arrangements in groups of boroughs where the Government was not satisfied that any other arrangements would be appropriate.

I L E A and the waste disposal authorities were new, statutory, authorities. But one of the most remarkable features of G L C abolition was the spawning of a dozen or more new voluntary joint committees, each of which consisted of a patchwork of boroughs.

Three voluntary waste disposal committees were set up by boroughs to organise waste disposal within their areas. These groupings received the Government's approval to create such voluntary committees. Boroughs which did not set up approved voluntary arrangements of this kind were placed by the Government in one of the statutory waste disposal authorities mentioned above.

In addition to these voluntary arrangements for waste disposal (which largely involved Conservative controlled boroughs), a range of single-interest voluntary committees was formed by boroughs (largely under Labour and Alliance control). Some of the new committees comprise no more than seven boroughs (e.g. the Technical Services Joint Committee)

89

while one involves all 33 boroughs (the London Research Centre).

Whether or not an individual household enjoys the benefits of services provided by one or all of the voluntary joint arrangements is little more than an accident of where it is situated. Individuals living in a borough like Camden would be in a position where their authority could take advantage of several voluntary organisations. On the other hand, in neighbouring Barnet, there would be membership of only the London Boroughs' Joint Ecology Committee.

Services and resources provided by the voluntary committees cover disability, ecology, nuclear policy, technical services, housing, research and intelligence and transport. In many cases, the individuals and functions concerned had previously been parts of G L C provision. The London Strategic Policy Unit was set up explicitly as a 'G L C in Exile', with a full-time staff of well over 300. L S P U was intended to provide research and campaigning material for boroughs represented on its controlling committee in areas such as transport, ethnic minorities and the police.

However, the Labour boroughs' attempt to create voluntary successor bodies to carry on ex- G L C activities provided considerable scope for conflict between the staff of the new organisations and those of the boroughs. There was some duplication of functions, for example between L S P U and the Association of London Authorities, where both organisations provided research and briefing for members. Equally, there were signs that the Central Technical Unit (see Technical Services Joint Committee) was engaged in functions that boroughs' own officers provided. But the most difficult conflict arose during late 1987 and early 1988 as several boroughs which contributed towards a number of voluntary committees found themselves in severe financial difficulties. As a result, it was decided to abolish the L S P U, and thus to save contributing boroughs three quarters of a million pounds each per year. Other voluntary part-London committees may come under similar pressures during 1988 and 1989, though the smaller (and therefore cheaper) units are generally more likely to survive than larger, costly bodies. The Central Technical Unit was closed in mid-1988.

There were broadly two reasons for boroughs creating joint arrangements. The first of these was a desire on the part of Labour and Alliance controlled boroughs to keep going some forms of multi-borough activity following the demise of the G L C. Conservative authorities pursued precisely the opposite objectives, and generally kept out of voluntary joint committees. The party political argument about joint action mirrored the debates during the passage of the Local Government Act 1985 about the need for London-wide committees to keep running some ex-GLC services.

The second reason for joint action was a desire to provide services or technical support with greater efficiency than would have been possible for a single borough. Statutory and voluntary arrangements for waste disposal are the best example of this search for efficiency. London-wide arrangements for fire and civil defence and for grants to voluntary organisations (considered in Chapter 3) are larger examples of the search for geographical efficiency within the post-GLC system.

Part-London or London-wide voluntary committees are operated under section 101 of the Local Government Act 1972, while committees set up by statute are operated under various sections of the 1985 Act or under secondary legislation. Perhaps the best example of the two kinds of committee is provided by the London Research Centre. LRC operates in two parts: the Intelligence Programme is a statutory committee involving all London boroughs (set up under section 88) while the Research Programme is a voluntary committee involving only 16 boroughs and operates under section 101.

There are, finally, a number of joint authorities and committees which pre-date the abolition of the GLC. These include the Lee Valley Regional Park Authority which, as its name suggests, brings together a number of authorities (including some outside Greater London) to plan and administer recreational services along the River Lea. Committees of London boroughs also exist for judicial services, involving magistrates courts, probation and careers.

Taken with the London-wide joint authorities and committees described in the previous chapter, the part-London authorities and committees make up well over thirty borough-based joint arrangements. Though some of these arrangements (e.g. Magistrates' Courts Committees) pre-date GLC abolition, the majority have been set up under statute or voluntarily to replace part of the GLC empire. An analysis of the extent of cross-membership and inter-agency co-operation was not possible in the preparation of this book. However, it is clear that strong London-wide relationships remain. These relationships are maintained by political party membership; by the fact that many officers of the new voluntary arrangements previously worked for the GLC; and by the continued existence at County Hall (or nearby) of a large number of units. In short, reports of the death of London-wide government have been somewhat exaggerated.

Docklands Consultative Committee

The DCC is a voluntary association with nine members: the Boroughs of Greenwich, Lewisham, Newham and Southwark, the Inner London Education Authority, the newly established Tower Hamlets Neighbourhood Committees for Wapping and the Isle of Dogs, and two community organisations, the Joint Docklands Action Group and the Docklands Forum. It was set up after the abolition of the GLC in order to carry on the work of the Council's Docklands Committee. The Committee co-ordinates members' policy responses to moves by central government and the LDCC, undertakes research and publicity on issues in the Dockland area (including publication of the occasional free newspaper *The Docklander*), and provides assistance to local and community groups. DCC is currently setting up a comprehensive database through which it monitors employment, housing and property market trends.

The Committee, whose six-weekly meetings rotate round the member boroughs, has an eight-person secretariat (seven full-time equivalents) called the Docklands Support Unit with Dr Bob Colenutt as Team Leader. The Unit is based in Stratford where it shares office accommodation with the London River Authority. Newham, as lead borough, provides full administrative support and administers staff salaries. The Committee is financed from contributions of £35,000 per borough, and £15,000 from ILEA. The scale of contribution to be paid by the Tower Hamlets Neighbourhood Committees proved difficult to resolve. The two community organisations have full voting rights but do not contribute financially.

Greater London Enterprise

Greater London Enterprise is a company limited by guarantee dedicated to assisting businesses to become profitable and to generate good job opportunities. It was owned by the GLC until abolition, and is now jointly owned by twelve boroughs: Brent, Camden, Ealing, Greenwich, Hackney, Hammersmith and Fulham, Haringey, Hounslow, Islington, Lambeth, Lewisham, Newham and Southwark. GLE provides investment funds for projects and companies of particular importance to London, as well as managing investment in industrial sites and properties to assist industrial development. It can also provide resources for the research and development of products and management advice.

GLE employs 65 staff. Its resources are provided by local authority contributions and private sector funds. Its offices are located at the

Elephant and Castle. Meetings are not open to the public, nor would its administrative actions be subject to examination by the Local Government Ombudsman.

Inner London Education Authority

Background

The Inner London Education Authority (ILEA) provides education in the twelve inner London boroughs and the City of London. Education has been run across this area continuously since 1904, by the London County Council from 1904 to 1965, by the Inner London Education Authority as a statutory sub-committee of the Greater London Council from 1965 to 1986, and by ILEA as a directly elected authority since April 1986.

Before 1904, education in London was administered by the London School Board. At the time that education was being transferred from boards to elected local authorities, the London County Council was given control of the service in its area. When the LCC was abolished in 1965, its powers were transferred to boroughs and to the GLC. Because it was thought impossible to split the education functions of the LCC between the inner boroughs in the same way that education was being given to Outer London boroughs, ILEA was set up.

In its first period of existence, from 1985 to 1986, ILEA was a statutory 'special' committee of the GLC, with its membership consisting of all the GLC members for Inner London constituencies, plus one member representing each Inner London borough council. Although the Authority had a separate administration, its finances and administration were tightly bound up with those of the GLC. Moreover, ILEA shared County Hall with the GLC.

When the GLC was abolished, there were a number of important consequences for ILEA. First, as the Authority existed as a special committee of the GLC, with most of its members being elected for the GLC, a new legal framework was obviously needed. Second, the Authority's administration would have to be made independent of the GLC. Third, some services were taken over from the GLC. Fourth, the Government wanted the London Residuary Body to sell off County Hall, which would entail ILEA finding a new home. Fifth, some financial reorganisation was necessary.

Membership and organisation

The Local Government Act 1985 set up ILEA as a new, directly elected, local authority. In the earlier stages of the debate about abolition, the Government made it clear that they wished ILEA to be a joint board, with membership derived from the Inner London boroughs. However, opposition within the Conservative Party to this idea was sufficient to make the Government change its mind. ILEA has elections every four years for two members for every Parliamentary constituency within its area. Membership in 1986/87 consisted of 45 Labour members, 11 Conservatives and 2 Alliance. The Authority's administration was made self-sufficient by taking on some of the ex-GLC staff. Staff were taken on in the biggest numbers from the property services, building, personnel and finance departments.

The services taken on by ILEA at abolition (as opposed to the administrative burden) were few in number and relatively small in scope. The major transfers were the Geffrye and Horniman Museums, the London-wide supplies purchasing arrangements, and the direct labour building and engineering functions. In total, they added some £15m to ILEA's revenue budget, plus some £120m of trading services. In addition, there were extra costs arising from the loss of the shared administration with the GLC.

The education service is administered in ten divisions, each of which consists of one or two boroughs (see Map 7), though all major decisions affecting education provision are taken at County Hall. In 1987/88, ILEA budgeted for 58,540 (full-time equivalent) staff, of whom 29,040 were teachers, 6,620 were clerical and administrative, 2,010 school-keepers, 11,560 manual workers and 9,310 in other posts. In addition, 5,900 were employed by ILEA polytechnics, plus about 3,720 in trading services and locally employed by schools.

The abolition of the GLC left ILEA as the biggest inhabitant of the sprawling County Hall complex. The LRB and a number of successor units to the GLC also occupied space, although the LRB intended to move them all out as soon as possible. ILEA was the only certain long-term resident of County Hall. But the LRB, in consequence of Government demands, intended to sell off County Hall. A planning inquiry determined that County Hall should continue to be used for local government purposes. However, the Environment Secretary stated that such a purpose would not be acceptable to him. So it appears inevitable that ILEA will have to leave County Hall. The cost of moving the Authority to a new headquarters is reckoned to be at least £200m.

Finance

The financial consequences for ILEA OF GLC abolition are summarised above. Because ILEA receives no block grant, on account of its large rate base and high spending levels, the removal of the GLC did not lead to a redistribution of grant or London Rate Equalisation Scheme resources which affected ILEA. Nevertheless, ILEA remains an important automatic redistributor of resources from Central London to the rest of Inner London.

The Local Government Act 1985 determined that all the new joint boards and ILEA which were set up as a consequence of abolition should be ratecapped for their first three years of existence. Although ILEA had already been subject to limitation under the Rates Act 1984, the abolition legislation subjected ILEA to further rate limitation for at least the years 1986/87 to 1988/89.

The 1985 legislation also required the new Authority annually to consult the Inner London boroughs and the City about its spending and financing for the coming year, and about any proposals to open, close or alter a school. Finally, the 1985 Act gave the Government the power to review the Authority's exercise of its education functions before 31 March 1991. Following the Government's decision during 1987 to allow boroughs to opt out of ILEA, it was announced that the power to review the Authority would be repealed.

The ILEA spent £1,025m on revenue items in 1987/88, plus £26m (gross) on capital. The respective figures for 1987/88 are £1,265m and £23m. Revenue spending is financed by a precept on all Inner London boroughs, which ensures that each authority contributes according to its rateable value.

In common with other education authorities in England and Wales, the ILEA is responsible for educating pupils aged 5 to 16 (i.e. the years of compulsory school attendance), plus under 5s provision and further education outside the universities. ILEA is a high spending authority by national standards. For example, in 1986/87, average expenditure per primary school pupil was £1,227, compared with the Outer London average of £881 and the England and Wales average of £788. Average secondary school spending per pupil in 1986/87 was £2,042 in ILEA compared with £1,357 in Outer London and £1,201 throughout England and Wales.

The future

Because of these high expenditure levels, because of concerns expressed about the quality of education in Inner London, and perhaps because of its strong Labour control, there has been simmering pressure to abolish or reform ILEA. Many Conservatives had misgivings about its creation in 1965 and about its recreation in 1986. In 1980, a report from a group within the Conservative Party, chaired by Kenneth Baker (who was then a backbench MP), proposed that ILEA should be broken up between the Inner London boroughs. In the event, there was no reform. Following the decision to continue with a single authority for the provision of education in Inner London at the time of abolition, the pressure to reform ILEA remained.

Subsequently, the Conservative Party's 1987 election manifesto promised that individual boroughs would be given the opportunity to opt out of ILEA. Westminster, Wandsworth and Kensington and Chelsea each announced that they would apply to leave. The legislation to facilitate opting out was introduced into Parliament in autumn 1987, with 1990 being the expected date of this further change.

A powerful group of backbench Conservative MPs, led by Michael Heseltine and Norman Tebbit (both ex-Cabinet ministers), successfully used Parliamentary procedures early in 1988 to put pressure on the Government to abolish ILEA outright. Kenneth Baker, now Education Secretary, moved amendments to the Education Reform Bill 1987, which led the Commons to vote to abolish ILEA and set up the boroughs as education authorities. Thus, in 1990, London is expected to see its second major structural reorganisation within five years.

Judicial Services

London local authorities, like those elsewhere in Britain, have certain responsibilities for the administration of justice, particularly in relation to magistrates' courts, coroners' courts and the probation service. However, arrangements for judicial services differ from the norm because of the special status of the Metropolitan Police and the after-effects of the abolition of the Greater London Council.

Magistrates' courts are administered, under the provisions of the Justices of the Peace Act 1979, by magistrates' courts committees made up of local justices of the peace, the Keeper of the Rolls ex officio, and a judge co-opted by the Committee. The commission areas of these committees correspond generally to the counties of England and Wales and are provided with courthouses, office accommodation and expenses by their county councils as 'paying authorities'. London can be seen on Map 11 to have six such commission areas, four in Outer London and two within. The paying authority for the two Inner London Commission Areas is, and has long been, the Receiver of the Metropolitan Police. The Greater London Council used to be the paying authority for the

Outer Areas. This responsibility was transferred in 1986 to the 20 Outer London boroughs.

Coroners are independent judicial officers appointed and paid by local government (generally the county councils). Greater London is divided into seven coroners' districts, excluding the City and Temples, which are within the jurisdiction of the City Corporation (see Map 11). Formerly the responsibility of the G L C, the coroners' courts are now administered by the London boroughs under the supervision of the Home Office.

The probation service is administered on an area basis by Probation Committees comprising local magistrates, a number of judges and justices appointed by the Lord Chancellor, and co-opted members including one from each local authority in the area. Greater London is divided between an Inner London area which – as with the magistrates' courts – is managed by the Receiver of the Metropolitan Police by direction of the Home Secretary, and four outer areas that match the Magistrates' Commission Areas. The work of the Outer London Probation Committees is funded 80 per cent by the Home Office and 20 per cent by local authorities.

Lee Valley Regional Park Authority

The Regional Park Authority manages an area of open space covering just under 10,000 acres which stretches across three counties: Essex (40 per cent), Hertfordshire (24 per cent) and Greater London (36 per cent). The Greater London portion lies within the London boroughs of Tower Hamlets, Newham, Waltham Forest, Hackney, Haringey and Enfield. The Park Authority was established on 1 January 1967 as a statutory body to manage this area, which includes a number of sports facilities, and organise recreational activities. Prior to G L C abolition, the membership of the Park Authority consisted of 28 indirectly elected councillors to represent the following local authorities: G L C (8), Essex County Council (4), Hertfordshire County Council (4), the 6 L Bs listed above (1 each), and Broxbourne, Epping Forest and East Hertfordshire District Councils (2 each). Funding for the Park Authority was provided by a precept on the G L C and the two other counties (within a ceiling set at the product of a 0.42p rate), with the G L C contributing about 80 per cent of the net total (£5m in 1984/85).

Membership and financial arrangements were altered at G L C abolition in order to make good the loss of the council's contribution to the running of the Park Authority. While the six L Bs whose boundaries contain parts of the Authority continue to nominate one member each, the remaining 27 London boroughs now jointly elect an additional eight representatives, thus preserving the original balance between London and non-London authorities, with 14 members each. The precept paid by the G L C has now been replaced by a direct levy on the L Bs, which still amounts to 80 per cent of the Regional Park Authority's running costs.

London Boroughs Disability Committee

Established in 1986 as a Voluntary Joint Committee, the Committee works to advise and assist its member authorities in the provision of services for blind and disabled people. It has eleven members – Brent, Camden, Ealing, Hackney, Haringey, Islington, Lambeth, Lewisham, Newham and Southwark – and Camden plays the role of lead borough, paying salaries and providing administrative support.

The Committee has a unit of 23 full-time staff, the London Boroughs Disability Resource Team, a direct descendent of the G L C's Disability Resource Team. In addition to the day-to-day advisory work of its specialist staff, L B D R T publishes leaflets and posters, organises training courses and conferences, and arranges for local government reports and papers to be taped or brailled. It was due to move from County Hall during 1988.

The Unit is funded through annual contributions of £60,000 from the constituent councils, which with other minor sources of revenue provide for a budget of approximately £750,000.

London Boroughs Nuclear Policy Committee

The Committee brings together the twelve London Labour-controlled boroughs which have declared themselves nuclear free zones: Camden, Ealing, Greenwich, Hackney, Hammersmith and Fulham, Haringey, Hounslow, Islington, Lambeth, Lewisham, Southwark and Waltham Forest. It was set up in 1986 as a joint voluntary committee, with Camden as the lead borough.

The Committee oversees the work of the London Nuclear Information Unit, based at 141 Euston Road. The Unit's four full-time staff conduct research on civil defence and nuclear waste issues in London, especially the transport of nuclear waste through the capital. They provide specialist advice and support for the nuclear free zone councils and aim to promote public awareness of nuclear hazards.

The Unit's operating costs of £120,000 are raised by a levy of £10,000 on each member authority.

London Boroughs Training Committee (Social Services)

The Committee annually provides 250 training courses for 7,000 social workers, housing managers, educational welfare workers and others. It was founded in 1965 at the demise of the London County Council to co-ordinate training in their new social service responsibilities for the London boroughs. As such it is an early precursor of the joint arrangements set up twenty-one years later at G L C abolition.

The Committee's training programmes attract membership from health, housing and education authorities besides its original clientele amongst social services departments. The City of London is a member as are all London boroughs with the exception of Barking, Barnet, Bexley, Hillingdon and Tower Hamlets. More than ten district health authorities also belong, and various voluntary sector agencies, making a London-wide consortium of 62 members in all. Subscribing members receive training and consultancy services free. L B T C also undertakes a variety of externally funded research and consultancy projects, including at present a major D H S S project on drug-taking, and another on problem drinking for the D H S S and the Alcohol Education and Research Council.

The Committee employs 26 staff and has a budget of £0.75m, a third of which is contributed by research contracts.

London Boroughs Transport Committee

The Transport Committee is a joint voluntary grouping of London boroughs set up to administer the night-time and weekend ban instituted by the G L C on movements by heavy goods vehicles on most roads within the capital's boundaries, under the Greater London (Restriction of Goods Vehicles) Traffic Order 1985. The Committee's present membership is composed of one representative from each of 22 L Bs (15 Labour, 2 Conservative, 3 Alliance, one hung council and the City of London – see Map 23), with L B Richmond acting as the lead borough. Also, L B Enfield makes use of the Committee's arrangements through an agency agreement, but without voting rights on policy matters.

The London-wide Lorry Ban had already proved a highly controversial policy measure even before the Committee took charge of it. The Ban was introduced by the last Labour G L C administration following the recommendations from a two-year inquiry commissioned by the Council

(Greater London Council, 1983) to look at ways to reduce the impact of heavy lorries on London's environment, and in response to long-standing demands from both environmental lobbyists and ordinary residents along the worst affected routes. It consists of a ban on movements by heavy goods vehicles weighing over 16.5 tonnes between 9 p.m. and 7 a.m. on weekdays, after 1 p.m. on Saturdays and all day Sundays, within an area covering almost all of Greater London, except on the Department of Transport controlled trunk roads and other 'exempt' roads designated by the GLC and its successor authorities. There are also exemptions permitted for vehicles engaged in essential services, collections and deliveries, provided that operators take certain steps to reduce noise emissions, including the use of specified equipment or 'hush kits'.

The GLC's decision to impose the Lorry Ban was opposed by the Department of Transport, as well as lorry operators, retailers and other business interests. The then Secretary of State for Transport, Nicholas Ridley, issued a directive blocking implementation of the Ban until a new public inquiry, but was overturned by the High Court, where this veto was condemned as 'unreasonable, irrational and unlawful'. This ruling was upheld in the Appeal Court, and the Ban finally came into effect on 30 January 1986. The main tasks associated with administration of the Ban by the Council consisted in the design and deployment of 2,500 signs informing lorry drivers of the prohibition on roads outside and leading into the perimeter of the Ban, and the issuing of exemption permits (displayed on vehicles) to some 3,500 firms operating 30,000 lorries. Enforcement was carried out by the Metropolitan Police, which was reluctant to devote more than a 'minimal' effort because of its other priorities and lack of manpower.

The fate of the Ban after GLC abolition remained undetermined for a considerable amount of time, and even its legal status is still unclear, especially as to whether individual LBs may revoke or modify provisions of the original traffic order, or if this requires unanimous agreement by all 33 LBs. Both the Department and most Conservative LBs remain opposed to the measure as ineffective and an additional burden on the capital's economy. The Conservative majority within the London Co-ordinating Committee finally won acceptance for the proposal to turn over administration of the Ban during 1986/87 to the London Residuary Body (LRB), pending a review of results in June 1986. At that point, a study by the Association of London Borough Engineers and Surveyors, commissioned by the LBA, did show a 20 per cent reduction in night-time lorry traffic on London roads covered by the Ban, but admitted that evidence as to the Ban's effectiveness was still inconclusive. Meanwhile, the DTp lifted the Ban from the 65 miles of new trunk roads which it had acquired from the GLC (Map 22), an action being challenged in the courts by LBs Richmond and Camden. The LRB for its part had adopted a policy of granting exemption permits to all applicants, without checking on compliance by these operators with noise abatement conditions, stating that it did not have the resources to do so.

While the Ban was thus subject during this initial year following abolition to a process of erosion, the boroughs were still heavily divided over new arrangements. The majority of LBA boroughs opposed keeping the Ban, with the exception of Alliance-controlled LBs Richmond and Sutton, and also Conservative-run LB Kensington and Chelsea. The Labour boroughs within the ALA, on the other hand, all favoured joint administration by the boroughs of a London-wide ban, as did the City of London, and a majority within the London Planning Advisory Committee (LPAC). Finally, in October 1986, 22 boroughs were able to agree on a joint voluntary scheme under section 101 of the Local Government Act 1972, and the Transport Committee held its first meeting in December 1986. Other boroughs may at some point enter into agency agreements with the Committee similar to LB Enfield's, or intend to enforce the Ban on an individual basis, as in the case of the City of Westminster. Five Tory-controlled boroughs in South London led by LB Bromley, however, are also attempting to form an alternative committee on their own, which would continue to issue lorry operators with permits during an interim period, but in the long run seeking a legal ruling which would allow them to revoke the Ban within their areas.

The Transport Committee began to implement the Lorry Ban on behalf of its members as of April 1987. Membership entails a three-year commitment to the scheme. The Committee has a revenue budget in 1987/88 of £855,000 and a capital budget of £525,00, to which participant members contribute on a per capita basis. There is a staff complement of 17, plus four uniformed enforcement officers. Work has begun on tightening the conditions attached to the issue of exemption permits, bringing them into line with EEC regulations on noise emissions, and on completing the signing of roads. Both tasks, however, may be complicated by the existing fragmentation among the LBs over the Lorry Ban issue. The LBTC boroughs, for example, might be forced in the end to erect new signs along their boundaries with non-participant boroughs, setting out different conditions to those of their neighbours, which is likely to create confusion for many operators. In these conditions the Metropolitan Police would find it difficult to co-operate on enforcement.

The Secretary of State for Transport has refused, however, to consider imposing a more uniform scheme on all boroughs.

London Canals Committee

L C C is a voluntary joint committee of all London local authorities along the routes of the Grand Union and Regent's Canals, Westminster and Kensington and Chelsea excepted. Hackney is lead borough. It carries on the work of the former London Boroughs Canals Consultative Committee, set up by the G L C in 1966, which achieved by strategic co-ordination a major transformation of London's run-down canals and derelict, inaccessible towpaths.

At present the Committee has no staff of its own, and relies upon the technical support of two groups in the boroughs of the eastern and western sectors. Its budget is modest, each borough contributing just £400 to cover the cost of preparing papers and running the meetings. Proposals to enlarge the contribution and provide full-time staff support are under discussion.

London Ecology Committee

Established in 1986 as a voluntary joint committee, the L E C involves all but ten local councils in London. The non-joiners are five inner authorities in the western sector (Merton, Wandsworth, Kensington and Chelsea, Westminster and the City) and five outer boroughs to the east (Bromley, Bexley, Havering, Redbridge and Enfield). The Committee has four co-opted members representing the Countryside Commission, the London Wildlife Trust, the Urban Spaces Scheme and the Nature Conservancy Council. The lead borough is Camden.

The purpose of the Committee, and its executive arm the London Ecology Unit, is to provide ecological expertise and promote public awareness of nature conservation in London. The Unit's nine professional staff, backed up by three administrators, maintain an Ecological Records Centre for London and produce a variety of technical and popular publications in addition to their specific work as ecological consultants in planning, land management and education.

Camden, as lead borough, employs and services the London Ecology Unit, charging £27,500 for administrative support in 1987/88. The Committee's total expenditure in 1987/88 was just under £350,000. The cost of running the Unit and its various agreed projects is shared equally between participating boroughs, with contributions from the Countryside Commission and contracts from the Nature Conservancy Council. Non-joining boroughs can buy data from the Unit's database, which is London-wide.

London Housing Unit

The London Housing Unit is run by a voluntary joint committee of 13 boroughs: Camden, Greenwich, Hackney, Haringey, Islington, Lambeth, Newham, Southwark, Tower Hamlets, Waltham Forest, Ealing and Hammersmith and Fulham. Its work falls in two broad areas: policy development and publicity. Recent work has centred on the problem of homelessness and the boroughs' use of bed and breakfast accommodation. L H U was behind a working party on homelessness which decided to set up a unit within the London Research Centre to create a database on bed and breakfast accommodation in Greater London. This database is intended to assist individual boroughs in achieving value for money. L H U is also seeking to reduce the extent to which boroughs 'swap' homeless people by moving them to hotels in other boroughs. Work is also proceeding on racial harassment and on tenant-managed co-operatives. Publicity effort includes the publication of *London Housing News* every six weeks.

L H U is also involved in lobbying on issues such as housing reform legislation. Much of this lobbying work is undertaken through the Association of London Authorities' Housing Committee, with which L H U has strong informal links.

The Unit attached to the Committee employs 14 staff, and is based at Holborn. It spent £400,000 in 1987/88, which was rather less than in 1986/87. Borough contributions are a flat charge per authority. Meetings of the Committee are open to the public.

London On-Line Local Authorities

L O L A provides computer services for Haringey, Hillingdon, Tower Hamlets and Hackney. It was set up in 1971 to provide computer services in the constituent boroughs. These services include rent and rate collection, payroll facilities and payments to creditors. Boroughs are charged for work undertaken on their behalf. There is a joint committee of elected members from the four boroughs to oversee the operation of the scheme.

London River Authority

The London River Authority is a voluntary association, with a core membership of London boroughs, river users, community groups, trades unions, and recreational and educational interests. A full-time staff of three share premises in Stratford with the Docklands Support Unit.

Its predecessor was the long-established Thames Consultative Planning Committee of the G L C, which brought together all riparian London boroughs and river interests for consultation over matters such as access to Thames-side steps and planning guidelines for the waterfront. After unsuccessful post-abolition attempts to maintain the Committee with the City Corporation in the lead role, the London River Authority re-established a framework for co-ordination, though on the basis of a more restricted membership of six London boroughs, all Labour-controlled and all except Hounslow and Lambeth located downstream of the Pool of London. The local authority members contribute the greater part of the authority's income through a subscription of £10,000 annually.

L R A's principal policy concern is to prevent irreversible damage to the economic and communications potential of the Thames as a result of the private residential property boom along the waterfront. Its meetings serve as a forum for a wide range of interests and groups and it publishes research on current issues such as the growing threat to commercial activity on the waterfront of the downstream Thames.

The London Planning Advisory Committee (L P A C) has set up an officer-level Thameside Working Party which complements the work of L R A, though with the difference that it embraces all the riparian boroughs.

London Strategic Policy Committee

The Committee was set up in March 1986 as a voluntary committee of 8 London boroughs – Camden, Greenwich, Hackney, Haringey, Islington, Lambeth, Lewisham and Southwark. Ealing joined subsequently. Camden took the role of lead borough. Its immediate purpose was to provide for continuity in the work of various policy teams within the G L C, which were reconstituted under the Committee on abolition as the London Strategic Policy Unit (L S P U). The Unit specialised in issues of women, race, the police, transport, planning, local economic policy and recreation.

The Unit had 344 staff and its running costs in 1987/88 amounted to £7.1m. The participating boroughs contributed equally towards its budget. A decision to dissolve the Committee and wind up the Unit was reached in September 1987 as a result of financial constraints on the member boroughs, and it closed on 31 March 1988.

London Welfare Benefits

London Welfare Benefits exists to encourage the take-up of welfare benefits by those entitled to them. It works with voluntary organisations and with welfare rights officers from local councils, providing training courses, information packs, briefings on current legislation, and translated information and claim forms for ethnic minorities.

Established in 1987 as a voluntary joint committee of London boroughs, London Welfare Benefits has ten member authorities – Brent, Ealing (the lead borough), Greenwich, Hackney, Haringey, Hounslow, Islington, Lambeth, Lewisham, Southwark and Waltham Forest. Camden and Merton have also contracted to use the services of London Welfare Benefits but are not members of its steering committee.

The Committee employs 37 staff. Its budget for 1987/88 is £715,000 made up from flat-rate contributions of £65,000 for each full member and a modest income from services.

Technical Services Joint Committee

The Technical Services Joint Committee, which ran the Central Technical Unit, was a joint committee of seven London boroughs (Greenwich, Hackney, Lambeth, Lewisham, Newham, Southwark and Tower Hamlets) providing a building and design service for boroughs and other public bodies in Greater London. It offered the services of architects, surveyors, structural engineers, quantity surveyors, and mechanical and electrical engineers. Its clients included the London Fire and Civil Defence Authority, the Thames Water Authority, the Arts Council, the London Residuary Body, housing associations, and, of course, the boroughs.

The lead borough for this Committee was Hackney. The Unit employed about 230 people, and was based in Wandsworth. The 1986/87 budget was £9m, which was financed by fees from member boroughs and from other bodies. The unit was closed in June 1988.

Waste Disposal Authorities

The Waste Disposal Authorities (W D As) are responsible for the transport, treatment and final disposal of over 3 million tonnes of household
and commercial waste collected by the London boroughs or delivered at
public waste disposal sites (civic amenity sites) in Greater London each
year. Prior to abolition, the G L C was responsible for the disposal of all
public sector waste in London and was the largest single waste disposal
authority in Europe. This function involved total revenue expenditure of
£63.3m in 1984/85, and capital expenditure of £15.7m. The Council
operated 20 waste transfer stations, where most of the waste collected is
packed into economical loads for transport (roughly half of it by rail and
river, and the rest by road) to landfill sites, over 90 per cent of them
outside the boundaries of Greater London itself. An additional 10 per
cent of public sector waste was burned by the G L C at its incineration
plant in Edmonton, the heat being used to generate electricity and
earning income for the Council of £4.5m in 1984/85.

Waste disposal was one of the most problematical functions affected
by G L C abolition. The Government originally proposed to devolve
responsibility to the borough councils, with voluntary co-operation
between L Bs where necessary, but giving the Secretary of State for the
Environment reserve powers to enforce statutory joint arrangements if
he was not satisfied that adequate service could be maintained (section
10, Local Government Act 1985). The G L C and other critics pointed to
the economies of scale and technical advances which the Council had
obtained after it replaced the ten joint waste disposal authorities which
existed prior to the G L C's creation in 1965, and argued that a single
London-wide authority was essential. The Government came to accept
the need for such an authority in the case of waste planning and
regulation, as well as disposal of hazardous waste and other specialist
tasks, and these were passed to a new London-wide statutory agency, the
London Waste Regulation Authority (L W R A), as described above in
Chapter 3. For disposal of ordinary waste, the Secretary of State was also
forced to intervene after only 8 out of 33 London boroughs were able to
agree among themselves on forming voluntary groups. In the end,
16 W D As were created, composed in the following way (see Map 15):

Four statutory joint authorities:

1. **East London Waste Authority** (L Bs Barking and Dagenham*,
   Havering, Newham and Redbridge).
2. **North London Waste Authority** (L Bs Barnet, Camden*, Enfield,

Hackney, Haringey, Islington and Waltham Forest).
3. **West London Waste Authority** (L Bs Brent, Ealing, Harrow, Hillingdon, Hounslow* and Richmond-upon-Thames).
4. **Western Riverside Waste Authority** (LBs Hammersmith and Fulham, Kensington and Chelsea and Wandsworth*).

Twelve individual L Bs as W D As, linked together into three voluntary groups:

1. **Central London Group** (the City of London, Tower Hamlets and the City of Westminster*).
2. **South London Group** (Bromley, Croydon*, Kingston-upon-Thames, Merton and Sutton).
3. **South East London Group** (Greenwich, Lewisham* and Southwark).

In addition, waste disposal in L B Bexley is carried out by means of an agreement between the borough council and neighbouring Kent County Council.

The main difference between the statutory joint W D As and the voluntary groups is that staff and facilities in the former are entirely separate from the individual members. Income is raised mainly by a levy on each member borough. Within the voluntary groups each individual council maintains its own staff and facilities with arrangements for contracting services from neighbouring councils and co-ordination of certain functions, such as negotiation of contracts with private firms, when required. L Bs Merton and Sutton, for example, pay L B Croydon a rate per tonne for use of its waste transfer station. Membership of both the statutory joint W D As and the joint committees overseeing voluntary groups is composed of two elected members nominated from each council. In all cases, individual boroughs have become responsible for the 40 civic amenity sites in Greater London, along with management of accompanying recycling centres.

The W D As now operate within the London-wide planning and regulatory framework provided by the London Waste Regulation Authority (L W R A), responsible for licensing all waste disposal activities. It is difficult to establish any clear trends in the performance of the new authorities since abolition. Many of them have been preoccupied with the renegotiation of contracts with the private firms handling waste transport, and arrangements with other local authorities both in and outside London for use of waste transfer stations and landfill sites. The

* Lead borough.

fragmentation into 16 separate authorities is unlikely to have strengthened their bargaining position compared to the GLC in this respect, and
the overall cost of smaller-sized contracts is likely to have increased.
Capital investment in new facilities appears to have been reduced
compared to the level maintained by the GLC, and the statutory joint
WDAS are dependent on a capital allocation from the DOE. One
long-term problem confronting all of the new WDAs in the near future is
the shortage of available landfill sites within easy reach of London,
which will force them to either move farther afield (at greater cost) or
attempt to develop new methods of disposal. It is by no means certain
whether they have sufficient resources to meet such a challenge.

CHAPTER 5

The Boroughs

Introduction

Within the new system of administration of Greater London created by the Local Government Act 1985, the London boroughs gained prominence as the sole remaining tier of representative, multipurpose local government within the capital. But the reorganisation of London government, along with other recent changes affecting the status of local government in general, has also meant new problems and pressures for the boroughs. While the boroughs have assumed new powers and responsibilities previously belonging to the GLC, in many policy areas their degree of discretion is now circumscribed both by ministerial controls and by the presence of new London-wide agencies described in the preceding chapters. Meanwhile, the political, organisational and financial constraints on them are growing ever tighter.

The additional burdens which GLC abolition has imposed on individual boroughs in terms of service provision, as well as the increased interaction with other authorities and with outside agencies at the London-wide level, are likely to bring about considerable changes of internal organisation and style of management in coming years. Other measures now being implemented, such as the introduction of a community charge or poll tax to fund local expenditure, competitive tendering for local services, or reforms in education and housing, will also require major adjustments on the part of London boroughs. The initial period since the demise of the GLC has barely allowed the boroughs to begin settling into their new role, and the full impact of the new system is as yet unclear. This chapter seeks to describe the new functions taken on by the boroughs as compared to their previous role, and where possible attempt a broad evaluation of their performance in these areas to date.

The Boroughs' Role Prior to GLC Abolition

Within the local government system which existed in Greater London between 1965 and 1986, the London boroughs were already the predominant providers of local services relative to the upper tier body, the GLC. The Report of the Herbert Commission on Local Government in London, published in 1960, had recommended that the boroughs be established as the 'primary' local authorities within the capital. According to this concept, subsequently incorporated with some modifications with the London Government Act 1963, the boroughs would become responsible for the delivery of the bulk of services, especially those of more local and personalised nature, such as housing, social welfare and education (except in Inner London, where ILEA was set up to administer the schools). Created from amalgamations of the previously existing metropolitan boroughs and suburban county boroughs and districts, the 32 boroughs were intended to be of sufficient size and population to perform a large variety of functions efficiently, yet still small enough for the borough councillors and officials to be accessible to the local population and allow the new units to maintain a strong sense of local identity. The City of London, despite its tiny area and population, was allowed to retain its unique status and institutions, with similar responsibilities to those of the boroughs.

The more remote GLC, located in County Hall, was to carry out only those functions which needed London-wide provision for reasons of economies of scale (e.g. waste disposal) or because their complexity and interdependencies with other areas required a directing agency with a 'strategic overview' of the capital's problems (e.g. land-use planning and transport). The GLC's strategic role, however, often only entailed planning, co-ordination and a few key interventions, leaving the boroughs with the tasks of actual service delivery and day-to-day administration. In other areas, the GLC and the lower tier had concurrent powers, which meant in practice that either tier could carry out similar activities, often without any real interaction or co-ordination. In terms of overall spending on local government services in Greater London, the boroughs accounted for over 60 per cent of total net current expenditure in 1984/85, while the GLC's share was 18 per cent and the ILEA's 22 per cent. The extent of borough involvement with a given function, however, varied considerably, as shown in Tables 5.1 and 5.2.

Table 5.1   Functions of the London Boroughs following the London Government Act 1963

Functions carried out wholly by the London boroughs:

Rates collection	Registration of births, deaths and electoral rolls
Cemeteries and crematoria	Allotments
Caravan and gypsy sites	Environmental health
Personal social services	Libraries
Trading standards and consumer protection	Refuse collection

Functions held concurrently or divided between the boroughs and the GLC:

Education: provision by boroughs in Outer London, the ILEA in Inner London.

Housing: boroughs had main responsibility for provision but the GLC had its own housing stock and strategic powers in the case of large projects, housing outside Greater London, aid for slum clearance, and in establishing London-wide mobility schemes.

Planning: the strategic land-use plan – the GLDP – was drawn up by the GLC, local plans by the boroughs, while development control was exercised by the LBs with GLC intervention in major schemes.

Parks and open space: boroughs were responsible for local parks, while the GLC maintained several large 'strategic' parks and Green Belt holdings, and had a major role within the Lee Valley Regional Park.

Highways and traffic management: GLC was the overall strategic transport planning authority, the highway authority for construction and maintenance on 895 miles of metropolitan roads, and the traffic management authority for non-trunk roads; the LBs were highway authorities for 7,000 miles of local roads, and could put forward local traffic management schemes and parking regulations for GLC approval; and the Department of Transport controlled 143 miles of trunk roads in Outer London.

Licensing: mainly carried out by boroughs, but the GLC carried out licensing of places of entertainment, betting tracks, petroleum storage, as well as building control in Inner London.

Emergency planning and civil defence: major GLC role with some input from boroughs.

Museums, art galleries and support for arts: concurrent.

Grants to voluntary organisations: concurrent.

Sports and recreation: concurrent.

Economic development: concurrent.

Historic buildings and monuments: concurrent, but the GLC had special powers regarding listed buildings.

Promotion of tourism: concurrent.

The division of expenditure between the boroughs and GLC/ILEA is shown for 1984/85 in Table 5.2.

Table 5.2   GLC, ILEA and London Boroughs' Share of Net Current Expenditure by Service (1984/85 estimates in £m at Nov. 1983 prices)

Service	GLC/ ILEA	%	LBs	%	Total	%
Education	852.6	(45.1)	1,036.0	(54.9)	1,888.6	(100.0)
Libraries, museums and art galleries	3.6	(3.7)	93.1	(94.6)	96.6	(100.0)
Personal social services	—	—	606.4	(100.0)	606.4	(100.0)
Fire	122.2	(100.0)	—	—	122.2	(100.0)
Admin. of justice	68.2	(96.1)	2.8	(3.9)	71.0	(100.0)
Highways and local transport	146.2	(49.6)	148.7	(50.4)	294.9	(100.0)
Passenger transport	256.8	(98.9)	2.8	(1.1)	259.6	(100.0)
Housing (non HRA)	35.1	(27.9)	90.7	(72.1)	125.8	(100.0)
Waste disposal	59.0	(100.0)	—	—	59.0	(100.0)
Waste collection	—	—	74.8	(100.0)	74.8	(100.0)
Envir. health	0.9	(1.1)	81.8	(98.9)	82.7	(100.0)
Sports and recreation	27.0	(31.6)	58.4	(68.4)	85.4	(100.0)
Parks and open spaces	16.5	(16.1)	85.8	(83.9)	102.3	(100.0)
Town and country planning	24.5	(32.2)	52.0	(67.8)	76.5	(100.0)
Cemeteries and crematoria	—	—	8.4	(100.0)	8.4	(100.0)
Rates collection	—	—	32.4	(100.0)	32.4	(100.0)
Other services	256.9	(57.2)	187.8	(42.8)	444.7	(100.0)
Debt charges	–206.5	(46.7)	–235.3	(53.3)	–441.8	(100.0)
Total current expenditure	1,562.3	(39.9)	2,351.1	(60.1)	3,913.4	(100.0)

Source: CIPFA, *Finance and General Statistics 1984/85*, Table 3.

This division of labour between tiers, while perhaps a logical and coherent one in view of the needs of a large metropolitan area such as Greater London, did involve a degree of duplication and mutual interference, which were intensified when the GLC and boroughs happened to be controlled by opposing parties or when their respective policies crystallised deep-seated conflicts of interest in relation to urban issues within the capital. Housing, for example, became a source of tension when suburban authorities under Conservative control were faced with successive strategic interventions by the GLC to promote council housing estates in their localities for working-class families. The GLC's powers, however, in the end proved to be too weak to allow it to impose this policy against determined borough resistance. During the 1970s it began to transfer its housing stock, much of it inherited from the LCC, to the boroughs, and its housing role became much more limited.

The sharing of planning powers also led to friction, where the G L C over-ruled the boroughs' decisions of planning applications or where basic disagreements emerged over major schemes, such as Covent Garden or Docklands. Many borough councils also opposed the G L C's transport strategies and experienced frustration in seeking G L C approval for proposed road and traffic management schemes, which are often refused or suffered long delays.

Dissatisfaction with the allocation of local government functions in Greater London partly influenced the Marshall Report (Greater London Council, 1978), which investigated a possible redefinition of the G L C's strategic role. It concluded that some of the G L C's executive functions in areas such as planning, housing and traffic management should be devolved downwards to the boroughs where they would be better managed, while at the same time reducing the need for a massive bureaucracy at County Hall. But the Report also urged that the G L C itself be reinforced by taking on new responsibilities from central government, including trunk roads and British Rail services in London, the capital's health services, stronger planning powers, a greater say in the affairs of the Metropolitan Police, and a new role in economic development and in the allocation of public finance, including the distribution of housing development funds and rate support grant (within a total for Greater London set by the D O E) among the London boroughs.

Fearful of the prospect of a more powerful G L C, most borough councils at the time opposed the conclusions of the Marshall Report. Even its recommendations on devolution of functions to the boroughs were never implemented fully. Proposals in 1980/81 to allow the boroughs to carry out local traffic management schemes without referral to the G L C, for example, were blocked by County Hall officials. Problems also emerged after 1980 regarding the return of the G L C's remaining housing stock to borough management, because of the backlog of badly needed repairs and renovation work on transferred estates. Meanwhile, the hostility of both the Conservative central government and many Tory boroughs to the policy initiatives pursued by the last Labour G L C administration from 1981 led to the proposals for abolition of the upper tier contained in the White Paper, *Streamlining the Cities* (Department of the Environment, 1983), and finally to the passing of the Local Government Act 1985. Transfers of additional functions to the boroughs would subsequently take place within the context of a reorganisation which sought to destroy rather than enhance the capacity of London's strategic authority.

Transfers of ex-GLC Functions to the Boroughs

Throughout the debate on GLC abolition, both in and outside Parliament, Conservative ministers sought to portray their reform as a decentralisation of powers from the upper tier to the local level, and insisted that the boroughs would be the main beneficiaries of the functions transferred from the GLC. To evaluate this claim it is essential to examine the detailed arrangements involved in each function, as well as the overall effect of reorganisation in Greater London on the boroughs' position relative to both central government and other agencies at work in the capital. Transfers of GLC services to the boroughs principally involved the following areas.

Planning

The boroughs took over in part the structure plan functions of the GLC, and will henceforth draw up a new form of land-use document for each borough, the Unitary Development Plan (UDP), which combines a short statement of general policies with more detailed, site-specific policies. The UDPs will eventually replace both the GLC's structure plan, the Greater London Development Plan (GLDP) and existing local plans. In drawing up their UDPs, however, the local planning authority must have regard to the Strategic Guidance produced by the Secretary of State for the Environment (with advice from the London Planning Advisory Committee, LPAC), concerning matters such as the general level of provision for housing development, major transport links, provision and location of major industrial and commercial development, and policies on the Green Belt and minerals extraction, as well as observing other national policies. In addition, the Secretary of State has powers to issue orders for the boroughs to commence work on UDPs, to synchronise their plans with other boroughs, or to 'call in' plans for approval.

This new planning system has yet to come into full effect anywhere in London, as consultations by the Secretary of State with other bodies are continuing in relation to the contents of the new Statutory Guidance, which will not become available in definitive form until 1989 at the earliest. The boroughs did assume immediate responsibility upon abolition for other functions related to planning such as derelict land reclamation and controls over minerals extraction. The GLC's duties relating to listed buildings, conservation areas and ancient monuments went to the Historic Buildings and Monuments Commission as explained in Chapter 2.

Housing

The boroughs were already the primary housing authorities prior to abolition, but the GLC had performed an important strategic role in this field. At one time the Council was in fact the largest single house-builder in Britain, but from the 1970s onwards it began to transfer dwellings within its housing stock to borough ownership, including both those units it had built itself and those it had inherited in 1965 from the late London County Council. Between 1980 and 1985 alone 160,000 dwellings changed hands in this way, leaving only the 5,500 dwellings in the 'new town' of Thamesmead (now transferred to a non-profit company, Thamesmead Town, as explained on pp. 52–53). After abolition, many boroughs were affected by the loss of the GLC's continuing programme of financial assistance for repairs and renovations on former GLC housing estates, which at borough insistence was included as a statutory obligation upon the Council in all housing transfer orders made by the Government from 1980 onwards. The legal force of this obligation to assist repairs and improvements was extinguished with GLC abolition, and the boroughs are now having difficulties in sustaining the renovation programme despite new post-abolition financial arrangements. The full impact of the removal of GLC support was cushioned somewhat during the immediate post-abolition period by forward funding of £78m for housing work which the GLC channelled to the boroughs through a private finance company, Satman Developments, and which successfully survived legal challenges by the LRB and Hillingdon.

The boroughs are also left with the problem of replacing GLC contributions towards revenue deficits on transferred housing (£72m in 1984/85), support for housing initiatives in the stress boroughs (£1.4m), area improvement grants to private homeowners (£6m to 3,000 homes located in 17 housing action areas and general improvement areas), loans to housing associations and co-operatives (£18m), and grants to voluntary organisations involved in the housing field (£4m) dealing with the special needs of the homeless and minority groups. However, all 33 boroughs agreed on a voluntary basis to set up the London Area Mobility Scheme (LAMS), while 13 boroughs at present fund the London Housing Unit to carry on the GLC's housing research activities.

Highways and Traffic Management

According to the Government's consultation document, *The reallocation of transport functions in London following GLC abolition* (revised version, July 1984), 'the main responsibility for London's roads and traffic would rest with the borough councils' (paragraph 6). Under the terms of the

Local Government Act 1985 (section 8 and Schedules 4 and 5), the
boroughs in fact became highway authorities for 830 miles of metropolitan roads and several of the Thames bridges, while the Department of
Transport added 65 miles to its existing 143 miles of trunk road network
in Greater London, along with responsibility for the Twickenham and
Kew Bridges, the Blackwall Tunnel, and the Woolwich Ferry (see
Map 22). At the same time, the boroughs took on traffic management
functions for all non-trunk roads (7,650 miles) within the capital. Their
freedom in exercising these highways and traffic management powers
has in practice, however, been severely constrained by the emergence of
new forms of both centralised direction and inter-authority co-
ordination.

As highway authorities, the boroughs are now responsible for both
maintenance work and new construction on the metropolitan roads
transferred to them, which includes associated structures such as
bridges, tunnels, flyovers and pedestrian subways. The GLC spent
£47.3m on road maintenance and operations and £37m on construction
and improvement of the metropolitan roads in its care in 1984/85.

As far as maintenance of ex-GLC roads is concerned, the boroughs
had already in fact been performing this work as the GLC's agents, and so
required little in the way of additional staff or expertise. They also
continue to act as maintenance agents for the DTp's newly acquired
trunk roads in London. Most of them do need to rely, however, on
outside technical assistance to monitor skid resistance and strength of
road surfaces, as well as other road conditions. The GLC's Road
Assessment Unit used to provide these services without cost to the
boroughs. After abolition, the LRB put the Unit and its equipment out to
tender, and the boroughs must now purchase road testing services from a
private company.

The boroughs' responsibilities for the upkeep of the Thames bridges
and other major structures may also prove onerous. Although the
Government proposed at one point that a single lead borough be made
responsible for the bridges and retain a team of specialists, in the end the
bridges were distributed among the riparian boroughs.

The transfer of maintenance responsibilities to the borough level has
meant, moreover, that the priority of repair work on road surfaces and
other structures of former metropolitan roads is no longer determined on
a London-wide basis, but now depends on conditions and the level of
resources in each individual borough, a situation which over time may
lead to wide variations in maintenance standards. A survey by the
Transport Unit of the London Strategic Policy Unit showed that in

1986/87 most boroughs were funding maintenance of former metropolitan roads at levels similar to the G L C in previous years, with 20 per cent of boroughs adopting even higher standards, and only one case of severe cuts in spending.

The boroughs' maintenance funding was affected, however, in both 1986/87 and 1987/88 by a miscalculation on the part of D O E civil servants, whereby a number of Inner London boroughs received a total of £22m in extra grant from central government for maintenance of ex-G L C roads which did not in fact run within their area, at the expense of Outer London boroughs which failed to obtain some of the grant funding owed to them for their new roads. A belated effort by the Secretary of State, Nicholas Ridley, to rectify this error was successfully blocked in the High Court by Greenwich. The Government has abandoned an appeal against the ruling.

The boroughs also took on a greater role in relation to new construction and improvement of London's highways following G L C abolition. Although the transport strategy pursued by the last Labour administration at County Hall was opposed to any significant increase in road capacity within Greater London, the G L C was engaged in several important schemes on its metropolitan roads, including the Rochester Way Relief Road (located in Greenwich, with an estimated cost of £75m at 1986 prices), the Hayes Bypass (Hillingdon/Ealing, £70m), and the North/South Route (Haringey/Enfield, £75m).

The first of these schemes became part of the D Tp's trunk road programme, but the other two were transferred to the boroughs. Both of them cut across borough boundaries and entail a substantial financial burden for the authorities taking charge, although they are eligible for extra funding (50 per cent of construction costs) from central government via the Transport Supplementary Grant (T S G) as road-building projects of 'more than local importance'. In the case of the North/South Route, the two boroughs involved decided to retain the services of the existing team of engineers previously employed by the G L C under an agency agreement with the L R B.

Beyond these inherited road-building projects, the boroughs have promoted new initiatives of their own, often involving schemes previously rejected or given low priority by County Hall. Merton, for example, unveiled schemes for relief roads and town centre improvements costing £36m a few days before G L C abolition took effect. Other authorities, such as Barking, Bexley, Bromley, Camden, Ealing, Enfield, Hillingdon, Sutton, Wandsworth and the City of London, have also recently put forward new road construction or improvement projects of their own. In all, the boroughs are now planning to complete 53 major schemes by 1996, entailing an estimated total cost of £421m (at 1986 prices).

According to the DTp, further road construction in London is needed in order to channel existing long-distance traffic away from sensitive local residential areas, but should not lead to an increase in overall traffic levels. But many observers believe that if the projects mentioned above, along with major new schemes proposed by the DTp for its trunk road networks are realised, they are likely to generate considerable amounts of additional traffic movements throughout the capital. This in turn could put still more pressure on the LBs to build and improve road capacity in their areas, even in the case of those boroughs that so far pursued alternative transport strategies such as improving facilities for public transport or for cyclists and pedestrians in order to encourage motorists to leave their vehicles at home and reduce congestion.

In their role as traffic management authorities for all non-trunk roads within Greater London, the boroughs are now responsible for making the legal orders regulating use of road space and parking facilities, as well as for the physical design, implementation and monitoring of traffic management schemes in their local areas. While relatively modest in terms of its demands on local authority resources (the GLC incurred £7.8m revenue and £12.5m capital expenditure on this function in 1984/85), traffic management is a complex issue which involved the GLC in continual controversy in its attempts to ensure the best possible use of existing road capacity in a context of generalised congestion, and to allocate priorities among the various and often conflicting interests present: buses v. private transport; pedestrians and cyclists v. motorists; local residents v. suburban commuters and heavy goods vehicles, etc.

Prior to abolition, the local authorities had already been involved with the GLC in determining details of traffic management schemes in their local areas, and in most cases the formal assumption of powers in this field has not posed serious problems for the boroughs. Altogether, they have taken on some 200–250 new staff (about 7 per borough on average) as a direct result of the transfer of this function, more than half of this increase being related to traffic order making within the borough solicitors' departments.

According to a survey by the Transport Group in the London Strategic Policy Unit (LSPU), 80 per cent of boroughs have experienced a considerable reduction (four weeks or more) in the time needed to process traffic orders as a result of the elimination of duplication between tiers. Half of them also report an increase in the number of new traffic management schemes created each year. There has been a shift in the type of schemes now being implemented, with a greater emphasis on pedestrian crossings (relatively cheap and popular with local voters), rather than the bus priority schemes and facilities for cyclists previously promoted by the GLC.

In regard to parking controls, the boroughs remain hampered, as was the GLC during its existence, by the fact that enforcement of these controls continues to lie with the traffic warden force employed by the Metropolitan Police, although the boroughs contribute a major portion of their means. The LBA and ALA have been lobbying the Home Office in favour of transferring the wardens and responsibility for enforcement to the boroughs, now that they had become responsible for parking regulations. These efforts have not yet been successful, although a review of arrangements for the warden force is in progress at present.

Borough councillors have generally welcomed the transfer of traffic management powers, as it affords them an opportunity to take direct credit before the electorate for measures protecting local residents from the adverse environmental impact of large flows of motor vehicles through their areas. The parochial outlook possible among elected members at the borough level, however, may prevent them from taking full account of the interests of other communities or the need to make provision for travel over longer distances, especially by commuters and commercial vehicles. Many traffic management measures have an impact beyond an individual borough's boundaries, while the effectiveness of others depends on co-operation between neighbouring boroughs (e.g. the creation of bus priority schemes on cross-borough routes) or at a London-wide level (e.g. policies limiting parking in congested centres, control of heavy lorry traffic, or modernisation of the traffic signals system).

In order to maintain a consistent and co-ordinated approach to key aspects of traffic policy, and ensure that major flows of road traffic within the capital are not disrupted, the Government sought to impose a number of restrictions and centralised controls on the boroughs' traffic management activities. The Local Government Act 1985 gives the Secretary of State for Transport powers to designate certain major non-trunk roads, so that boroughs are required to notify the DTp of any proposed schemes to regulate traffic or use of parking space along these designated roads, or even on adjoining roads if they affect traffic movement on a designated road (Schedule 5, paragraph 5). Within a one-month period following notification, the Secretary of State may exercise a power of veto over these borough schemes. At present, some

330 miles of former metropolitan roads have been designated in this way, and together with trunk roads in the capital they form part of a new 550 mile 'strategic road network' which has been defined by the D Tp for Greater London, largely catering to the needs of longer-distance, area-wide movements.

The Secretary of State is also authorised to issue general guidance to the London boroughs on traffic management, along with reserve powers to intervene directly where these guidelines are disregarded with adverse effects for traffic movement (Schedule 5, paragraph 6). After consultation, guidance of this type was issued in April 1987 (D Tp Circular 2/87), which set out basic principles to be observed by the boroughs in matters such as major roads with through traffic, road safety, schemes for pedestrians and cyclists, parking control, bus and other vehicle priority schemes, and signing on primary routes.

Finally, the abolition legislation laid an obligation on the London boroughs to consult with neighbouring local authorities concerning any proposals likely to have an impact on traffic in their area. In the event of a disagreement between authorities, the Secretary of State now has the power to arbitrate between them (Schedule 5, paragraph 7).

The Government's initial proposals for traffic management in London after G L C abolition also looked, at least in part, to voluntary joint arrangements created by the boroughs themselves to take charge of several important executive functions which the G L C had previously provided on a London-wide basis, and to co-ordinate approaches to various policy issues. Efforts to form such joint arrangements have had only limited success at best.

Concerning the executive functions, in many cases the boroughs are now dependent for specialised expertise on outside agencies. For example, they failed to reach any agreement on a structure to support the Traffic Control System Unit (T C S U), responsible for the computerised Urban Traffic Control system which co-ordinates traffic signals in central and inner London, as well as other maintenance and development work on signals. The Department of Transport eventually invoked reserve powers to take charge of the Unit, and it was at first run by the L R B as the D Tp's agent, and has latterly passed to the City of London as agent. Similarly, the D Tp assumed overall responsibility for the Greater London Transportation Survey, with the actual work being continued by private consultants. Other traffic surveys, accident analysis and road safety work are carried out by the London Research Centre, which is supported by a joint committee of boroughs, while research on traffic noise and the environmental impact of roads in London is provided by

London Scientific Services. The GLC Cyclist and Pedestrian teams, as well as other specialist groups have been disbanded, however, and few boroughs have retained comparable expertise as part of the permanent staff of their own engineering departments.

The degree of policy co-ordination achieved by the boroughs on a voluntary joint basis has also been disappointing. The London Boroughs' Transport Committee is responsible for implementation and enforcement of the Lorry Ban at night-time and weekends established by the GLC in January 1986, but several boroughs have already decided not to participate, as noted in Chapter 4. The LBA and ALA both have transport specialists and could facilitate common approaches on a wider range of issues, but their potential role is limited by the partial and partisan nature of their memberships and their lack of executive powers.

A somewhat more effective joint mechanism for road and traffic matters exists at the level of the boroughs' own professional officers. In the months prior to GLC abolition, the Association of London Borough Engineers and Surveyors (ALBES) produced a number of 'codes of practice' which aimed to ensure uniform standards were maintained by borough engineers throughout London in the design and implementation of road and traffic management schemes. But while useful in preventing chaos on the streets, meetings at officer level and codes of practice cannot provide policy decisions regarding priorities or the amount of resources to be devoted to traffic problems at the London-wide level, which would require participation of elected councillors from each borough.

Given the present degree of fragmentation among the boroughs and the powers retained by the DTp, the latter is likely to be the primary source of major policy initiatives regarding roads and traffic in London for the forseeable future. Borough input into decision-making at this level has so far been minimal. Before issuing guidelines this year on strategic traffic management within the capital, the Secretary of State did consult beforehand with the boroughs, via their local authority associations, the LBA and the ALA, as well as with the Metropolitan Police, but no important modifications of the DTp's directives came out of this process. The Greater London Advisory Consultative Committee in theory provides a means for borough representatives to discuss policies for London's roads with the DTp's junior Minister for Roads and Traffic, but up to now this body has had a rather desultory existence, meeting only once a year. A new London Road Safety Committee, announced by the Government prior to abolition, whose members were to include boroughs, the D Tp, the Metropolitan Police and national road safety organisations, has not yet been set up.

Public transport

This was perhaps the most highly visible area of the G L C's activities for most Londoners, and one with a considerable impact on their daily lives, especially after the Council assumed in 1969 overall policy and financial control over London Transport, the operator of the bus and Underground services in the capital. The G L C's role also involved funding in support of some British Rail services and facilities within Greater London (although it had no powers of direction over B R), and aid to a number of community transport schemes and other projects aimed at the needs of special categories of transport users. By 1984/85, G L C funding of public transport services had risen to £278m in revenue, and £145m in capital expenditure.

In July 1984, following the controversial ruling by the Law Lords in 1981 overturning the G L C's Fares Fair policy and other conflicts over the Council's stance on public transport, the Conservative Government enacted the London Regional Transport Act, which transferred control over L T services to a new quango, London Regional Transport (L R T), a body appointed by and under the policy direction of the Secretary of State for Transport. The remaining G L C powers over public transport which were passed on to the London boroughs following abolition are thus largely residual in nature, although some boroughs are making maximum use of the leverage they afford *vis-à-vis* L R T and other transport operators in the capital.

The present Government, however, has meanwhile announced its intention to use reserve powers contained in the Transport Act 1985 (section 46) to introduce deregulation of the bus services in London within the next few years, as it has already done throughout the rest of Britain. This would only require the Secretary of State to lay an Order before Parliament. Deregulation would end L R T's present monopoly over the provision of bus services in Greater London (at present private bus companies are only permitted to tender for routes under contract with L R T, in competition with the latter's own bus subsidiary, London Buses Ltd – L B L), and allow operators substantial freedom to determine their routes, level of fares and most other service conditions.

It is also possible that proposals to privatise certain sections of L R T Underground or B R rail networks within London might also be implemented in the near future, and has already begun in the case of some of L R T's ancillary services (e.g. catering, cleaning and computing). Both deregulation and privatisation may weaken the local authorities' influence over the quality of public transport provision in London.

The London Regional Transport Act 1984 contains a number of provisions specifying the relationship between L R T and local authorities in London (later amended in certain minor aspects by the Transport Act 1985). The transport authority is required to inform the boroughs on the general level of services, facilities to be provided, general structure of routes, and basic policy on the level of fares and charges (section 30), in addition to publishing an Annual Report (section 34).

Provision of such information, however, does not allow the boroughs any input into L R T's policies. Nevertheless all of the boroughs have created liaison arrangements with the District Manager of one of the six bus districts set up by L B L, either through informal contacts with borough officers or by invitations to attend formal meetings with local councillors, which permit information to be exchanged about local bus services and transport conditions. But few boroughs have been able to develop similar links with the Line and Area Managers for the Underground and B R rail services in their area. At the London-wide level, the London Strategic Policy Unit's Transport Unit monitored developments affecting public transport services on behalf of its member boroughs until it was wound up.

The 1984 Act also lays down a duty on L R T to consult with the boroughs before setting its policies or making decisions on a number of matters. This includes the preparation of L R T's Strategy Statements, which present its plans for the provision of public transport services in London over a three-year period, as well as the policies of the L R T subsidiaries and any arrangements agreed with B R and other operators (section 7).

Boroughs affected by closures of Underground lines or stations can demand to be consulted by L R T, and have the right to participate in inquiries on closures held by the London Regional Passengers' Committee (section 42). Similar rights exist in the case of B R rail services in London. The boroughs' views must also be sought by L R T on any proposals for new services, on 'relevant aspects', of alterations in existing services, and on any decision to discontinue a service (section 43). This requirement concerns both services run by L R T's own subsidiaries, and those which are contracted out to other operators. But the term 'relevant aspects' used in the Act is tightly defined as including only modifications of service routes, terminal and returning points, and stopping places for passengers, while 'discontinuation' of a service does not include withdrawal of services on particular sections of a route or at certain times or days. In practice, LRT consultation exercises over proposed service changes have given rise to widespread complaints from the boroughs (and in one case a successful legal challenge by Southwark), particularly over the limited time (28 days) allowed to them for making a response.

In addition to their rights to receive information and to be consulted on certain decisions, the L R T Act 1984 gave boroughs limited powers to enter into agreements with LRT for the provision and finance of transport services. These include the 'buying in' of extra services where LRT (or BR where similar powers exist) is unwilling to do so on its own (section 28). Brent, for example, financed the additional cost of a Sunday service along London Buses' 297 route, while Lewisham has funded four new bus routes called 'CentreLink' for Christmas shoppers travelling to its town centre. These powers may also be exercised collectively, as in the case of four South London boroughs (Lambeth, Southwark, Lewisham and Greenwich) who negotiated with BR to set up a new orbital South London Line between Abbey Wood and Clapham Junction, with frequent services and two new stations at Brixton and Brockley. The boroughs would be providing BR with an annual joint subsidy of £0.25m in revenue support to make up its losses in operating this service.

Financial support by the boroughs might also take the form of capital grants for equipment and infrastructure to LRT or BR, or the joint funding of local station refurbishments (as in the previously successful joint GLC/BR programme). The boroughs' capacity to finance new services and facilities, however, is in most cases likely to be extremely limited by ratecapping and other restrictions. In the event of deregulation of the bus services, the cost of supporting socially necessary but uncommercial routes may be even greater, due to the loss of cross-subsidy which still exists within the integrated system. LRT has recently imposed accounting practices on its bus subsidiary designed to eliminate such cross-subsidy.

The boroughs also have other powers at their disposal to aid transport operators. Perhaps the most important of these is the highway and traffic management powers acquired following GLC abolition, which include the creation of new bus lanes, bus laybys and other measures to assist the passage of buses through areas of traffic congestion (see previous section). The GLC maintained a vigorous programme in this field, instituting 227 measures throughout Greater London between 1981 and 1986, including a pilot project to give buses priority at traffic signals, as well as both 'with-' and 'contra-' flow bus lanes. LRT continues to advocate such measures, as congestion is a major cause of delays and financial loss for its bus services, but the boroughs are likely to encounter resistance from the D Tp (which retains the right to veto such schemes on 330 miles of 'designated' borough roads) and from the Metropolitan Police, due to the disruption to private car traffic caused by their introduction.

The creation of bus lanes on cross-borough routes also entails lengthy consultations with neighbouring authorities, while measures involving modifications to traffic signals require the technical expertise of the London Traffic Control System Unit (LTCSU). The latter, however, severely reduced its 1987/88 programme to introduce bus priority measures (which originally included 288 signalled junctions in Outer London, and now consists of only 56 junctions within LBL'S SELKENT network). Moreover, many boroughs are themselves now reluctant to introduce more bus lanes. In 1986/87, the boroughs created five new bus lanes in all, but at the same time removed four others, a net gain of only one.

Finally, the boroughs can provide support in the form of subsidies or even the purchase of fleets for local community transport services which make available vehicles for hire by local groups and charities. These are usually organised through the voluntary sector, although Islington, for example, set up the Dial-a-Ride service in the borough on a direct labour basis. At the London-wide level, the boroughs have formed joint arrangements for the Concessionary Fares Scheme, which funds the free and reduced-price travel passes for old-age pensioners and the disabled on LRT and BR services in London, and for the Taxicard Scheme subsidising the use of radio-taxis by the disabled.

The boroughs' role thus includes a variety of new powers and activities in relation to public transport, but their position is still weak in relation to the D Tp and the major transport operators, LRT and BR. They are also hampered by their lack of experience in dealing with this issue, and in some cases their own internal structures remain ill-adapted, with no single council committee having an overview of transport policy. In many boroughs, engineering departments continue to have a strong interest in roads and traffic management, but little expertise in public transport. Since GLC abolition, however, several boroughs have begun to reorganise themselves, forming new Transport Committees (e.g. Ealing), borough liaison groups with local passengers and/or transport staff (e.g. Lewisham, Lambeth and Hackney), or have begun to produce local plans for public transport provision in their area. At the London-wide level, the ALA, LBA, and LPAC provide some opportunities for boroughs to co-ordinate their responses, but lack statutory powers and suffer from political and geographical divisions.

Parks, open spaces and Green Belt land

The boroughs previously had concurrent powers with the upper tier
authority in this field, but have now taken on most of the considerable
landholdings and associated activities of the G L C, following an order of
transfer by the Secretary of State under clause 92(i) of the 1985 Local
Government Act. These holdings included 43 urban parks and open
spaces encompassing an area of about 5,500 acres, compared to total
public open space within Greater London of 42,800 acres (including
D O E-run Royal Parks, the boroughs' local parks, and the Lee Valley
Regional Park). The G L C also owned the freehold of 12,425 acres of
designated Green Belt land, both within and outside Greater London
under the 1938 Green Belt Act (including 1,075 acres devoted to
statutory smallholdings), as well as a contributory interest in an additional 27,500 acres managed by other authorities.

Although the Government's intentions were that responsibility for
these areas should in general pass into the hands of individual authorities, either the boroughs or the surrounding districts and counties, in
some cases more complex arrangements were required due to the size,
location, particular use or financial implications involved. Regarding the
urban parks and open spaces, in 1984/85 the Council spent £21.9m
revenue and £4.3m capital (including sports and recreation – see pp. 129–
30). Under the G L C, these areas were organised into 22 management
units, with nine units containing parks which sprawled across two or even
three boroughs. In some instances the Secretary of State simply divided
up the parks among the authorities involved, each taking charge for the
area within their boundaries. Blackheath (272 acres), for example, was
split between Greenwich (78 acres) and Lewisham (194 acres). On the
other hand, Victoria Park (218 acres), lying between Tower Hamlets
(148 acres) and Hackney (70 acres), was to have a joint management
committee and joint funding, with Tower Hamlets playing the lead role,
an arrangement viewed with enthusiasm by neither party. Even where
complexities of this nature have not arisen, the costs entailed by transfer
of these parks have often been burdensome, and in several cases (e.g.
Burgess Park in Southwark and Mile End Park in Tower Hamlets) have
already halted development work planned by the G L C.

One remaining source of difficulties has been the management of
Hampstead Heath, where a definitive arrangement had still to be
reached in the summer of 1988. The Heath is one of the largest open
spaces in London, with an area of 789 acres within the boroughs of
Camden (667 acres), Barnet (111.5 acres) and Haringey (10.5 acres).

Initially, the Government proposed that the Heath should be managed by a joint committee of the three adjoining councils. But because of its unique character and high running costs (now estimated at £2m per year), the DOE later argued that control by a single agency was needed, and recommended the City of London should take on this role. The City has the financial resources required and already has considerable experience in the management of open space within Greater London, including the vast area of Epping Forest (over 6,000 acres). This plan has been bitterly resisted by Opposition MPs, Camden and many local groups, and the Government finally decided to transfer control of the Heath to the LRB during the first year after GLC abolition (with the exception of the grounds surrounding Kenwood House, transferred to the Historic Buildings and Monuments Commission), pending further discussions on a long-term solution.

The Green Belt land previously owned by the GLC was transferred by the Secretary to over 20 different borough, district and county authorities. The Outer London boroughs thus received some 7,000 acres (compared to previous borough holdings of 75,000 acres) of land located within their boundaries or straddling their borders with the Home Counties. Outside Greater London, both the GLC's ownership and its contributory interest in lands were generally passed to the districts and counties. In those cases, however, where a London borough already shared a joint contributory interest with the GLC, the latter's share passed to the borough.

The GLC's involvement in these Green Belt holdings included conservation measures, estate management, encouragement of agricultural and horticultural enterprises, and the development of recreation and educational uses on land. The Council often participated in similar schemes by other bodies (e.g. the Herts/Barnet, Colne Valley Park and Lower Mole country management projects), and it was a powerful force in the defence of the Green Belt as a whole against encroachment by development. As the strategic planning authority within Greater London, it advised the boroughs on all planning applications affecting the Green Belt, and generally recommended refusal. Its contributory interests in the holdings of other authorities outside London also gave it an effective veto power over proposals to dispose of sites or allow development. In all, GLC management and control of the Green Belt entailed revenue expenditure of £1.5m and capital spending of £0.3m in 1984/85.

Economic development

The GLC, especially in its last years, had developed a number of interventionist policies directed at London's economy, in order to stimulate employment and encourage equal opportunities. These initiatives included the creation of the Greater London Training Board in 1981 and Greater London Enterprise (then known as the Greater London Enterprise Board or GLEB) in 1982, an Industrial Property Development Programme to refurbish existing and construct new industrial premises, the development of Technology Networks to help form links between University research and small firms, the provision of grants to employment projects, and the production of economic planning documents as well as strategies for individual economic sectors. The Council's Industry and Employment Programme totalled £45.8m in revenue and £21m in capital expenditure in 1984/85, most of it funded under section 137 of the Local Government Act 1972, which gives local authorities general powers to spend on behalf of the interests of their area and give financial assistance to business up to a maximum equal to the product of a 2p rate.

The London boroughs already had concurrent powers to give assistance to industry prior to abolition, and the Government saw no need to make specific provision for GLC activities in this area. Of existing GLC initiatives, Greater London Enterprise survived under voluntary arrangements, assisted by funding to employment and training projects through the London Borough Grants Scheme. But many individual boroughs have begun similar initiatives of their own in recent years, including the provision of grants, loans and loan guarantees to small businesses, training schemes, or the creation and refurbishment of industrial and commercial premises. All but three boroughs fund their own enterprises (for example Croydon Business Venture Ltd, Islington's North London Business Development Agency and the Wandsworth Business Resource Service). The funding available for economic policy initiatives remains restricted. One effect of abolition was to eliminate spending under section 137 by the upper tier of London government, thereby halving the amount of resources from this particular source. Some boroughs with inner city areas do have additional spending powers under the Inner Urban Areas Act 1978.

Funding for Arts and voluntary organisations

In addition to central government and other agencies such as the London Boroughs Grants Scheme (LBGS), Greater London Arts and the Trust for London, the individual London boroughs also share in the responsibility for continuing funding to the type of voluntary organisations previously supported by the GLC, an area where the boroughs already possessed concurrent powers (see p. 111). Of the total replacement funding from all sources of £83.5m in 1986/87, the individual boroughs provided £26.9 from their main grant programmes over and above their contributions to the L B G S of £26.4m in 1986/87 and £28.0m in 1987/88.

During the first year after abolition, the boroughs were able to maintain a relatively adequate level of funding for artistic and voluntary groups, because of additional R S G provided to them from central government, and because of resources made available to new London-wide bodies and to appointed bodies. Only 45 local groups previously funded by the G L C were forced to close down because their applications for main programme aid from the boroughs were denied, while another 18 found their funding severely reduced. Almost half of those that lost funding were located in four boroughs: Westminster (7), Wandsworth (5), Tower Hamlets (5) and Barnet (4). The City of Westminster refused to participate in any transitional funding arrangements, opting instead for a 'pound for pound' scheme, whereby the council would match funds raised by the voluntary sector from other sources.

In 1987/88, the situation was less generous for voluntary organisations, due to the tightening financial circumstances of many London boroughs, particularly those twelve boroughs which were ratecapped. The burden on all boroughs was increased on account of the tapering off of the D O E's share of transitional funding (see Chapter 3), the exhaustion of G L C forward funding, reductions in Arts Council funding, and inflation. According to a study by the National Council for Voluntary Organisations, the boroughs would be required to find an additional £10.6m in 1987/88 to make up for these factors, offset only by the creation of the small Trust for London. With many Labour boroughs now seeking massive reductions in expenditure, it appears unlikely that they can continue to meet this demand in forthcoming years.

Sports and recreation

The London boroughs inherited responsibility for a wide range of facilities and activities devoted to sports and recreation previously provided by the G L C, which in 1984/85 involved £14.5m revenue and £0.8m capital spending (in addition to amounts included under parks and open spaces discussed above). While the National Sports Centre at Crystal Palace was transferred to the Sports Council, most other major G L C installations went to the boroughs, including Brixton Recreation Centre (Lambeth), the Old Ford Manor Golf Course (Barnet), West London Stadium (Tower Hamlets), Herne Hill Stadium for cycling

(Lambeth), as well as other facilities such as many other smaller sports pitches, adventure playgrounds, swimming baths, horseriding facilities, etc. Along with these facilities, the boroughs also became responsible for organising sports coaching, safety on sports grounds, pre-school playgroups and entertainments in the special events, such as the Easter Parade (Wandsworth).

Miscellaneous transfers

A number of smaller GLC services were transferred to the boroughs at abolition. These involved entertainments licensing, building control (inner London only), tourism, local valuation panels, civic amenities sites and GLC provision for minority groups. Boroughs picked up these services with varying degrees of enthusiasm: those such as entertainments licensing were universally continued, while provision for minorities was generally picked up only by Labour boroughs.

Conclusion: What the Boroughs Do Now

Services which were originally given to the London boroughs and which have been unaffected by functional or structural reform include those listed at the start of Table 4.1, e.g. personal social services and environmental services. Following the transfer of housing from the GLC to boroughs either before or as a result of abolition, housing is now a full borough function. Planning and a number of other services, which were previously run concurrently by the GLC and the boroughs, are now run solely or largely by the boroughs. We have already described in detail the transfers made from the GLC after abolition. A brief description of current borough services is given below.

1. **Education** is the major service provided by the boroughs, although in Inner London, it is run through a single directly elected authority, the Inner London Education Authority (see pp. 93–96). The Government has proposals to allow inner boroughs to become separate education authorities. Education services include schools for children aged 5–16 and a system of further education for those beyond the age of 16. Some boroughs provide nursery education. Until 1989, eight polytechnics (higher education institutions similar to universities) will be controlled by local authorities in the capital. Inner London has five polytechnics, the outer boroughs three.
2. **Social services** is another significant borough service. As in other parts of Britain, London boroughs run services for the young and for

the elderly, including residential homes, social workers, home helps, foster parents and day centres. Local authority social service departments generally have strong links with local hospitals. New policy initiatives, such as 'Care in the Community', are having the effect of moving individuals out of health service care and into that of local authorities. In Inner London, there is inevitably a need for regular communications between social services departments and the Inner London Education Authority.

3. **Environmental health** has been solely a borough function since 1965. A range of services are described as 'environmental health' including pollution control, noise control, street cleansing, gypsy sites, inspection of premises selling food, pest control and infectious diseases.

4. **Libraries** are run by borough councils. Central boroughs (such as Westminster, Camden and the City) provide specialised library services which are used by many individuals from outside their areas.

5. **Housing** is, after education, the largest of the services provided by the boroughs. Unlike the bulk of local government services which are financed out of local taxation and government grants, housing revenue expenditure is largely financed out of charges for services (i.e. rents). But in authorities like Camden, Islington and Lambeth, substantial amounts of local ratepayers' money (over £30m per borough in 1987/88) is used to hold down rents. Council house building has been very much reduced since the late 1970s both in London and elsewhere in Britain. Local authorities in Inner London suffer acute pressure on their resources as a result of their statutory obligations to provide accommodation for the homeless.

6. **Arts, leisure and recreation.** Although these were a concurrent set of services run by both the boroughs and the GLC, the bulk of spending was always undertaken by the boroughs. This spending includes support for arts organisations and the provision of facilities like swimming pools, parks and other sports areas.

7. **Refuse collection** has always been a borough function, involving the removal of commercial and domestic rubbish. As explained above, the GLC used to be responsible for waste disposal, a duty transferred at abolition to consortia of boroughs.

8. **Planning** is a borough function, though they must draw up local plans having regard to strategic guidance produced by the Environment Secretary. Planning involves not only the production of local plans, but also decisions on individual planning applications to take down, build or change structures.

9. **Roads and street lighting.** All local roads (not major roads or motorways) are borough functions, as is street lighting. Boroughs are also responsible for regulating parking and traffic management. However, the Transport Secretary has considerable reserve powers concerning roads and traffic (see pp. 115–122).

In addition to these major service groups, London boroughs are responsible for consumer protection, licensing of premises and services, markets, cemeteries and crematoria, and some trading services. A full breakdown of which authorities and institutions run which public service in London is given in the Directory.

CHAPTER 6

Representing London

Who Speaks for London?

Previous chapters have documented the geographical and functional fragmentation of London's government. The discussion now turns to the question of who speaks for London as a whole? Who, for example, negotiates with central government on behalf of London's councils? Who represents London abroad? Who entertains visiting dignitaries? Who formulates the positions taken by the political parties in London?

In this chapter we examine four means of representing London. First we look at the local authority associations; second at individual authorities who play a leading role in London; third we turn to political organisation in the capital; and finally we consider matters of ceremony. There are other contenders for inclusion in a discussion of representation which have been omitted. London is associated closely with the monarchy and though the discussion examines the role of the Lord Lieutenants, the monarchy itself, above all a national institution, is not discussed. Second, the media play a vital role in the shaping of political debate and the dissemination of ideas and opinion. London has its newspapers, radio and television programmes and is the location of the national press and broadcasting networks. Much national news originates in London. The definition of representation adopted here, however, is a narrow one and excludes vehicles which lie outside government and politics in the strictest sense.

Local Authority Associations

Local authorities up and down the country belong to associations which represent their collective interests, particularly to central government. Almost all London boroughs belong to the Association of Metropolitan Authorities (AMA) which represents councils in the capital and the major

conurbations. In addition London has a tradition of separate representation. The origins of this lie in the uniqueness of London's problems and
its long history of two tier local government. The boroughs were obliged
to organise themselves to deal with the powerful upper tier authority, first
the London County Council (LCC) and then the Greater London
Council (GLC). The Metropolitan Boroughs Committee and, after
1965, the London Boroughs Association (LBA) developed a considerable presence in London government. The London Government Act
1963 defined a number of roles for bodies 'which appear to the Secretary
of State to be representative'. In addition to its role as spokesbody and
negotiator on behalf of the boroughs, the LBA was also a co-ordinator
and provider of services such as the distribution of grants to voluntary
bodies and the housing mobility scheme.

Until 1983 the LBA represented the interests of all the London
boroughs. It was never, though, able to speak clearly and strongly for the
interests of London as a whole on many contentious issues. London
contains different and conflicting interests which divide geographical
areas (especially Inner and Outer London) and social groups. Unlike the
democratically elected upper tier authority, the voluntary LBA could only
operate on the basis of a compromise between these elements. Central
government's proposals to abolish the GLC and the metropolitan counties demolished this fragile consensus. A number of Labour boroughs
left the LBA when it adopted a pro-abolition stance and, together with
the GLC, set up an alternative representative body, the Association of
London Authorities (ALA). By default the LBA became the voice of
Conservative London. One outcome of the break-up of the old LBA was
to make untenable a proposal widely canvassed at the time that the LBA
should take over some of the London-wide functions of the GLC. The
White Paper, *Streamlining the Cities* (Department of the Environment,
1983), devoted only five lines to the question of representation which
centred on the view that it was not a problem.

It has been argued that the GLC and MCCs have an essential role in
representing, to Government and generally, the wider interests of their areas.
The Government consider that the borough and district councils are quite
capable of performing this role acting together voluntarily. (para 2.30)

The capacity is not in doubt, but the sectional nature of the views
projected has shifted the locus of negotiation and bargaining and thereby
changed the probability of acting in certain ways and following certain
policies.

The Association of Metropolitan Authorities

The formal objectives of the A M A are as follows:

1. To watch over, protect and promote the interests, rights, powers and duties of its member authorities as they may be affected by legislation or proposed legislation or otherwise.
2. To provide a forum for the discussion of matters of common concern to its member authorities and a means by which joint views may be formulated and expressed, particularly in negotiations with Government departments.
3. To provide (in conjunction, where appropriate, with the other local authority associations) such central services for its member authorities as it may consider to be appropriate.

All the London boroughs except Bromley belong to the A M A, together with the City and I L E A. London accounts for almost half the membership of the A M A which also includes the 36 metropolitan districts outside London. The nineteen joint authorities for fire, police and transport, created after abolition, are corporate members with reduced voting rights. The A M A has its headquarters in London with a staff of about 50. Full Association meetings take place in London and so do many committee meetings. The press and public are admitted to both though there are provisions whereby items can be heard in private.

Full member authorities can send up to three delegates to A M A meetings but each council has only one vote. The A M A has twelve committees, mostly with 30 to 40 members to which local authorities elect councillors on a regional basis. There are checks which ensure that no council is over-represented on the committees. Officers of member councils act as advisors. The A M A has 88 vice-presidents who are peers, M P s and M E P s from the main political parties, elected annually. They form a key link with Parliament.

Local authorities pay a subscription to the A M A. In the year 1986/87 the full subscription was £20,800, half price for corporate members. The A M A has a total income of about £1.8m, the greater part from subscriptions but some from publications, events and rents.

The A M A is controlled by Labour at the present time. Although London authorities are numerically important the A M A has a very strong role in representing the interests of the provincial cities. Northern cities play a prominent role in the leadership but there are two key links for London. At the present time the leader of Croydon both chairs the L B A (see below) and is the leader of the opposition on the A M A. The leader of

Islington chairs the ALA and is a deputy chair of the AMA.

There is an agreement between the AMA and the LBA concerning which issues should be dealt with by which Association. Issues which relate only to London are the province of the London associations. The committee structures of the AMA and LBA emphasise different sets of services. In part this is a political emphasis but the difference also reflects the wider membership of the AMA and the peculiarity of London government, for example its lack of responsibility for policing.

The London Boroughs Association
Functions
The formal objectives of the LBA are as follows:

1. To protect and advance the powers, interests, rights and privileges of the constituent Councils and to watch over those powers, interests, rights and privileges as they may be affected by legislation, or proposed legislation or otherwise.
2. To discuss questions of London government, and to advise and assist the constitutent Councils in the administration of their powers and duties.
3. To express the views of the Association and to consult with appropriate bodies or persons whenever deemed advisable.

It is therefore a forum for discussing common problems, and a means of co-ordinating activity and expressing a corporate view to Government and other bodies. It is no longer a service-providing body, in the way it was before abolition when it ran a housing mobility scheme and paid a small number of grants to voluntary bodies.

Membership
Eighteen boroughs and the City belong to the LBA, the majority of them Conservative controlled:

Conservative authorities:

Barnet	Redbridge
Bexley	Wandsworth
Bromley	Westminster
Croydon	
Enfield	Alliance authorities:
Harrow	Richmond-upon-Thames
Kensington and Chelsea	Sutton
Merton	Tower Hamlets

Labour authorities:	Authorities with
Barking and Dagenham	no overall control:

Independent authorities:
City of London

Havering
Hillingdon
Kingston-upon-Thames

The location of the member authorities, shown on Map 5, demonstrates the fragmentation of the L B A's constituency. It covers two-thirds of the geographical area of London and about 56 per cent of its population.

The Association has 60 members who are appointed by its constituent councils. Much of the work of the L B A is carried out by its committees: General Purposes, Housing and Works, Social Services and Education. Each member council appoints three members to the Association who in turn appoints them to its committees. Outer London boroughs appoint members to the Education Committee; the chair, vice-chair and opposition leader of the Education Committee sit on the full Association. Councils send representatives of the majority party if there is one; hung authorities send a mixed delegation. The Association has a clear Conservative majority. The chairman is elected annually by the full Association.

Budget
The L B A's annual budget amounts to rather less than £250,000. Each member authority pays an annual subscription which for 1987/88 is £12,750. This is a considerable increase on the 1986/87 subscription of £9,450. The increase was caused by the loss of a number of boroughs which became Labour controlled in the local elections.

Most of the budget is used to reimburse boroughs who employ staff on the L B A's behalf. The Association pays their salary and a sum which covers overheads such as postage, telephones and accommodation. Other much smaller areas of expenditure are printing and publications.

Staffing
The Association and its committees are serviced by honorary clerks, all of them chief executives of London boroughs. The contribution of the honorary clerks, their assistants and secretarial help amounts to the equivalent of ten to eleven full time staff.

The Association is dependent for professional advice upon officers working within the London boroughs. When the L B A represented all London boroughs this advice was provided by the relevant association of London chief officers. That advice has now to be channelled in two

directions: to the LBA and the ALA. The LBA does receive papers from
chief officers associations as a whole but it also has a number of ad hoc
arrangements whereby it receives advice from groups of officers which
will not include those overtly advising the ALA.

Public access
Issues are normally brought to the LBA by the boroughs, central
government or other public bodies. Local groups and members of the
public are expected to approach their local borough who will take the
issue foward to the LBA if it has London-wide implications. The press
are invited to meetings of the full Association but it is not normal practice
for the public or press to attend committees.

The representative role of the LBA
The LBA generally adopts a reactive stance. At the present time its
political sympathy with central government inhibits the presentation of
strong public views on many issues; its political position, however, gives it
an effective weight with a Conservative government. The ALA, on the
other hand, maintains a very high public profile and it is possible that the
LBA may be edged towards raising its own profile.

Despite its predominantly Conservative and Outer London membership the LBA feels that it does represent the interests of London as a
whole, albeit by putting first the interests of its own members. For many
of those authorities their sense of London is a peripheral one. They cover
outer suburbs and in some cases free-standing communities whose
identification with the metropolis is less than wholehearted. Together
with the very wealthy central boroughs which belong to the LBA they feel
that they are net contributors and as such should have a say over areas
which are net consumers of resources.

On many issues the LBA and the ALA take different positions; on a
large number of others they take a common view and work jointly to
pursue it. This is made possible by the commonality of professional
advice upon which each draws, and by mutual recognition of the other's
legitimacy as a representative body, which enables the leaders of the two
associations to work together.

The Association of London Authorities

Functions
The ALA states its objectives as 'to protect and promote the interests,
rights, powers and duties of all its member authorities and to seek proper
levels of government financial support for London in general and

member authorities in particular'. In order to do this the ALA:

Provides a forum for London boroughs to come together to discuss issues of common concern and formulate policies and to generally ensure that members have the resources and powers needed to operate effectively and efficiently. . . . It seeks to publicise as widely as possible its members' case. On behalf of its members, it actively lobbies Parliament in conjunction with other local authority associations and interest groups and works to ensure that the democratic principle of local government is protected.

Membership
Fifteen boroughs and ILEA belong to the ALA. They are all Labour boroughs. Tower Hamlets, which became Alliance in the local elections in 1986, left the ALA subsequently. The boroughs are:

Barking and Dagenham	Hackney	Lambeth
Brent	Hammersmith and Fulham	Lewisham
Camden	Haringey	Newham
Ealing	Hounslow	Southwark
Greenwich	Islington	Waltham Forest

The membership of the ALA represents the stressed inner ring of London between the prosperous central business district and the outer suburbs. In population terms the boroughs involved represent about 45 per cent of London's total.

Structure
Member authorities nominate a representative, usually the council leader, to the full Association. Beneath the Association are thirteen committees, to which members are also nominated, covering the main local authority services and areas of concern to the member authorities such as employment, race, the police, women, and lesbian and gay issues. The chair and vice-chairs are elected annually by the full Association.

Budget
The budget for 1987/88 is set at £848,330, in the previous financial year being £794,845. Member subscription is the main source of income. For 1987/88 the subscription has been set at £58,051 (the ILEA pays twice the borough sum, i.e. £116,103). A small income from ALA activities, such as sales of publications, is anticipated in the current year. Salaries and accommodation are the main expenditure heads.

Staffing
The ALA employs approximately 30 staff in its central office. They

provide administrative support as well as research and policy development. All staff are paid through Islington's payroll system. Like the LBA the ALA draws upon officers within member boroughs for professional advice.

Public access
The ALA has published and promotes a charter for open government and consistent with this the public are admitted to meetings and have access to the budget, accounts and papers.

The representative role of the ALA
The ALA is proactive and pursues the campaigning role which it adopted at the time of abolition. It is politically out of sympathy with the present Government and has no privileged access to it. It compensates by pursuing a relentless public campaign in support of its views and proposals. It courts publicity, produces documents and leaflets to distribute to support its stance and puts considerable effort into lobbying. The ALA has focused strongly on central government policy towards local government expenditure with which it disagrees on the grounds that it wrongly ignores the needs of its member authorities which contain disproportionate levels of unemployment, deprivation and physical decay.

Behind this public stance the ALA, like the LBA, is involved in wide-ranging discussion with central government and other bodies, putting forward the case of its member authorities. The suspicions and lack of legitimacy which surrounded the ALA when it was first founded appear to have gone and the ALA is seen as both representative and authoritative by both Government and other bodies.

The ALA is the voice of Labour London. While putting forward views which reflect the priorities of the inner authorities where Labour is in power it considers that on London-wide issues it is putting forward a genuine London-wide view.

The ALA is linked into what has been termed the 'GLC in exile'. Immediately after abolition, it worked closely with the London Strategic Policy Unit and other bodies funded by a similar set of boroughs as those belonging to the ALA. The ALA acts as the campaigning arm for work produced by these bodies. Through this network the ALA has until recently had considerable resources behind it.

Outer London Districts Metropolitan Police Consultative Association
The Association represents those non-metropolitan district councils

which fall within the Metropolitan Police District, but outside the Greater London area. Eight districts are wholly or partly in this position, and these are members of the Association: Broxbourne, Epsom and Ewell, Reigate and Banstead, Spelthorne, Elmbridge, Epping Forest, Welwyn Hatfield, and Hertsmere. Each district currently contributes £30 per year towards the costs of the Association.

The Association has an annual consultative meeting with the Receiver of the Metropolitan Police to discuss the Met's budget. This meeting, as well as meetings from time to time with Home Office ministers and officials, takes place jointly with the London Boroughs Association and the Association of London Authorities. Meetings also take place between the O L D M P C A and Metropolitan Police representatives to discuss operational matters such as crime prevention and traffic. Meetings involve both members and officers.

Other local authority groupings

Groups of boroughs sponsor statutory and voluntary authorities whose remit is London-wide or significantly wider than a single borough. Unlike the local authority associations they focus on particular issues or services. Many of them are described elsewhere in this handbook such as the London Planning Advisory Committee (L P A C) or the London Research Centre. Their role is not primarily representative but they cannot be ignored in any discussion of representation. Many of the functions of the former G L C are now lodged officially and unofficially with such bodies in line with the thinking of the White Paper, *Streamlining the Cities*, cited elsewhere. They are the obvious source of a voice for London on the issues upon which they focus.

As we have seen in earlier chapters, these groupings fall into two main categories. On the one hand there are those described in Chapter 3, in which all boroughs participate and which took over the key executive responsibilities of the G L C such as fire and civil defence, waste disposal and research and intelligence, as well as services formerly provided by the L B A such as housing mobility and grants to voluntary bodies. In the same category comes the London Planning Advisory Committee which seeks to provide guidance to central government on what strategic policies are needed for London. L P A C has the responsibility of identifying the interests of London in relation to development planning – a role which has proved difficult to fulfil in the light of the political divisions it must bridge. All these bodies operate at member level and some have faced some difficulty in developing goals and policies acceptable to the different areas and parties they represent.

The other groupings fall into the category of the 'G L C in exile'. These are the bodies described in Chapter 4, supported by groups of Labour boroughs, focusing on issues which central government has not recognised as legitimate subjects for local authority concern, such as policing, women and nuclear policy, as well as issues upon which the boroughs concerned had views at variance with Government, such as housing and strategic planning. They operate at both member and officer level and are often relatively generously staffed in comparison with the groupings in the first category. The biggest grouping set up was the L P S U (London Strategic Policy Unit) which had an establishment of around 340; others are much smaller, for example the L B N P C (London Boroughs Nuclear Policy Committee) has only three staff. Their role is to provide an alternative, socialist, London-wide view on key issues. The outlet for many of their reports and proposals is the A L A, although from the start there was a degree of competition between L P S U and A L A, both working on similar issues. Their future must, however, be in doubt at the present time. To subscribe to the full range of 'G L C in exile' groupings would cost a local authority around £1m per annum. Hard-pressed ratecapped Labour authorities may reduce their support in the coming year leaving only a small core of staff undertaking policy work linked in directly to the A L A.

Professional bodies

Local government is highly professionalised and large numbers of officers belong to professional associations which often have London regional branches. In addition chief officers in London form their own associations such as A L B E S (Association of London Borough Engineers and Surveyors), L F A C (London Financial Advisory Committee of treasurers), or L A D S S (London Association of Directors of Social Services). These bodies, listed in the Directory, are often the source of professional advice to the local authority associations and directly to central government and others seeking their opinion. They represent the London professional view on matters relating to their services. Their non-political status precludes a high public profile but their views are authoritative and legitimate in the eyes of politicians and central government. Much of the face-to-face negotiation between boroughs on wider issues occurs through such bodies and their working parties.

Individual Boroughs

No borough would claim that it spoke for London as a whole but a number of boroughs play a strong role in London government and in some cases act as opinion-leaders for others. The way they play such roles is very varied. Some are known publicly through flamboyant leaders but the more powerful ones often play their roles less openly. Some, such as the City of London, play a continuing special role; others such as Bromley have developed a role in relation to the politics of the times.

The Corporation of London

The boundaries of the City of London were set in Saxon times when a swathe of land surrounding the Roman walled city was annexed. Its present structure and powers date back to a charter of 1191 which sanctioned the appointment of a Mayor, a role which has endured almost 800 years. The City of London covers only approximately one square mile and has a resident population of under 6,000. However it contains the heart of the nation's financial sector: 300,000 people work there, mostly in banking, insurance, financial and business services – all growing sectors. The City is also a main area for tourists and has developed significant cultural facilities.

The City was bypassed in the reforms of London government in the 1960s. The Herbert Commission on London government recognised the anomalous position of the City but considered that its historical and ceremonial importance to London and the nation outweighed the advantages of modernisation. The City also stands apart politically: it has a unique system of elections and offices and remains outside the party political framework. Its standing in London-wide politics is therefore unusual. The City helps to represent business interests at home and abroad. It also plays an important ceremonial role in London through the office of the Lord Mayor of London, as described on p. 150.

The City has never sought to lead London on political issues but its non-partisan viewpoint has enabled it to play a balancing role on certain occasions. It attempted to moderate the aggressively pro-abolitionist stance of the L B A in the correct belief that it would lead inevitably to its disintegration, which in the City's view was not in the long-term interests of London. In 1986 the political composition of the boroughs changed to a very fine overall balance so that the voting decisions of Alliance boroughs, those with no overall control and the City took on a new importance. Conservatives have looked upon the City as an ally on bodies such as L P A C but its representatives have maintained a pattern of independent voting on the issues in front of them.

At abolition the City consciously reassessed its position and rejected the notion of picking up some of the representative roles previously discharged by the G L C because of the political overtones that would have been attached to them.

Some 99.5 per cent of the rate revenue collected by the City comes from the non-domestic sector. The City of London is unique in retaining a business vote although only some 10 per cent of the rates are paid by business with votes. The City's close relationship with business also has a diplomatic aspect. Many distinguished visitors come to the City for financial services and to do business. The Corporation is able to receive and host such visitors in conjunction with the business community. The Corporation maintains discreet contacts with the Foreign Office and with embassies concerning distinguished visitors to London. For many heads of state and lesser visitors, banquets and receptions are arranged by the Corporation which have a primarily diplomatic function. Such a role is made appropriate because of the City's non-partisan status and is made possible by the private funds which the Corporation has to pay for such visits and the facilities, such as the Guildhall and the Mansion House, which it has to house them. Such hospitality is provided on behalf of London as much as on behalf of the nation.

The City of Westminster

Westminster can also lay claim to history and antiquity, tracing its origins back to an Act of 1585. Unlike the City of London it became an ordinary London borough in 1965 and is characterised by partisan politics. Westminster contains large parts of London's central retail and commercial area, many very fashionable areas, most of its theatres, Whitehall, Parliament, Westminster Abbey and many of the monuments and buildings which comprise tourist London. Many of the parts of London which Londoners would call 'town' lie in Westminster.

Westminster is Conservative and projects strong views on issues. It is clearly influential in Tory London, although it maintains a somewhat independent line and one which at times differs significantly from that espoused by the majority of Conservative boroughs which represent the outer suburbs. Westminster, however, plays a pivotal role in London.

Its location is important. It is the most central authority and an obvious place for meetings involving borough representatives. Nevertheless it is not a lead borough for any purposes. Because it contains Parliament, large numbers of M Ps and politically influential figures live within Westminster. The council itself is part of a complex network of influence linking it to key areas of decision-making in London and in central government. It also becomes involved in ceremony and diplomacy. A large number of embassies are located in the borough and state visits occur within the borough in which the council is involved formally as a welcoming body. It has received international gifts such as statues or fountains which are gifts to London.

Westminster has traditionally played a key role in the LBA by providing the secretary to the Association. Indeed, LBA is physically located in Westminster City Hall. Since the demise of the GLC it has also taken on the role of providing a clerk and accommodation for the Lord Lieutenant of London. Westminster not only facilitates representation but is often called upon to represent London. It is a frequent source of media comment and is often approached by overseas people who want to know about local government in London.

Leadership among the Conservative boroughs

Sir Peter Bowness, leader of Croydon and chairman of the LBA, is clearly one of the key figures in Conservative London at the local level. Other boroughs and their leaders also stand out as opinion-formers. Bromley is an active borough on the right of London politics. It took the lead in promoting abolition at the LBA and challenged the GLC subsidised fares policy in the celebrated 'Fares Fair' court action of 1981. Bromley also holds the chair of the LFCDA, the London Area Mobility Scheme and the London Waste Regulation Authority.

Westminster's leading role has been discussed above; together with Wandsworth it has been keen to promote radical Conservative policies for local services. Both boroughs would see themselves in the vanguard of reforms.

Camden

Camden provides 'pay and rations' to most of the units comprising the 'GLC in exile' as well as to some broader-based successor bodies. In some cases this was a continuation of work it was involved in when an active member of the LBA. Camden is also ideally located as a venue for boroughs to meet, and is the most centrally located Labour borough.

Camden was very active in the ALA when post-abolition arrangements were being made and seems to have volunteered freely to take a lead role in supporting successor authorities. Such enthusiasm could be interpreted as a bid for power within the ALA and leadership of Labour London if it had led to Camden securing the chairs of the successor bodies. In the event the chairs were more widely distributed and Camden has had to devote considerable managerial resources to setting up the successor bodies without being reimbursed by the voluntary joint committee charging system which only pays for staff and overheads. It may also face the prospect of overseeing the difficult task of winding up some of these bodies in the future.

Leadership among the Labour boroughs

Leadership among the Labour boroughs is fragmented. Unlike their Conservative counterparts, many Labour boroughs see merit in setting up mechanisms for joint action. This very interest can generate its own rivalries. Additionally, there are many ideological strands within London's Labour politicians which can give rise to shifting and complex patterns of alliances to gain and maintain power within the Labour scene.

In the last years of the GLC Ken Livingstone became powerfully identified as the whole voice of Labour London and indeed of London as such. After abolition attention focused on a new group of a high profile black leaders – Bernie Grant of Haringey, Merle Amory of Brent and Linda Bellos of Lambeth – associated with radical and outspoken attitudes. The 1987 General Election took several of London's best known Labour figures out of local politics and into Parliament, leaving mature leadership among the London Labour boroughs still largely in the hands of Islington and its leader Margaret Hodge who chairs the ALA. Islington has been involved with most of the issues close to the heart of Labour in London and has taken a lead role not only in the ALA but also in ensuring the continued existence of the London Research Centre.

Leadership among the Alliance boroughs

The Alliance boroughs are few and recently elected. Liberals are the dominant force. Richmond is the most solidly Alliance council and the most active borough at the wider level. It occupies the chair of the London Boroughs Grants Committee and the LPAC as well as being lead authority for the Grants scheme.

The Political Parties

Prior to abolition the political parties needed a level of organisation which could choose candidates and provide political support for activities at County Hall. The GLC area is still an entity for the political parties both for the indirectly elected bodies which have replaced the GLC in some services, and for London borough matters.

The Conservative party

The constituency is the key organisational level in the Conservative party. At the grass roots members work at the ward or, where numbers permit, at the polling district level. Representatives are elected from this level to the executive council of the constituency association, the party's governing body at the local level. The party does not organise formally at the borough level, although ad hoc borough meetings and structures may be formed.

Greater London is one of eleven regional areas into which the Conservative party divides the country for organisational purposes. The main body at this level is the Area Council, comprising 504 members, six from each of the constituencies within the Greater London area. It elects its own officers – a chairman, two deputies and two treasurers. Its main role relates to organisation and co-ordination although it also provides a forum for political debate based on resolutions proposed by constituency parties. It meets twice a year.

The constituencies also send representatives to a number of specialist committees at the area level which report to the Area Council. These include the Area Women's Committee, and committees concerned with local government, education, Conservative trade unionists, and the Conservative Policy Centre. The Local Government Committee is a discussion forum for party policy in London and is essentially advisory.

Each region has a regional office, the Greater London Office being situated within Conservative Central Office for convenience. The London office has three full-time party workers, all experienced ex-constituency agents. There is a chief agent who looks after the area organisation and two deputies who support the constituencies, one concerned with the constituencies south of the river and one concerned with those to the north. Their help is particularly needed by constituencies without full-time agents.

The Greater London Office works closely with the London Boroughs Association. It organises a meeting for all council and minority group leaders five or six times a year. This is the forum for discussion of matters relating to the London-wide successor bodies such as LFCDA, the Grants Scheme and the waste disposal bodies.

The Labour party

Wards are the primary units of Labour organisation and elect representatives to a General Management Committee at the constituency level to form the main decision-making body of the Labour party at the local level. The constituencies within each borough elect representatives to a Local Government Committee which is responsible both for writing the borough manifesto at election time and maintaining control over councillors on the relevant authority in between times.

Above the constituency level the Labour party has a network of regions. The Greater London Region, more popularly known as the London Labour Party, has a Regional Executive Committee of 57 which meets approximately every six weeks and is elected by an annual conference of the region. Its composition is typical of Labour party structure. Sixteen places are reserved for the constituency parties, sixteen for affiliated trade unions and the remainder divided between the representatives of local government bodies such as the ALA, ILEA and LFCDA, and representatives of the Socialist Societies, the Co-operative Societies and Women's Groups. The regional party has a number of committees which handle campaigns and organisation, policy, women and the Young Socialists.

Formerly the Regional Executive was the key body which related to the GLC. Now its role is more advisory but it continues to supervise Labour councillors and Labour policy on successor bodies and ILEA as well as providing a policy framework with which the local government committees can work. The London Labour Party entered popular consciousness in the late 1970s when it was captured by the left and started to promote the policies on which new Labour leaders came to power at County Hall and in a number of boroughs. In recent years its political stance has shifted towards the centre following defeat of the left-wing candidate in the Greenwich by-election and the obvious electoral liability of the 'loony left' epithet ascribed to London Labour politics.

The region has a full-time staff of around fifteen, more than would be found in other regions, who are employed by the National Executive Committee and work from offices a few doors from Labour's own headquarters. Labour leaders and councillors can draw upon extensive policy support from the ALA and the 'GLC in exile' which has been discussed earlier in the chapter.

The Social and Liberal Democrats

In Spring 1988 the Social Democratic Party and the Liberal Party agreed to merge to form the Social and Liberal Democrats, subject to the agreement of a simple majority of their respective members. The constitution of the new party reflects elements of the organisation of the two parties.

The SDP had a strong national organisation which in many matters interacted directly with its individual members bypassing intermediate levels. The main local level of organisation was the area which was generally coterminous with boroughs. In London there were 34 area parties, two boroughs being divided into two areas. Delegation to constituency and ward groups was permitted. However, the area level was the key policy-making level outside the national arena of the Council for Social Democracy and the National Committee.

The area of the former GLC was designated a region with a regional council to which area parties sent delegates. The regional council had neither jurisdiction over the areas within it nor policy-making powers, although it was able to discuss policy issues and put items on the agenda of the Council for Social Democracy. Apart from the discussion of London-wide issues, the regional council also had a co-ordinating and organising role. The SDP supported regional government for England and campaigned for regionalisation through its regional councils.

In addition to a council and an annual assembly the SDP also had a number of standing committees at the regional level. They covered such matters as crime and policing, inner cities, transport and housing. These and other ad hoc committees were open to any individual member who cared to join.

The SDP had no full-time support at the sub-national level. The national party headquarters, situated in central London, acted as a postbox and provided resources for regions to use. All organisational and policy work was done on a voluntary basis. The numbers of SDP members elected to councils have been few and none have been involved at a London-wide level.

Liberal party organisation on the other hand was heavily influenced by ideals of decentralisation giving rise to variety at the local level. Like the SDP the Liberals had a regional tier of organisation. The London region was coterminous with the former GLC area and had both an organisational and a policy-making role. The regional council had a general oversight of Liberal activity in London and was particularly concerned with issues for London government.

Beneath the region was the main organisational level in the Liberal party, the constituency. Beneath that was ward organisation. There was no organisational level that corresponded to boroughs although co-ordinating committees were set up at this level to deal with the selection of candidates. The main relationship between Liberal councillors and their parties was at constituency level.

The national party established and paid for a network of full-time regional organisers. The London regional organiser and his staff operated from an office in South London. Liberal councillors, like their SDP counterparts, were supported by a national body, the Association of Liberal Councillors, based in Yorkshire. Within London contact between councillors was based on informal systems. Successor bodies such as LPAC also provided a forum for contact between Liberal members on different councils.

The primary unit of the new party is the local party which is based on the Parliamentary constituency or two or more adjacent constituencies. Local councillors are represented on the executive committee of the local party which must have a democratic process for agreeing local policy and selecting candidates for local government elections. Co-ordination at the borough or other local authority level is provided for and so is the setting up of branches at ward level under the general supervision of the local party.

Above the local party is the regional party. The former GLC area is the only English region which is defined in the party's constitution. The role of the regional party is to co-ordinate, support, organise and campaign. It may also, through a regional conference 'make definitive policy on issues which relate exclusively to the region.'

Duly ratified by the general membership of the founder parties the new constitution came into effect on 1 March 1988. Interim arrangements have since come into force to allow members to reorganise themselves. The proposal to merge the SDP and the Liberals caused a major split in the SDP during 1987 which resulted in a breakaway anti-merger party led by David Owen continuing to organise as the SDP.

Ceremonial London

Some of the figures who represent London are not political but ceremonial. Mayors belong with the monarchy in the dignified part of the constitution leaving chairmen and leaders of local authorities with effective power. Dignified elements of a system of government nonetheless play their part.

The Lord Mayor of London
The office of Lord Mayor of London is ancient and the processes of election are unique and complex. The electorate consists of freemen and liverymen, i.e. those associated with guilds. To become Lord Mayor a person must have occupied other municipal offices in the City, namely those of Alderman and Sheriff. The Lord Mayor is elected annually and

takes an oath of office amidst great pageantry known as the Lord Mayor's Show held on the second Saturday in November.

The Lord Mayor is the chairman of the Corporation of London but effectively delegates this task to the Town Clerk – the equivalent of the chief executive. He or she is briefed regularly on Corporation affairs but his or her major role is played outside the authority. The Lord Mayor has an extensive programme of social engagements both within the City and elsewhere at home and abroad in the course of which he or she delivers some 1,000 speeches a year. The Lord Mayor has a programme of overseas travel which is determined by current interests of business, the City and Government. The travel programme is partially supported by the City's private funds. Members of the Corporation and officials will travel with the Lord Mayor. The 1987/88 programme included trips with a diplomatic purpose such as attendance at Berlin's 750th anniversary, with a trade and business purpose such as to Latin America and the United States, and with a representative purpose such as attending the conference of capital cities in Ottawa.

The Lord Mayor of London is popularly seen as a powerful and benevolent position eliciting large numbers of requests from individuals for personal advice and assistance.

The Lord Mayor of Westminster

The Lord Mayor of Westminster is a less ancient but equally public office. Duties involve formally welcoming visiting heads of state to Westminster, sometimes in conjunction with royalty, and attending functions at the many embassies located within the borough. Thus although in status similar to the mayor of any other borough, the Mayor of Westminster has a far greater public ceremonial role. In recent years Westminster has facilitated the development of such a high profile office and has encouraged more international involvement. Unlike the Lord Mayor of London the Lord Mayor of Westminster can claim to repre- sent a modern local authority which delivers public services within the heart of London.

The Lord Lieutenant of London

The Lord Lieutenants are a remnant of knight service. The origin of the role was military. Lord Lieutenants are appointed on a county basis including the Greater London area. The Lord Lieutenant was the local representative of the monarch and was charged with raising troops and maintaining order. He also had the task of keeping the court records. The present occupant, Field Marshal the Lord Bramall of Bushfield, maintains the military tradition although his predecessor was a woman without military connections. The Lord Lieutenant deputises for the monarch, for example by presenting awards, and is present to guarantee the safety of the monarch on state occasions within his county. Traditionally the incumbent financed him or herself but both the GLC and now Westminster have provided assistance for staff (a secretary and a driver) and hospitality.

The Town Crier of London

Peter Moore, the current Town Crier of London, announces public events, leads parades, opens festivals, and travels widely around the world to lend a touch of pageantry to overseas business promotion. The post, a modern revival, was formerly administered by the GLC Arts and Recreation Committee and is currently administered by the London Borough of Merton.

CHAPTER 7

The Finance of
Local Government in London

Local authorities in Greater London operate within a legal and financial framework which corresponds closely to that in the rest of England and Wales. The services provided by local authorities are very similar (with the exception of police and public transport) to those provided elsewhere in the country. The sources of funds to pay for services are also the same as elsewhere. However, the amount spent by London authorities and the extent to which different sources of revenue are used are often radically different in London than in other authorities.

Local government in Greater London spent about £6,650m in 1986/87. Of this, £6,050m was revenue expenditure, while about £1,000m (including spending financed out of asset sales) was spent on capital. London authorities generally spend more than average on both revenue and capital items.

Expenditure

Current

The major service provided by local authorities in London, as elsewhere, is education. Current expenditure in London on local authority education was about £2,000m, or some £300 per head of population in 1986/87. Other major services include social services (£680m); police (£825m); highways and transport (£190m); and refuse collection and disposal (over £100m). Police spending is controlled by the Metropolitan Police rather than by local authorities. Much of public transport expenditure (not included in figures above) is undertaken by London Regional Transport. In recent years, current expenditure patterns have changed to some extent, with greater emphasis given to areas like social services at the expense of environmental services and housing. There have been marked differences between changes in real spending from borough to borough.

153

For example, a number of inner London authorities like Hackney and Westminster have changed their political outlook in recent years, even though political control has not changed. A new, more radical administration in Hackney (and in some other Labour boroughs) has sought to increase real spending rapidly, whereas in Westminster, Wandsworth and some other Tory boroughs, the controlling party has attempted to find new methods of service delivery and thus to reduce net spending.

Changes in overall current and capital expenditure by individual boroughs up to 1986/87 are obscured by the abolition of the Greater London Council, which led to expenditure being transferred to boroughs. Some boroughs took over much more ex-G L C spending than others, which means that 1986/87 spending cannot readily be compared with that for earlier years. However, comparison of 1985/86 current expenditure with that for 1978/79 shows clearly how individual boroughs have pursued very different spending policies. In this period, Hackney increased its budgeted current spending by 172 per cent, Camden by 147 per cent and Greenwich by 141 per cent, while Westminster's spending rose by 95 per cent, Kensington and Chelsea by 82 per cent and Wandsworth by 71 per cent. In Outer London, the percentage change varied from 131 per cent in Brent to 56 per cent in Merton. Over the same period – 1978/79 to 1986/87 – general inflation in the economy amounted to 87.5 per cent.

Capital

Housing, rather than education, is the major area of capital spending in London and throughout England and Wales. Out of a total of about £1,244m capital expenditure in London 1985/86 (roughly £185 per head of population), roughly three-quarters was devoted to housing. Other significant areas of capital expenditure (though in each case representing only between 5 and 10 per cent of spending) are education and highways/ transport.

Because data about capital expenditures are not available until well after the end of each financial year, figures for 1986/87 were still unpublished in mid-1988. The redistribution of services because of abolition will make 1986/87 and future capital spending figures difficult to compare with those for earlier years. Spending per head in 1985/86 varied from £279 in Haringey, £270 in Camden and £240 in Lambeth to £61 in Barking and Dagenham, £56 in Sutton and £48 in Richmond. The average capital spending per head in London was just under £130.

Income

Current

Local authorities derive their income to fund revenue expenditure from local taxation (the rates), government grants and from fees and charges. Most analysis of local authority expenditure excludes that part of spending which is funded out of fees and charges. The remaining spending is known as 'net' expenditure. This section concentrates on the income to finance net expenditure.

Rates are a local property tax, levied on all domestic and non-domestic property. In London, as elsewhere, authorities are free in most cases to set the level of their rate poundage. Rate income must be sufficient to finance all expenditure which is not supported from other sources (e.g. grants and charges). London authorities have, in many cases, large concentrations of property with high rateable value. The overall rateable value in London is £303 per head, compared with the average for England and Wales of £157. In the centre of the City, rateable values are very high indeed, with Camden at £668 per head, Westminster at £1,789 per head and the City at £47,200. The lowest rateable value per head in London is in Bexley (£144).

Other things being equal, the wide variations in the tax bases on individual boroughs would mean that the rate of tax in, say, Westminster would inevitably be lower than in Bexley because of the former's large rateable resources. Boroughs in the centre of the capital would be able to rely heavily on their non-domestic rate bases to finance high levels of expenditure at a relatively low cost to domestic taxpayers.

The grant system is designed by the Government to take account of variations in authorities' rateable resources. The block grant, which is the major element within the Rate Support Grant, compensates authorities for differences in their rateable resources and their spending needs. In addition to these equalising objectives, block grant is also used by the Government to discourage spending by local authorities: as spending increases, so grant is removed.

Because of their very large rateable resources, some London authorities receive no block grant. The size of the rate base is such that the grant system assumes that all spending can be supported locally. The Cities of London and Westminster are in this position. In other authorities, a combination of a relatively high rate base and high spending leads the authority to lose all its block grant. The London Fire and Civil Defence Authority and Camden lose all their grant in this way.

In addition to block grant, with its equalising and spending disincentive objectives, there are a range of other grants. A 'domestic rate relief grant' operates to maintain the rate poundage charges to house-holders at a level below that charged to non-domestic ratepayers. 'Specific' grants are paid to authorities to finance areas of provision where the Government wishes to keep detailed control over how money is spent (e.g. on the police). There has been a considerable growth in the use of specific grants in recent years, particularly in education. Finally, there are significant grants for housing purposes, which are kept separate from general local authority financing.

Capital

Local authorities must keep separate current and capital accounts. The financing of capital expenditure is significantly different from the funding of current spending, largely because of the use of borrowing to finance capital. Borrowing, revenue contributions and capital receipts are the major sources of income to finance capital spending. In addition, authorities have come increasingly to use leasing to fund capital items.

Capital expenditure is influenced by the Government by use of a system of capital controls. Authorities are given annual allocations of capital spending within blocks for main services. There is freedom to move an allocation from one block to another, and to move a proportion of the total allocation from one year to the next. Authorities are free to use a proportion of any receipts from capital assets to add to their capital allocation, and thus increase their spending power.

Within the total allocation, authorities are free to finance spending by borrowing, revenue contributions (e.g. rates and Rate Support Grant), capital receipts or by leasing. Borrowing has become less important as a funding item in recent years, while income from capital receipts and the use of leasing have grown. These trends have occurred both in London and throughout the rest of England and Wales.

Rate Limitation

The use of block grant in an attempt to discourage expenditure by local authorities was described above. In fact, block grant did not bring local government spending down to the Government's planned levels, even when a system of expenditure targets and grant penalties had been superimposed on the original grant arrangements. The Conservatives promised in their 1983 election manifesto to cap the rates of high spending authorities. After the passing of the Rates Act 1984, ratecapping (as it came to be known) was operated in each year from 1985/86.

London authorities have featured prominently in ratecapping from the start. In 1985/86, 11 out of 18 authorities selected for limitation were in London, including the Greater London Council and the Inner London Education Authority. In 1986/87, 8 out of 12 selected authorities were in London. Because of sections in the Local Government Act 1985, the ILEA and the new London Fire and Civil Defence Authority were ratecapped along with all other new joint authorities created after abolition. By 1987/88, 40 authorities were ratecapped overall, 20 (including ILEA and LFCDA) under the Local Government Act 1985 and 20 under the Rates Act 1984. Fourteen out of 40 were in London. In 1988/89, 12 out of 37 ratecapped authorities were in London.

Five Labour-controlled Inner London boroughs (Camden, Lewisham, Lambeth, Hackney and Southwark) have been capped in each year since 1985/86, as has ILEA. The GLC was capped in 1985/86, before it was abolished.

After initial attempts by most ratecapped authorities to resist the new law, authorities have sought to work within the system. Because rate limitation works by capping the rate or precept, rather than expenditure, it is possible for authorities to manipulate their spending and financing in such a way as to maximise spending within a given rate limit. This manipulation, which had initially been encouraged by attempts to avoid penalties within the block grant system, came to be known as 'creative accounting' (see below).

Ratecapping has not led to the reductions in spending which the Government must originally have hoped for. Comparisons of 1984/85 spending with that for 1985/86 showed little slowing in budget growth. Beyond 1985/86, comparisons are made difficult by the redistribution of services which accompanied abolition. However, there is no evidence of redundancies or manpower reductions resulting from ratecapping. During 1987, however, it became clear that a number of ratecapped councils would have, finally, to make spending reductions. Several boroughs announced major budget cuts for 1988/89.

Creative Accounting

The growth of creative accounting as a reaction to block grant and to rate limitation has been alluded to above. Such creativity has also been used to finance larger capital spending programmes. The scale of this creativity was far greater in London than elsewhere in the country. At its simplest, creative accounting means shifting the point at which particular items of current or capital expenditure appear in local authorities' spending figures. Many London authorities have shifted the incidence of tens of millions of pounds worth of spending into future years. 1988/89 and 1989/90 are widely seen as the years when the appearance of this spending will create difficulties for authorities, though even in 1987/88 the first signs of financial difficulties were becoming apparent.

The Audit Commission in its report *The Management of London's Authorities: Preventing the Breakdown of Services*, published in January 1987, estimated that a group of eight deprived London boroughs (Brent, Camden, Hackney, Haringey, Islington, Lambeth, Lewisham and Southwark) had accumulated almost £750m worth of creative accounting moves, while another, slightly less deprived group (Hammersmith and Fulham, Greenwich, Kensington and Chelsea, Newham, Tower Hamlets, Waltham Forest, Wandsworth and Westminster) had just under £250m worth of creative accounting. Press reports suggest that many further moves have been made since the Audit Commission undertook its work.

If financial difficulties are to be avoided in those boroughs which have indulged in extensive creative accounting, the Government will have to alter the distribution of block grant and increase the capital allocations of the relevant authorities. If such changes are not made, the boroughs concerned will face huge cuts in current and capital expenditure, or, possibly, insolvency. Further Government action against creative accountancy was announced in March 1988.

The London Rate Equalisation Scheme

The earlier sections on current income discussed the issue of the wide variations which exist between the rateable values of individual London boroughs, and of the need to equalise between these variations. At present, block grant achieves a considerable degree of equalisation. In a number of authorities in central London with exceptionally high rateable values per head, no block grant is received, because the grant system works in such a way as to assume that the whole of, say, Westminster's expenditure can be funded from its own rate base.

However, the law determines that no authority shall receive less than zero block grant. That is, there are no negative grants, so an authority with exceptionally high rateable resources will find that it will simply receive no block grant, however high its expenditure. If the system were to equalise fully, the grant system would have to work in such a way as to take resources away from those councils with the highest resources: there would have to be negative grants.

Table 7.1   London Rate Equalisation Scheme: Contributions and Receipts 1985/86

Contributions	(£m)
City of London	47.016
Westminster	26.272
Receipts	
Camden	14.086
Greenwich	4.099
Hackney	4.594
Hammersmith and Fulham	4.467
Islington	6.657
Kensington and Chelsea	9.071
Lambeth	7.480
Lewisham	4.355
Southwark	7.370
Tower Hamlets	5.675
Wandsworth	5.434

Source: CIPFA *Finance and General Statistics 1985/86*, Table B.

The London Rate Equalisation Scheme is an attempt to make an allowance for the advantage which the 'no negative' rule gives to authorities with very high rateable values such as the Cities of London and Westminster. A similar scheme has operated for many years.

In the years from 1981/82 to 1985/86, the LRES operated only within Inner London. The City of London and the City of Westminster each contributed resources into a pool which was then distributed to the other Inner London boroughs. Contributions by the two Cities were set by the Secretary of State in 1981/82, and then increased in line with inflation thereafter. The receipts of the other eleven inner boroughs were determined by their respective rateable values, with the authority with the largest rateable value (Camden) receiving the biggest share. The contributions to and receipts from LRES in 1985/86 are shown in Table 7.1.

The abolition of the GLC led the Government to extend the LRES. The GLC's precept, levied on all London ratepayers as a common poundage, had also played a significant part in achieving resource equalisation in the capital. Removal of the GLC would, other things being equal, have led to a large gain to ratepayers in the Central London

Table 7.2   London Rate Equalisation Scheme: Contributions and Receipts 1986/87

Contributions	(£m)
City of London	105.452
Westminster	77.732
Receipts	
Camden	3.772
Greenwich	7.189
Hackney	7.981
Hammersmith and Fulham	7.896
Islington	11.643
Kensington and Chelsea	16.106
Lambeth	13.133
Lewisham	7.669
Southwark	12.960
Tower Hamlets	10.076
Wandsworth	9.684
Barking and Dagenham	2.433
Barnet	5.633
Bexley	2.856
Brent	4.574
Bromley	4.619
Croydon	6.334
Ealing	5.120
Enfield	4.398
Haringey	3.206
Harrow	3.195
Havering	3.468
Hillingdon	4.278
Hounslow	4.489
Kingston	2.624
Merton	2.801
Newham	3.184
Redbridge	3.326
Richmond	2.983
Sutton	2.692
Waltham Forest	2.860

Source: C I P F A *Finance and General Statistics 1986/87*, Table A.

boroughs of Camden, Westminster and the City, while elsewhere in the country ratepayers would have been made worse off. The reason for this shift of resources into central London was the fact that the three central London authorities received no block grant, and could not therefore have their grant reduced to compensate for the cash gain they enjoyed when the GLC precept no longer had to be paid, and when, in effect, they no longer had to contribute towards the cost of GLC services elsewhere in London.

The three central boroughs were thus included in a second equalisation arrangement. In 1986/87, the contributions to this second scheme were £56.321m, £50.278m and £11.108m for the City of London, the City of Westminster and Camden respectively. The total of these amounts was distributed to all other boroughs, including those in Outer London. Unlike the first equalisation scheme, where receiving authorities were paid LRES in addition to their block grant, the second scheme operated in such a way as to reduce the block grant entitlements of receiving authorities. In effect, receipts from the new equalisation scheme were offset against authorities' block grant receipts. Offsetting the new LRES payments in this way had the effect of sharing the benefits of the additional contributions of the central London boroughs with all other grant-receiving authorities in England.

Camden, which received resources from the original equalisation arrangement, is a contributor to the new scheme. In fact, it enjoys a small net receipt from the two combined schemes. The City and Westminster now make much larger contributions than before abolition. Other inner boroughs have receipts from the two arrangements, while Outer London boroughs receive from the new scheme only. The contributions and receipts in 1986/87 are shown in Table 7.2.

The contributions to the second equalisation arrangement were set in cash in 1986/87 so as to include the effects of payments made by the City of London and Westminster towards certain London-wide expenditure. Contributions to the second arrangement would remain the same in succeeding years, while the contributions to the first scheme would continue to be uprated in line with inflation from year to year. Both LRES arrangements are expected to continue in future years, or until local government finance is reformed. LRES is operated under section 66 of the London Government Act 1963.

Reference

Department of the Environment (1983). *Streamlining the Cities*. Cmnd 9063.

CHAPTER 8

Londoners' Perceptions of London Government

This chapter, after some initial observations upon research into citizens' attitudes towards local government, distils the major findings of the many studies made of the attitudes of citizens throughout Greater London towards local government in the capital between 1985 and 1987. The studies are listed in detail in an appendix at the end of the chapter.

Research into Citizens' Attitudes

The final three or so years of the life of the GLC cemented a marriage of seemingly ill-suited partners: on the one hand, local authorities (most of them Labour ones, and some left-wing Labour ones like the GLC itself) who were anxious to ascertain opinions of their electorates towards their image and activities; on the other, two of the major market research organisations who were keen to sell the methodology, resources and technical expertise to conduct the necessary survey research.

There has long been a tradition among progressive local authorities (including the GLC when Labour-controlled) of seeking the electorate's preferences and views on certain local policy issues, although this concern seems in the past to have been confined largely to London local authorities (Husbands, 1985). Moreover, government inquiries into local government reform have, since the Redcliffe-Maud Commission of the late 1960s, conducted research on attitudes to local government. The most recent to do so has been the Widdicombe Inquiry, initiated by the Department of the Environment in February 1985 to conduct a general review of a range of aspects of local government (Department of the Environment, 1986).

By the beginning of the 1980s several local authorities were also experimenting with studies of local electors' opinions and, when the threat of abolition hardened, the GLC became a major user of this type of research, as did several Labour-controlled London borough councils threatened with ratecapping. At the same time occasional studies on similar and related subjects were commissioned by others, notably newspapers and television companies. During its brief life the *London Daily News* produced further London-wide studies, both on attitudes to London government and also on other issues that affect Londoners. Television companies such as Thames Television and London Weekend Television, the latter with its 'The London Programme', have produced several studies on particular issues, either London-wide or among special groups or locations of London.

Of the five major political polling organisations in this country, two have been particularly associated with research on attitudes to local government: Harris Research Centre and Market & Opinion Research International (MORI). Both these were used extensively by the GLC during its public campaign against abolition. The pace of research on this subject has slowed since the GLC's demise, perhaps because of fears about the ramifications of the Local Government Act 1986 against politically motivated expenditure, despite the fact that section 5 of this Act, which requires local councils to keep a separate account of their spending on publicity, did not come into force in April 1986 with the rest of the Act. The operation of this section was delayed pending the satisfactory conclusion of negotiations between representatives of local government and the Department of the Environment over what was to be counted as publicity. Nonetheless, it seems certain that the inclusion of such provisions in the Act has made some local authorities less keen to commission this type of research than was once the case. Marplan, NDP, Gallup and Audience Selection, which had previously undertaken work for local authorities, have not done so recently. Only MORI continued to conduct a number of studies for local authorities during 1986 and 1987.

Continual involvement in this research area has refined methodologies, particularly in the standardisation of questions, until the point where Harris and MORI are each able to offer a basic local government evaluation package to interested clients. After the demise of the GLC, several members of its Public Relations Branch that had been largely responsible for the widely acclaimed media campaign against abolition – including the director Tony Wilson – established their own business (called Issue Communications) intending to market, along with the Harris Research Centre, the skills that they felt they had acquired in promoting the GLC's cause but, more particularly, in measuring citizens' reactions to local government. Wilson (1987) claimed that the Public Relations Branch and Harris developed 'public opinion techniques of a sophistication hitherto unknown in local government' since 'previous surveys had generally failed to probe public attitudes and perceptions to the degree required to make the results really useful'. At the time of writing no full surveys under the aegis of this initiative had been commissioned.

Attitude Studies Conducted in Greater London

A huge number of local government related studies were conducted across Greater London during the final years of the GLC. Between October 1983 and March 1986 there were at least nineteen publicly available studies of attitudes to the abolition of the GLC and to related issues – eleven conducted by Harris or MORI for the GLC itself (see Waller, 1987) and eight conducted for *The London Standard*, Thames Television News, London Weekend Television, the BBC or the Association of London Authorities. In addition, a study commissioned by *The London Standard* from BJM Research and conducted in September 1985 – for comparison with an earlier survey done by the same firm for *The London Standard* in 1981 – contained a question about the abolition of the GLC, although its results were not made publicly obtainable at the time.

This chapter examines studies conducted between mid 1985 and May 1987. It has been difficult to compile a comprehensive list of all studies available in the public domain that have been conducted in Greater London between these two dates; however, the appendix to this chapter makes claim to a reasonably full coverage.

Certain themes emerge from the surveys that were carried out around the time of GLC abolition. The *London Attitude Survey: July 1985* of July 1985 and the *National Attitude Survey* of November–December 1985 were part of a package commissioned by the GLC from Harris Research Centre in order to provide post-GLC institutions such as Labour boroughs, the London Strategic Policy Unit and other sympathetic bodies, with a large database upon the political preferences and opinions of Londoners, not merely about London-based but also about national issues.

The first question of the July survey was a standard one asked in most national level polling: 'In your opinion, what are the main problems facing the country today?' Respondents were asked whether certain problems affected Londoners more than others, as well as good and bad aspects of living in London. A major purpose of the study was to elicit detailed reactions on specific questions and there were numerous probe-instructions given to interviewers. Only towards the end of the survey were questions asked about the GLC. Harris's conventional question on approval or disapproval of abolition elicited a 19 to 64 per cent response against abolition (with 17 per cent 'don't know') – about the norm at that time for the distribution of responses on the question.

The November–December survey was in fact a vast compendium of data largely on attitudes to national political questions: on images of the parties and of their leaders (Ken Livingstone included), on party loyalty and likelihood of switching, on a range of national policy issues and, at the end of the study, on a number of policy orientations associated with the practices of the G L C, such as pressing companies to employ more from ethnic minorities and more women, forcing companies to invest locally rather than abroad, and so on. On the latter items there was usually a very clear balance of approval for the G L C's stance, although there were notable exceptions.

Of Londoners questioned 46 per cent indicated some measure of approval for stopping public spending on civil defence, 43 per cent disapproved, either 'to some extent' or strongly. Pressing companies to recruit more from ethnic minorities attracted 48 per cent disapproval, 44 per cent approval. On a question concerning employing more women, 44 per cent disapproved while 50 per cent approved. Gays and lesbians, as could have been expected, were not a popular cause: on the item 'provide services such as meeting places specifically for gays and les-bians', 48 per cent strongly disapproved and 15 per cent did so to some extent. Only 7 per cent strongly approved, whilst 22 per cent approved to some extent.

The *London Daily News*'s 'Life in London' survey of January–February 1987, some of whose results were published in the newspaper in the week after its launch, provided important data on Londoners' attitudes in post-G L C London; it also contained more general data about life in London and towards London (see also Peschek, 1987). Although the abolition of the G L C has produced no subsequent public outcry and no large-scale visible effect, it is interesting to note that – when prompted on the matter – only 5 per cent of respondents felt that the quality of life had improved since abolition, whereas 35 per cent felt that it had deteriorated; 47 per cent answered 'no change'. The most missed item was the services offered by the G L C, mentioned by 36 per cent of those answering 'worse'. Even among Conservative voters 'worse' responses exceeded 'better' ones by 18 to 10 per cent.

Of respondents, 50 per cent, including 34 per cent of Conservative voters, said that there should be an elected council for London; 34 per cent of Londoners, and 52 per cent of Conservative voters, opposed this. Although the ratio of 50/34 represents some shift from the 60/65 to 25/20 ratios of disapproval-to-approval found by those studies done before the abolition, it is nonetheless significant that, nearly a year after the demise of the GLC and without the pro-GLC publicity being disseminated at the earlier time, approval for an elected council for London still greatly exceeds disapproval. Moreover, only 20 per cent of respondents felt that the present system of local government in London is the best one. The old GLC system was favoured by 42 per cent. In answer to a question, 'Should there be an elected leader for London?', 56 per cent answered positively. As for people's perceptions of living in London, even among those in the outer boroughs, as many as 66 per cent considered that they lived in London; in the sample as a whole the percentage was 80 per cent.

The two *Women in London* surveys conducted in January 1986 and March 1987 also merit discussion in some detail. They were products of the GLC's interest – sustained by the London Strategic Policy Unit – in the position of women and in the use of local government to deliver services of particular value to them. Accordingly, their purpose was to 'examine attitudes towards the representation of women, to identify women's priorities and to ascertain how they feel about themselves and the problems they encountered'. The samples deliberately over-represented women in relation to men, although the data were re-weighted in order to present findings that would be representative of the population as a whole.

In the January 1986 survey there were questions about attitudes to service delivery after GLC abolition. Of women 37 per cent and of men 38 per cent believed that the interests and needs of women in London would be served less well once the GLC had been abolished; 41 per cent of the reweighted sample thought that it would make no difference. Among women, 59 per cent saw the need for a single public body to look after and speak for women's needs and priorities, while 59 per cent also agreed that their local council could do a lot more for women. Moreover, 58 per cent of women and 55 per cent of men agreed that their local council did not know enough about the needs of local people. Only 18 per cent of the total reweighted sample felt that the local council cared about people like them.

Those commissioning the March 1987 study were reluctant to ask about perceptions of service delivery to women explicitly in the context of the absence of the GLC; in the light of results from the 'Life in London' survey just a month or so earlier, this was a perhaps unnecessary nervousness that the results might have shown complacency about abolition of the GLC. However, on a general question about the need for a single public body to look after and speak for the needs and priorities of women in London, 64 per cent of women and 43 per cent of men (54 per cent overall) answered that such a need existed. Many questions of the previous year's study were replicated and showed little significant change in aggregate responses. Now 23 per cent felt that their council cared a lot about people like them, while 58 per cent thought their local council could do a lot more for women in their borough. In addition 43 per cent said that their council did not realise that men and women have different needs.

In general, the mood of post-GLC London – with respect to a capital-wide authority – seems a reluctant acceptance of the present situation, as judged by the absence of any serious political movement to restore the GLC or to make its absence a major issue in the June 1987 election campaign. However, although the matter has low salience, a year after the disappearance of the GLC a far higher number of Londoners wished for some comparable elected body than were content with the *status quo*.

Appendix: Checklist of Attitude Studies

The list below of attitude studies conducted in Greater London between mid 1985 and mid 1987 is organised in the following way:

1. those conducted in the period before the abolition of the GLC (i.e. mid 1985 to March 1986);
2. those conducted in the period since the abolition of the GLC (i.e. April 1986 to May 1987);
3. those continuing series of studies that span the pre- and post-abolition periods.

Within each of these categories are listed in order:

(a) studies that are the main focus of this report in that they contain substantial information on public attitudes to local government and to London from Greater London-wide samples, even if they may also contain data on other matters;
(b) studies that are tangentially interesting in that they contain relevant questions on attitudes to local government but for a sample drawn from a population within only some part of the Greater London population (e.g. an individual borough);
(c) studies devoted largely or exclusively to subjects other than attitudes to local government, albeit conducted among Greater London-wide samples.

There are sometimes no known studies in one or more of these latter categories for the time periods defined above. No attempt has been made to catalogue the many studies that sought data on matters other than attitudes to local government among the citizens of individual boroughs or among specific population groups; for example, various local crime surveys and studies of victims of racial attacks have not been listed. Nor are included those studies using methods other than surveys of individual adults, e.g. crime-incidence studies, such as one on the London Underground. Surveys cited above are asterisked.

1. Studies conducted in the pre-abolition period from mid 1985:
   (a) Studies on attitudes to local government in London among Greater London-wide samples:
       (i) *London Attitude Survey: July 1985*, conducted by Harris Research Centre for the Greater London Council from 13 to 29 July 1985 (sample size: 1,511).*
       (ii) *National Attitude Survey*, conducted by Harris Research Centre for the Greater London Council from 9 November to 7 December 1985 with a national sample (size: 3,192) and a London sample (size: 1,459).*
       (iii) *Final Day Poll*, conducted by Harris Research Centre for the Greater London Council from 22 to 24 March 1986 (sample size: 1,104).
   (c) Studies across Greater London on subjects other than attitudes to local government:
       (i) *The Londoner Survey*, conducted by BJM Research Partners Group Limited for *The London Standard* in September 1985 (sample size: about 2,500). (See *The London Standard*, 30 September 1985, pp. 22–23.)

2. Studies conducted in the post-abolition period from 1 April 1986:
   (a) Studies with substantial data on attitudes to local government in London among Greater London-wide samples:
       (i) *Life in London*, conducted by Harris Research Centre for the *London Daily News* from 30 January to 8 February 1987 (sample size: 2,141).* (See *London Daily News*, 2 March 1987, pp. 18–19; 3 March 1987, pp. 22, 29; 4 March 1987, p. 17.)
   (c) Studies across Greater London on subjects other than attitudes to local government:
       (i) A survey on Londoners' attitudes to the police and to crime in

London conducted by NOP Market Research Limited for the Metropolitan Police from 5 June to 5 July 1986 (sample size: 2,932). (See *London Daily News*, 13 April 1987, p. 1.)

(ii) A 'sex after AIDS' survey conducted by Harris Research Centre for the *London Daily News* from 31 March to 1 April 1987 among adults aged between sixteen and forty-five (sample size: 764). (See *London Daily News*, 7 May 1987, pp. 18, 27.)

3. Continuing studies that span the pre- and post-abolition periods:
   (a) Studies with substantial data on attitudes to local government in London among Greater London-wide samples:
      (i) *Women in London, January 1986*, conducted by MORI for the Women's Committee Support Unit of the Greater London Council from 15 to 19 January 1986 (sample size: 699 women and 315 men), and *Women in London: A Survey of Women's Opinion, March 1987*, conducted by MORI for the Women's Equality Sub-Committee of the London Strategic Policy Unit from 27 February to 4 March 1987 (sample size: 711 women and 317 men).*

   (b) Studies that contain substantial data on attitudes to local government within some part of the Greater London population:
      (i) *1987 Residents' Attitudes Survey, January–February 1987*, conducted by MORI for the London Borough of Richmond-upon-Thames among adult residents of the borough from 19 January to 8 February 1987 (sample size: 827), this being the third such survey by MORI in the borough; the first was conducted in November 1984, shortly after the Alliance assumed borough control, and the second was done in January 1986. In addition, in the near future MORI is likely to embark on a similar survey in Waltham Forest and may also repeat earlier such surveys done in Camden and Islington.

   (c) Studies across Greater London on subjects other than attitudes to local government:
      (i) Since 1980 London Regional Transport has operated a series of surveys tracking attitudes towards its management and towards the provision of public transport in London; that of June 1986 was the eleventh such survey (sample size: 3,011).

References

Department of the Environment (1986). *The Conduct of Local Authority Business*. Report of the Commission of Inquiry into the Conduct of Local Authority Business.

Husbands, C. (1985). 'Attitudes to local government in London: evidence of 20th September 1984'. *The London Journal*, II, 1, pp. 59–74.

Peschek, D. (1987). 'Image'. *Local Government Chronicle*. March 13.

Waller, R. (1987). *Moulding Public Opinion*. Beckenham: Croom Helm.

Wilson, A. (1987). 'What does the public know of local government?' *Local Government Chronicle*. March 6, pp. 16–17.

CHAPTER 9

London Government: Past, Present and Future

This chapter briefly surveys the past organisation of London government, the present structure, and two possible general schemes which are supported by the major political parties for the future of London government. The working definition of London in this chapter is the continuous built-up area in the conurbation surrounding the historic core of the Cities of Westminster and London. This definition, while admittedly vague, is preferred because it is nevertheless more objective and operational than the even more nebulous definition of London as a community.

The Past: Metropolitan Systems

Most people would agree that London is a metropolis with social and economic interdependencies which call for appropriate administrative and political institutions. There has been disagreement over two issues:

1. the boundaries of metropolitan interdependence, and
2. the appropriate structures of metropolitan government.

The first issue raised the question: 'Where is the boundary of London drawn?' This is a matter of obvious concern for local politicians who represent different social constituencies on the ground. The second area of disagreement raises the question, 'What degree of democratic and administrative decentralisation should exist in the metropolis?' This query not only concerns local but also national politicians, because how it is answered affects central–local government relations.

Since liberal democracy was fully established in the UK, i.e. since full adult suffrage was introduced in 1928, there have been only three ways in which London has been governed. These three patterns have represented different possible answers to the two key issues of the boundary of London and the appropriate degree of decentralisation.

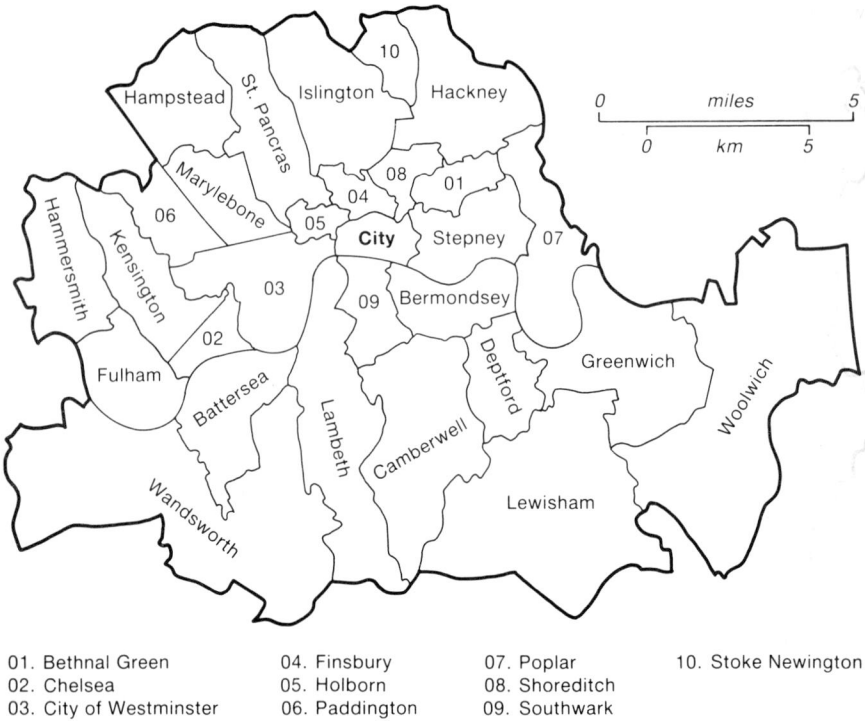

01. Bethnal Green   04. Finsbury   07. Poplar   10. Stoke Newington
02. Chelsea   05. Holborn   08. Shoreditch
03. City of Westminster   06. Paddington   09. Southwark

Figure 9.1   Inner London before 1965

Figure 9.2   Outer London before 1965 ▶

HERTFORD

Watford RD

miles 0 — 10

kms 0 — 10

HERTFORDSHIRE

MIDDLESEX

ESSEX

LONDON COUNTY COUNCIL

SURREY

KENT

01. Barnet UD

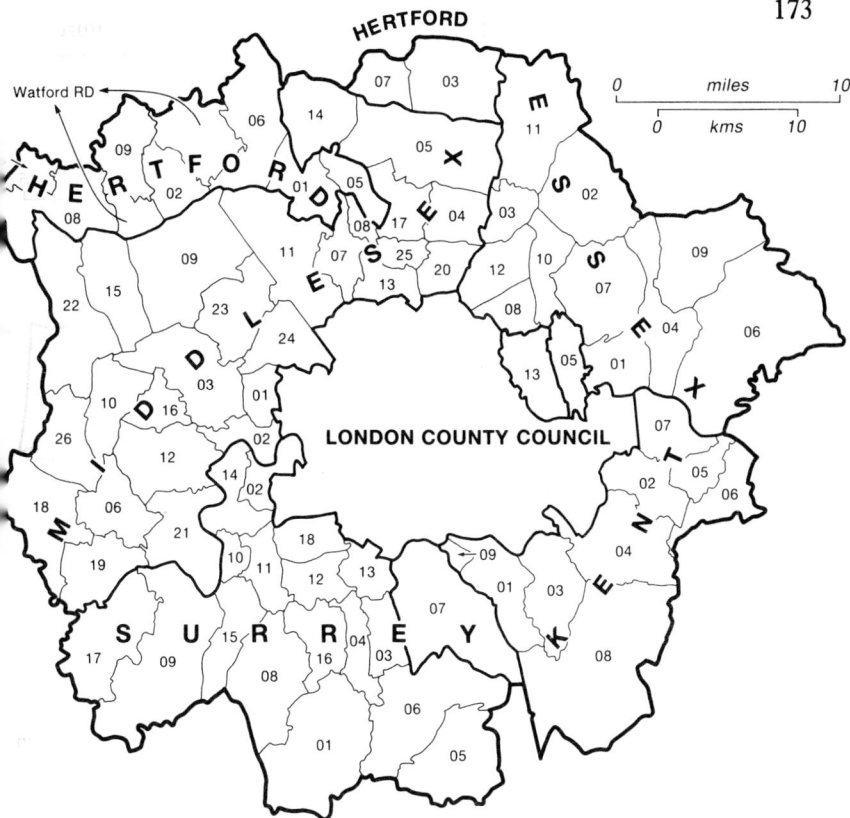

Herbert Commission Review Area

Counties and County Boroughs

Urban and Rural Districts and Municipal Boroughs

ODLESEX

Acton MB
Brentford and Chiswick MB
Ealing MB
Edmonton MB
Enfield MB
Feltham UD
Finchley MB
Friern Barnet UD
Harrow MB
Hayes and Harlington UD
Hendon MB
Heston and Isleworth MB
Hornsey MB
Potters Bar UD
Ruislip-Northwood UD
Southall MB
Southgate MB
Staines UD
Sunbury-on-Thames UD
Tottenham MB
Twickenham MB
Uxbridge MB
Wembley MB
Willesden MB
Wood Green MB
Yiewsley and West Drayton UD

HERTFORD

01. Barnet UD
02. Bushey UD
03. Chestnut UD
04. Chorleywood UD
05. East Barnet UD
06. Elstree RD
07. Northaw PH
08. Rickmansworth UD
09. Watford MB

ESSEX

01. Barking MB
02. Chigwell UD
03. Chingford MB
04. Dagenham MB
05. East Ham CB
06. Hornchurch UD
07. Ilford MB
08. Leyton MB
09. Romford MB
10. Wanstead and Woodford MB
11. Waltham Holy Cross UD
12. Walthamstow MB
13. West Ham CB

KENT

01. Beckenham MB
02. Bexley MB
03. Bromley MB
04. Chislehurst and Sidcup UD
05. Crayford UD
06. Dartford MB
07. Erith MB
08. Orpington UD
09. Penge UD

SURREY

01. Banstead UD
02. Barnes MB
03. Beddington and Wallington MB
04. Carshalton UD
05. Caterham and Warlingham UD
06. Coulsden and Purley UD
07. Croydon CB
08. Epsom and Ewell MB
09. Esher UD
10. Kingston-upon-Thames MB
11. Malden and Coombe MB
12. Merton and Morden UD
13. Mitcham MB
14. Richmond MB
15. Surbiton MB
16. Sutton and Cheam MB
17. Walton and Weybridge UD
18. Wimbledon MB

Until 1965 London was governed by the institutions which had been established in the late Victorian era. This dual system was structured by simple premises. The inner core of London was organised in two elected local government tiers, with the area-wide upper tier authority, the London County Council, having by far the greater functional responsibilities and administrative resources (see Fig. 9.1). The LCC, as it was known, remains internationally famous among scholars of comparative public administration as the grandfather of metropolitan government. By contrast, Outer London was organized on the basis of counties, county boroughs, and urban and rural districts. Their size, resources and administrative capacities varied considerably; there was also considerable duplication and overlapping in jurisdictions (see Fig. 9.2). The two Londons, outer and inner, corresponded, albeit very roughly, with the major axis of cleavage in British politics. Outer London was dominated by the Conservatives, Inner London by Labour. The pre-1965 system reflected more than anything else the culmination of historic, pragmatic and incremental adjustments to the numerous organisations which had performed government functions in the pre-democratic era. The system was latterly criticised by planners, administrators and academics as being anomalous, incomprehensible and in need of fundamental reorganisation. But it was largely the Conservatives' political ambition in the 1950s to strike a blow at Labour's LCC heartland which led to its demise in the London Government Act, 1963.

From 1965 until 1986, London was governed by a modernised and rationalised two-tier directly elected metropolitan system. Elements of the previous system survived, notably the organisation of education in the Inner London Education Authority, and the archaic and undemocratic government of the City of London. An area-wide authority, the Greater London Council, was established for the purposes of providing 'strategic' or metropolitan-wide functions in housing, urban planning, fire services, traffic, and the like. Public transport was later added to these functions. The 32 London boroughs which were carved out, with little respect for tradition (unusual by English standards), were established beneath the GLC, and were given more local, managerial, direct service and implementation functions (see Map 1). The system which emerged from the 1965 reorganisation reflected the political dilution and transformation of the ambitions of the planners and non-partisan reformers. The upper tier was left much weaker both in its range of functional responsibilities and autonomy than had been envisaged by enthusiasts for wider metropolitan government. The GLC was heavily dependent upon the boroughs for successful implementation of whatever programmes it chose to pursue, and was constrained by central government. It was sandwiched between central government and the boroughs. This weakness was exacerbated by the fact that political control of the GLC alternated between Labour and the Conservatives, whereas many boroughs, for most of the time, were bastions of one-party rule. Labour dominated Inner London, and the Conservatives Outer London. The GLC suffered from a combination of organisational weakness and political vulnerability. Because of particularist and local resistance, mainly by Conservative-dominated suburban boroughs, the GLC proved incapable of achieving many of its original objectives – especially in housing, planning and road-building – and by the mid 1970s was increasingly exposed to the charge that it was redundant. However, it can plausibly be argued that the Conservative pledge to abolish the upper-tier authority in the 1983 general election again owed more to politics than to considerations of administrative rationality (O'Leary, 1987).

Finally, London is currently experiencing its third governmental system in the democratic era. Since 1986 it has been organised on a stripped-down version of the previous two-tier metropolitan system. The elected metropolitan tier has been abolished and most of its functions and personnel transferred to central government, unelected quangos, statutory joint boards of borough representatives, and to the boroughs themselves. Metropolitan-wide government still exists but is now fragmented among diverse unelected and indirectly elected organisations. The ILEA is exceptional in that it survived reorganisation and was also made a directly elected authority, though it too is now under threat of imminent abolition. The London government system as a whole has also been subjected to the twin drives of the current Conservative administration since 1979: centralisation and privatisation. The financial and policy autonomy of borough governments in spending on housing, social services and education has been reduced, and central government has encouraged local authorities to move toward market and quasi-market policy-making systems in place of the more established bureaucratic mechanisms of public administration. The current government of London remains a modified metropolitan system but is clearly in a state of flux.

The Present: Unstable Metropolitanism

The most striking feature of the present organisation of London government as described throughout this Handbook is that it is fundamentally

unstable. The Conservatives, who have instituted and implemented all of
the major reorganisations of London government in this century, are
unhappy with the surviving embers of the GLC – notably ILEA – and
ambitious to implement completely their streamlined market model of
small-scale local government. They are also demonstrably anxious to
remove local government functions from the public to the private sector,
to relocate other functions, notably education, elsewhere in the public
sector, and, as they understand it, to depoliticise local government. The
Conservatives are also keen to attack Inner London Labour strongholds,
which remain as sporadic, albeit disorganised, centres of political and
ideological resistance to present philosophical trends. To the modern
Conservative these institutions are not just convenient electoral
scapegoats but are regarded as serious obstructions to the revitalisation
of Great Britain. For Conservatives the reorganisation of London
government has only started. Since 1979 they have moved dramatically
away from support for any idea of metropolitan government: the notions
of 'strategic' planning in a metropolis and local public sector intervention
and administration in transport, housing, land-use and education are not
consonant with the doctrines of neo-liberal political economy.

The dispositions of the Opposition parties, both Labour and the
Liberal- SDP Alliance, also suggest that the status quo is unstable. The
entire Opposition condemned the abolition of the GLC and have
frequently complained about the problems it has created. Although the
Opposition was much less cohesive in attacking the Conservatives'
privatisation drive in local government they have also been united in their
condemnation of the centralisation of public administration, both in
London and elsewhere in the country. However, while the Opposition
were agreed that the Conservatives were wrong to abolish the GLC, since
then they have by no means been advocates of a return to the previous
arrangements. They do not want just to restore the GLC, although that
may figure in part of a wider re-design. The Opposition, like the
Conservatives, have moved some distance from their past commitment
to the idea of metropolitan government. Some have moved to the
opposite extreme of advocating regional government.

The Future: The End of Metropolitanism

Political decentralisation, in principle, can extend from just one single
centre in which all political authority and resources are concentrated, to
an infinite number of discrete tiers. Similarly the number of functions
served by each centre of authority can range from one to infinity. The two

future models of decentralisation for London which are discussed here have been selected from the theoretically infinite number of possible designs on the basis that they are on the political agenda, are administratively feasible, and are compatible with key cultural and ideological alignments in both London and the UK. As the foregoing discussion has suggested, there are two emergent and competing ideals for the future organisation of London government, the *market model with the strong centre* and the *regional model*.

The other obvious possibility for London government is the *unitary model* – with all its many variations. In the full unitary model there is only one tier of directly elected local government with multi-functional responsibilities in each spatial unit and no intermediate elected or unelected tiers of government other than that of central government. The key problems with all variants of the unitary model for London government are obvious. One London-wide authority, however defined, would be extremely powerful, and so large as to defeat some of the objectives of decentralisation. By contrast, several unitary authorities in London – of whatever size and construction – would face all the problems of co-ordination and interdependence which in the past and the present have created the need for metropolitan-wide government whether elected, indirectly elected, or unelected, voluntary or imposed. We can neglect the analysis of unitary models here because they are not on the political agenda and would only come onto the agenda in the event of the future Royal Commission. Bereft of the support of any current political party, the unitary model does not seem to have a good future, despite its cogent advocacy by Ken Young of the Policy Studies Institute and now Director of INLOGOV, and Professor George Jones of the London School of Economics and Political Science.

Nor are either of the other two ideals ever likely to be wholly realised as there is always a gap between political aspirations and their implementation. However, it is worth spelling out their salient features, and their most obvious merits and drawbacks, precisely because they are very likely to shape the future of London.

The Market Model and the Strong Centre

The modern Conservative party has attempted to move towards a more market-type model of local government. Many of the thinkers behind modern Conservative ideals have regarded local government as monopolistic and bureaucratic suppliers funded by general taxes, and therefore as generically prone to the wasteful over-supply of services. The government's White Paper which preceded the abolition of the GLC displayed such views by suggesting that the GLC was spending more than was necessary to provide basic services, in pursuit of unspecified goals: 'The upper tier authority has a large rate-base, and an apparently wide remit. This generates a natural search for a "strategic" role which may have little basis in real needs' (Department of the Environment, 1983).

Policy-makers within the Conservative government appear to have been influenced by the market-type model of local government ex-pounded by 'Public Choice' theorists of the American New Right. These believe that in the best of local government worlds citizens should be able to adjust their public service-local tax mix by 'voting with their feet' to local authorities whose tax mix best meets their preferences (Tiebout, 1956). The implication of this model is that if there are more, single-purpose, and smaller local authorities in the London area, then the greater will be the degree of consumer control over the local authorities. However, supporters of a more market-orientated kind of local govern-ment accept that it is not feasible to have as many authorities as there are individual preferences. And they realise that decentralisation, by itself, does not guarantee an accurate picture of citizens' preferences. The voting system, the organisation of local government and inter-governmental relations can seriously distort the articulation of voters' wants. Moreover, over-decentralised local government can result in losses of economies of scale.

These qualifications mean that it is possible to support the idea both of a more free-market approach to local government *and* of metropolitan-wide government, provided that such government is financed, wherever possible, by specific levies or from user-charges, and provided that quasi-market mechanisms such as contracting out are used to encourage efficiency. However, there remains considerable pressure with Con-servative thinking to reduce the role of central government, new quan-gos, the new London-wide authorities and the boroughs in the direct public provision of services in London. To this end, Mrs Thatcher's third administration can be expected to consider a number of further reforms.

First of all, education is to be simultaneously centralised, fragmented and marketised. The education reforms legislation of 1988 implied almost as profound a reorganisation of local public services as did GLC abolition. The service is increasingly to be financed by earmarked funds from central government. Schools will be offered the possibility of opting out of local government control and into control by the DES. Effectively, power would go to the DES and governors/heads. ILEA is to be fragmented, with its polytechnic supervisory functions being altogether removed from its ambit.

Second, London boroughs, especially Inner London Labour-controlled ones, are likely to experience increased central controls over their finances and compulsory contracting out of services. The central government will in part be responding to the high levels of indebtedness in such authorities. It may continue to bypass the boroughs when trying to promote economic development by setting up further special agencies like the London Docklands Corporation and by extended promotion of deregulated enterprise zones. Moreover, it is not implausible that for both administrative and political reasons the Conservatives will be tempted to reorganise the boundaries of Inner London authorities. The effects of final crises through the collision between Labour's local socialists and Conservative retrenchment from Whitehall will create the opportunity for further fragmentation and parcelling. In this case the Government will continue to encourage boroughs to combine voluntarily to contract out to private suppliers, especially in such activities as waste disposal. It is even possible that a Ministry for London, in which Inner London is governed directly from Whitehall, will be considered as a possible response to the 'ungovernability' of the inner city. And third, we can expect that certain major services, such as London Transport and the Thames Regional Water Authority will become prime candidates for privatisation.

The ideal of privatised local governments run by streamlined councils – consisting of little more than elected councillors with teams of financial, computer and legal advisers engaged in the management of contracts – clearly appeals most to many Conservatives who regard it as a route to greater freedom and efficiency. But there are four major drawbacks to this model for London government.

First, the market model with a strong centre has been, and is likely to be, unpopular, making its implementation problematic and intensely conflictual. In the absence of electoral reform and agreement over boundaries the system is only likely to last as long as the Government does – thereby encouraging further bouts of adversarial politics.

Second, the move to greater use of market forces throughout London government is likely to exacerbate metropolitan inequalities.

Third, the market ideal explicitly downplays the importance of government regulation of the environment and of social costs, and suggests that where local authorities have common interests they will co-operate with one another without any need for co-ordination by a higher-level regional or metropolitan authority. If they do not co-operate they will produce sub-optimal welfare outcomes, but if they do try to co-operate every authority will have the incentive to free-ride on the contributions of the others. In principle there are only two optimal solutions to this dilemma. Either voluntary co-operation emerges over the long run through social learning or coerced co-operation by the centre is essential. It is worth recalling that it was precisely the evidence of the failure of voluntary co-operation in London's past which was used as an argument by Conservatives for the establishment of the GLC (Smallwood, 1965; Rhodes, 1970) in the 1960s. And the current joint boards provide plentiful fresh evidence of the difficulties with voluntary co-operation. In the recent reorganisation the Government had to opt for coercion through provisions for the Department of the Environment or the Department of Transport to intervene where necessary to compel co-operation between boroughs. The government's belief that the new joint boards would be more efficient and effective than the GLC does not fit the evidence (Flynn and Leach, 1984). These facts suggest that the Conservative case against metropolitan government *per se* is not over-whelming, even on its own terms. When co-operation fails coercion may be the best solution. And if there has to be metropolitan government because of metropolitan-wide problems the critical question is: why should it be the central government which chooses and compels the mode of co-operation in the metropolis? A consistent 'new right' theory would hold that where possible the relevant consumers-citizens should not have their welfare controlled by people who are not elected to represent their preferences. The Conservatives' strategy for London is not consistent in this respect. The legitimacy of the centre's decision-making powers in the metropolis will be continually at issue, quite apart from the administrative load which will be placed on the centre.

Finally, it is often argued that the market model with the strong centre neglects the existence of explicitly regional public problems which create a case for a distinct regional level for the management of public policy. This criticism is the starting point of the second possible future model of London government.

The Regional Model

The Labour party and the Liberal-SDP Alliance, albeit to differing extents and with very important differences over the issue of electoral reform, have both moved in favour of a regionalist organisation of local government in the UK. What are the principal assumptions behind this emergent regionalism?

First, it is believed that the existence of distinct city-regions or regional economies, spatial units with high interdependencies, notably in housing, transport, land-use and labour markets, creates a prima-facie functional case for a tier of government distinct from either traditional local or central institutions.

Second, it is argued that a regionalist solution to the organisation of decentralised government provides the most democratic and effective mechanism for dealing with administrative overload and complexity. On the one hand much central government field administration and various quasi-governmental agencies, such as the National Health Service, the Water Authorities, British Rail and London Transport, are effectively free from democratic accountability at any level, and lack any compelling managerial justification for being nominally controlled by Whitehall. They could, in principle, be subordinated to elected, or indirectly elected, regional governments. On the other hand a regional tier of government, organised over a wider and coherent spatial area, in principle, offers the prospect of easier and more effective co-ordination of recognised regional issues than that provided through the voluntary co-operation of smaller and more numerous local governments. The latter are likely to be in competition with each other for resources and keen to export their difficulties in ways which will produce overall reductions in welfare.

Third, regional government is seen as a mechanism for creating a more powerful counter-balance to the central government than that which has been provided by local governments in the past. Regional governments will draw support from wider electoral and financial bases, and, provided the distribution of functions between centre and region is carefully organised they will have an excellent chance of obtaining the legitimacy, stability and capacity to resist centralisation.

Fourth, it is argued that there are distinct regional identities, shared cultures which transcend other forms of stratification, which ought to be reflected in democratic political institutions. Such recognition might enhance the legitimacy of the political system.

Finally, regionalists generally are in favour of maintaining local governments rather than abolishing them or subjecting them to central-ised controls. They seek an extra tier of democratic government not the substitution of one tier by another, through the confederational orga-nisation of the regional and local governments, and they believe that regionalist solutions will strengthen local government by removing many

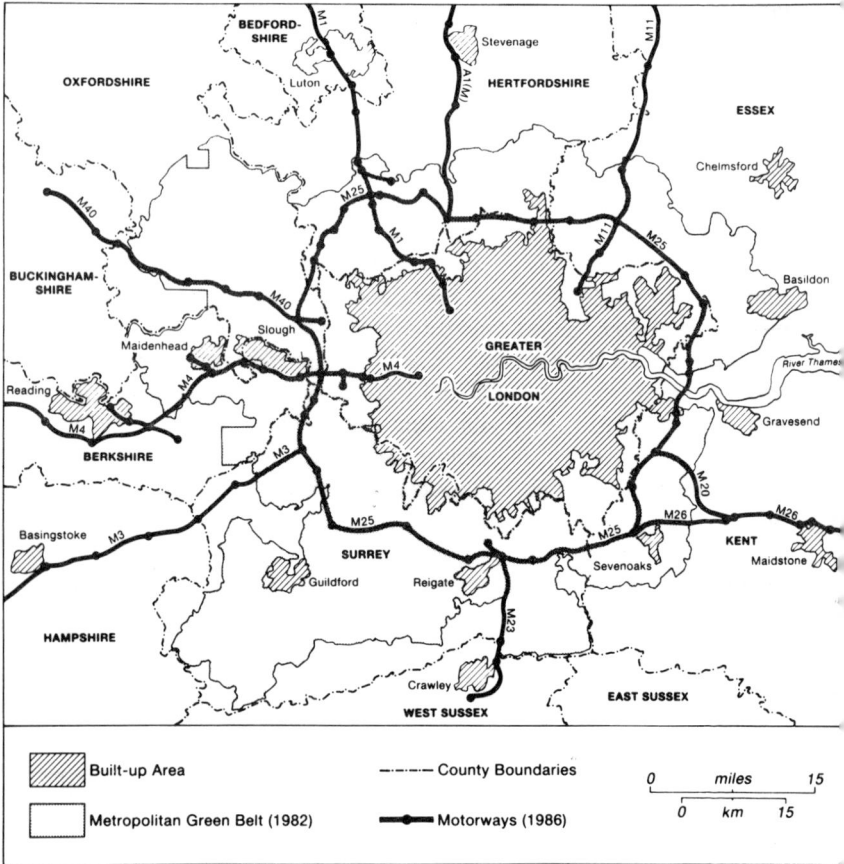

Figure 9.3   The London Region as defined by the Metropolitan
              Green Belt

unnecessary sources of conflict between centre and locality.

These assumptions are all contestable. But regionalist philosophies have made some headway in discussions of the future of London government among the Opposition parties. There are, however, three difficulties which the Opposition parties share in considering the implementation of the regionalist ideal for London, and one which divides them.

The first difficulty is the most straightforward: what region is London in? The minimalist answer to this question is obvious: the Greater London area – or the old G L C boundaries. This solution amounts to a restatement of the case for metropolitan government. And within the Labour and Alliance parties there are some advocates of a revived but strengthened G L C – with a new functional allocation of powers and greater capacity to implement strategic plans. The intermediate answer to the question is based upon the commuter region – which might include all the territory within the boundaries of the M25 and the Green Belt (see Fig. 9.3) or go beyond these boundaries to incorporate satellite dormitory and new towns. The maximalist position, based on the logic of economic interdependencies, presumably will include the Home Counties, East Anglia and Kent within the appropriate boundaries of a South East Region (see Fig. 9.4). The size of the regional unit clearly matters considerably for administrative and political reasons. The wider the definition of the region the more likely it is to increase the cultural, economic and political dominance of the South East of England within the U K – and the more likely it is to be controlled by the Conservatives. A large South East region will imperil support for regionalism elsewhere, and in the absence of electoral reform, will be against the party political interests of the Opposition parties.

The second difficulty is: what functions should the region have? The maximalist position of permitting the region to pass laws, make policy and raise taxes as it wishes, subject only to explicit prohibitions, is incompatible with British constitutional convention, and is almost certainly a non-starter. However, the Opposition parties have moved towards support for a local income tax. Most regionalists also have a favoured list of functions in London which they believe are appropriately managed at the regional level: transport, land-use, waste-disposal, water supply, health services, public health and safety, and environmental regulation, to which policing, economic development, employment creation and education are sometimes added. These are functions, it is argued, where interests so transcend the constituent parts of London and its environs that they require a strategic authority for their articula-

Figure 9.4   The South East Planning Region

tion and aggregation. Regionalists argue that such a multi-functional regional authority need not be bureaucratically top-heavy. Provided that it is given sovereign legal authority over its plans, it could manage implementation at arms length, through existing public agencies and/or contracts with private agencies.

The third difficulty compounds the first two: how will the creation of the region affect the rest of the governmental and intergovernmental system? Regionalism creates obvious political and organisational tensions. Localists fear that the creation of powerful regions will largely take place at the expense of local government. They believe local government is already eviscerated by centralisation, reduced to an administrative apparatus of Whitehall, and already too large, by European standards, to be genuinely local. Regionalism to them represents the termination of English local government. By contrast, 'centralisers' fear that the creation of powerful regions will take place largely at the expense of Whitehall and ministers, exacerbate the considerable turbulence in intergovernmental relations, and potentially block the centre from achieving its programmes – including regional equalisation and equalisation of service provision.

Only one set of these anxieties can effectively be alleviated. Most regionalists in the Opposition parties do not want the creation of a South East Regional Government or Greater London Council to take place at the expense of local government. Therefore they emphasise that regional functions should largely be ones which are currently exercised by the centre or quasi-governmental agencies, or in the case of London, functions formerly exercised by the GLC. They also want the bulk of personnel to be employed by local government rather than the region, separating out, as far as is possible, policy-making to the region and implementation to the local authorities. And critically, most regionalists see a case for the restructuring of the London boroughs and the City Corporation to make them fit better with any proposed regional authority.

Several proposals for such restructuring have been floated, though mostly it should be noted by non-regionalists. One school of thought has advocated the amalgamation of the Inner London boroughs to create a core London authority, reminiscent of the London County Council (Fig. 9.1), capable of managing the inner city. By contrast, another suggests that all the London boroughs should be abolished and carved up into five wedges of similar size and resources, akin to the London Fire Divisions (Map 14).

The fourth difficulty is controversial both within and across the

Opposition parties: how should the region be elected? There are two
issues at stake here. The first is whether the regional government should
be directly elected or indirectly elected, and the second is whether the
voting system should be reformed. The enthusiasts of direct elections
argue that they are more democratic and more legitimate and will give
the new regions a fighting chance of survival. The advocates of the
indirect election of elected local councillors to the regional authority
believe that such procedures are more likely to harmonise regional–local
relations and relieve anxiety at the centre about the emergence of a rival
power-centre. The issue of electoral reform divides the Opposition
parties, with the S L D and S D P favouring proportional representation
and the Labour party at present still in favour of the plurality rule
mechanism. Labour is in a painful dilemma. The application of proportional representation throughout London local government would
weaken Labour's domination of certain areas – especially Inner London.
But the wider the boundaries of the region in which London government
is situated the more likely Labour is to benefit from proportional
representation and to suffer from the plurality rule. The general election
result of 1987 may perhaps concentrate Labour's mind on the rationality
of its position and on the subject of electoral reform.

The regionalist ideal has many coherent arguments and enjoys support within the Opposition parties. It has major difficulties in design and
implementation which its enthusiasts recognise: the issues of appropriate boundaries, functions, intergovernmental relations and the election
system being the most obvious. However, there are further drawbacks
which must enter into judgements of its feasibility. With the unflattering
exception of Northern Ireland, regionalism is wholly novel to British
political tradition. A South East Region is not a popular demand, this
being a region that paradoxically has a much clearer definition in the eyes
of the rest of the United Kingdom than of its own population. And here's
the rub. A London Region will be regarded elsewhere as another
instrument for developing the privileged economic position of the South
East. The bigger the region the more widespread will be such suspicions.
The argument that the South East needs regional government to cope
with the problems of affluence and localised poverty whereas other areas
need regional government because of their relative deprivation will
sound more than a little odd – especially for those concerned by
national-level inequalities. Finally, the regionalists will also face the
problem that there will be no consensus for their model, although it is
less likely to cause the depth of controversy and conflicts that the
implementation of the market model promises. Nonetheless, the Con-

servatives can be expected to oppose regionalism with all the support they can muster.

Summary

The future design of London government will be neither the product of administrative rationality or academic reflection, nor the by-product of allegedly inexorable economic or social processes. Rather, it will be shaped largely as a product of party political interests, political ideologies, party conflicts and coalitions. The two most likely configurations are the market model with a strong central government role in London, and some variation on a regional model which will include a reorganisation of the London boroughs. At present the former configuration seems more likely to shape London's future than the latter. But whichever ideal is partially realised we may be confident that for the foreseeable future there will be no going back to the previous modes of metropolitan government.

References

Department of the Environment (1983). *Streamlining the Cities*. Cmnd 9063.

Flynn, N. and Leach, S. (1984). *Joint Boards and Joint Committees: An Evaluation*. University of Birmingham, Institute of Local Government Studies.

O'Leary, D.B. (1987). 'Why was the G L C Abolished?' *International Journal of Urban and Regional Research*.

Rhodes, R. (1970). *The Government of Greater London: The Struggle for Reform*. London: London School of Economics.

Smallwood, F. (1965). *Greater London: The Politics of Metropolitan Reform*. New York: Bobbs-Merrill.

Tiebout, C. (1956). 'A Pure Theory of Local Expenditure'. *Journal of Political Economy*.

CHAPTER 10

Conclusion

One of the more telling shots in the propaganda war between the Greater London Council and the Government after the publication in 1983 of the White Paper *Streamlining the Cities* was a diagram of 'London-wide Planning Arrangements, Existing and Proposed', which featured in the GLC response to the White Paper and was much reproduced. In the 'existing arrangement' the GLC appears as a central exchange linked upwards to Government, outwards to the county councils, and downwards to the London boroughs. The diagram contains just 43 connections in all. The 'proposed arrangement' takes the form of a dense criss-cross web of over 600 communication lines joining boroughs to each other and to joint committees, boards, counties, public utilities and central departments.

Though the logical simplicity of the first diagram and the anarchic tangle of the second were equally exaggerated the underlying contrast was real enough. The one sure conclusion about London government since the abolition of the GLC is that its arrangements are complicated. In every service with the possible exception of housing, administrative structures have become more intricate and political responsibility harder to attribute. Nothing is straightforward about local government in London today.

For the boroughs, as suggested in the Introduction, the abolition of the GLC has been in some ways an invigorating episode, offering some compensation in an otherwise difficult decade of high staff turnover and severe financial problems. Londoners in general are more aware than five years ago of the separate identities and territories of the boroughs, thanks to newly marked boundaries in the streets and new political prominence or notoriety for local politicians in the media, both spurred on by the removal of the London-wide authority. If for the moment the present scene were viewed only through the eyes of the boroughs, especially the suburban boroughs, the conclusion might well be that this

188

fresh sense of political weight vindicates the Government's democratic argument for 'streamlining'.

Unfortunately what is good for the boroughs individually may be less so for London as a whole. The downside of borough self-confidence is a new and growing climate of parochialism on matters outside those freshly marked boundaries, a phenomenon likely to be aggravated by the intense fiscal pressures of the third Thatcher term. Parochialism is a common flaw running through all the various forms of joint arrangement between boroughs for London-wide service provision, given that it has been decided that such joint arrangements are most appropriate, and it affects both the way these services are organised and the pattern of their provision.

Statutory joint functions, which should by definition be robustly established, may be immobilised by the requirement in section 88 of the Local Government Act 1985 for a two-thirds majority for budget approval. Government deliberately compounded the problem in the case of the London Boroughs Grants Committee by requiring a positive resolution by every approving borough, a difficult requirement to meet given the symmetrical pattern of party control in London, with almost equal blocks of Labour and Conservative members separated by a small group of Alliance or hung boroughs. Even if such annual hurdles have been cleared, and that may take months, the joint boards remain cumbersome entities, with decision-making in their slow committee cycles slowed still further by intermittent attendance by members and their need to consult parent authorities whenever policy enters sensitive ground.

Though the voluntary joint committees are, by definition, less liable to immobilisation through internal policy disagreement than all-borough bodies, they have problems of their own. Voluntary, and hence variable, borough participation in their various services means that agencies such as the London Boroughs Joint Ecology Committee, the London Research Centre and the London Children's Regional Planning Committee are supposed to perform different sets of functions in different parts of London. There are good financial, geographical and political reasons for the discriminating approach of the boroughs towards joint participation. But seen from the Clapham omnibus, the resulting patterns may well appear irrational or irrelevant.

Implementation presents further difficulties. The notion of a lead borough running a service on behalf of all has proved less simple in practice than it looked on paper in section 58 of the Local Government Act 1985. A borough has little benefit to show for shouldering the burden of attributing and raising revenue, clerking meetings and managing the expenditure of a joint committee, especially a voluntary joint committee which lives in perpetual insecurity from year to year. The pattern of London-wide services is notably dependent upon the good offices of Camden's chief officers, who between them assumed administrative responsibility for seven joint committees after abolition. Now in a harsh financial predicament and faced with the need to redeploy or lose many staff, a local authority such as Camden is bound to look closely at the burden of the lead borough role.

There may be an increasing tendency to share the 'lead' role. While Hackney is the lead borough for the London Canals Committee, technical co-ordination of canal matters to the west of London has been devolved to Ealing, an hour's travelling distance away. The four members of the East London Waste Authority decided to split the task into four parts, Barking and Dagenham handling administration, Redbridge finance, Newham operations and Havering the technical branch. Once again, this approach may be rational for the participating authorities but it poses difficulties for the general public who pay for and use the joint service.

The tidiest pieces of administrative machinery in London today are the centrally appointed boards for transport, health, the police, Docklands redevelopment, and all the other services detailed in Chapter 2. Morale in these agencies is generally good. Their members, many of them from shared specialised backgrounds, have a defined functional remit. They are often generously remunerated and can in many cases draw upon support services closer to those of private directors than local councillors. These single-minded agencies have evident attractions yet one cannot help being uneasy at their proliferation in London, and at the prospect of still further powers and resources being reallocated to central government's nominees in the forthcoming reforms of housing and education. Elected local government is being diminished.

London's accumulating experience with this style of government confirms the two text-book objections to boards, (a) that seen in the round they are inefficient, being by their very nature ill-suited to co-ordinate the function for which they are entrusted with other functions which are not their responsibility, and (b) that they are essentially undemocratic and unresponsive. It comes as no surprise that there has been more than a hint of high-handedness in the relations between agencies such as the LDDC and LRT and local councils, communities and consumer organisations. Board members, able and committed though they may be individually, are not politicians. Unlike the elected local councillor, the salaried members of appointed boards have not canvassed on doorsteps, fought for votes, and endured the hurly-burly of public meetings or the ordeal of complaint in constituency surgeries. They meet (for the most part) behind closed doors, well protected from Londoners by a buffer of public relations officers. They are not accountable to the public they serve.

Surveying this scene – the complacency and narrow purpose of the appointed boards, the parochialism of local elected councils, and the great muddle of joint action in between – we have often been reminded of the original work of the Greater London Group, documenting and criticising the problems of a wholly inadequate structure of local government in London before the establishment of the Greater London Council in 1965. There are more than a few contemporary touches in that great and shrewd panorama, *The Government and Misgovernment of London* by William Robson, published in 1939. But whereas the 'chaos of authorities, functions and areas' anatomised by Robson was the product of a gradual, accidental accretion over decades, and could be contrasted with the potential of a reformed Greater London government, today's system is itself the product of reform, a reform inspired in part by the supposed failure of the London-wide elected authority for which Robson campaigned for so many years (see Hill, 1986).

However, there has been no return to the pre-1965 state of affairs. The design imposed by the Local Government Act 1985 is viable not because of any intrinsic sense in a system that divides a single, tightly integrated metropolis into 33 independent units, but rather because of the continuing legacy of the 1963 reform that made Greater London one. Though the Council was abolished in the spring of 1986, many of the services which it had built up continued to operate for at least two years subsequently, often from the same rooms at County Hall and with the same personnel. The newly autonomous London Fire and Civil Defence Authority has continued to draw on former GLC support services for its building programme through LRB, medical inspections (a major annual item for firefighters over 43) through ILEA, purchasing through ILEA, computer services through the Central Computer Service, scientific support through London Scientific Services, and building maintenance (in inner London) through ILEA. The Government's doctrinaire decision, taken against the recommendation of its own inspector, to allow the London Residuary Body to sell off County Hall to the private sector will break up this complex system of support services. Dissipating the overhead capital inherited from the GLC can generate only friction and overlap in the forseeable future, and stimulate a fresh

growth of arguments for new general structures of metropolitan government, both upper and lower tier, in the longer term.

The legacy of pre-abolition days survives in another, less palpable way.
The GLC was abolished but not 'Greater London'. Those familiar
metropolitan boundaries, first controversially set out by the London
Government Act of 1963, have become deeply entrenched in the
political and administrative reality of the capital. The 'London factor' has
if anything been reinforced by abolition of the GLC, which confirmed the
London boroughs' status as relatively wealthy, unitary and long-standing
authorities. There has been no talk in the suburbs of reunification with
the shire counties from which the outer boroughs were wrenched in
1964. One of the distinctive features of the system of government
described in this book is its self-containment. With a very few exceptions,
such as Bexley's preference to join Kent rather than its suburban
neighbours for rubbish disposal (see Map 15), London government
presents a remarkably compact appearance. It is a universe unto itself.
This 'Londonness' of London is, of course, reinforced by all those
agencies of central government, such as the Metropolitan Police,
London Regional Transport or English Heritage, which acknowledge
London's status as a special and distinct territorial entity.

Even though the distinctiveness of London is currently denied any
direct political expression, it remains strongly rooted in the professional
side of local government. Each of the specialised groupings of London's
local government officers listed in Part I I I of the Directory below meets
regularly to discuss policy and practice. Organisations such as the
London Region of the Society of Chief Personnel Officers (SOCPO) and
the London Branch of the Society of Local Authority Chief Executives
(SOLACE) – and the comparable organisations existing in every service,
from architecture and baths through to treasurers, security and valuation
– now have a unique status in the London system, in that they continue to
operate on a universal basis with members in all boroughs, inner and
outer, right, left and centre. At their monthly or six-weekly meetings
members discuss legislation (current and proposed), financial matters
and general policy, and hear visiting speakers from central government
or specialist bodies. Some of the larger associations have working groups
and a policy committee in addition to the general meetings.

In general the professional groups have avoided formal involvement in
London-wide arrangements, rightly recognising the importance of a
detached, professional forum in the turbulent and highly politicised
policy environment. There are some exceptions. The relevant associations nominate representatives to the Officers' Advisory Panel of the

London Planning Advisory Committee, and the 'Waste in London Group of Officers' (WILGO) advises the London Waste Regulation Authority. Waste is where the post-1986 arrangements appear on paper to be particularly complex and friction-prone, with parts of London charging each other for use of what used to be a single disposal system. The practicality of the system described in Chapter 2 is largely because of the insertion of an informal element of London-wide liaison at officer level. The Association of London Borough Engineers and Surveyors (ALBES) and of London Cleansing Officers (ALCO) have held a quarterly group meeting since GLC abolition, known as the Joint Officers Group (JOG). Clerked by an ALBES nominee, the JOG brings together the widest possible range of professionals with an interest in waste collection and disposal: the Chief Technical Officers of all London Boroughs, the LWRA, the DOE, and all the general managers of the statutory and voluntary waste disposal groups. The ALBES also initiated the Joint Highways and Transportation Group, which similarly convenes large meetings three or four times a year at which borough officers can talk face to face with representatives of the Metropolitan and City Police Forces, the Department of Transport, London Regional Transport and British Rail.

In this first edition of the *London Government Handbook* we have not attempted to provide systematic coverage of these informal professional groupings, though the main groups are listed in the Directory. Without premises or staff of their own, carried on the back of the regular responsibilities of their individual professional members, these organisations are not in the public eye and attempt to avoid pressure group and political lobbying. Yet their importance can hardly be overestimated. In the Byzantine scheme of government described in this Handbook, the professionalism of local government officers constitutes perhaps the single most important force for stability and continuity in the delivery of local public services to Londoners.

London continues to be heavily governed, despite the removal of its tier of county-wide government. With the exception of gas supply, all the public sector provision of services such as health, water, education, housing and transport remains with public bodies.

Directly elected local government is now weaker than before, while appointed bodies have become ever more numerous and important. In London, where transport and police are central government services, the local electorate is, as compared with the rest of Britain, uniquely distant from its public services. The more services are moved to the centre, the greater the possibility that in future London will have little or no effective local government. Whitehall, perhaps through a 'Minister for London' may become Londoners' democratic focal-point.

It is certain that the present arrangements for London government will not last long. The last vestiges of the LCC are being swept away with the abolition of ILEA. The capital is in transition from a system of local government where at least some personal services were locally determined to one where the centre will be far more powerful. A future government may decide to shift the balance back towards local people. This book describes the starting point from which short- and long-term reforms begin. The results of such reforms will affect the lives not only of Londoners, but of all the people of Britain.

References

Hill, C.E. (1987). *A Bibliography of the Writings of W.A. Robson*. Greater London Paper No. 17. Greater London Group: London School of Economics.

Robson, W.A. (1939). *The Government and Misgovernment of London*. London: George Allen and Unwin.

DIRECTORY

This Directory is organised in five sections. Part I contains an analytical table of the provision of public services in Greater London. Part II presents key information about organisations and is set out in the same order as Chapters 2,3,4 and 5, namely:

1. centrally appointed bodies;
2. London-wide local government bodies;
3. local government bodies for parts of London;
4. the boroughs.

Part III of the Directory is a list of Associations of Local Government Officers in London. Part IV lists London M Ps by borough. Part V gives basic data about the boroughs.

PART I
Provision of Public Services in Greater London

	Central government	Centrally appointed body	Centrally regulated private body	London-wide local government body	Part-London local government body	Borough
Ambulances		X				
Arts and libraries		X^1		X^1		X
Cemeteries and crematoria						X
Civil defence				X		
Consumer protection						X
Education (not universities)					X^2	X
Electricity		X				
Environmental health						X
Fire				X		
Gas			X			
Health		X				
Housing				X^3		X
Land drainage		X^{10}				X
Planning	X^4			X^4		X
Police	X					
Public transport		X				
Recreation		X^5				X
Refuse collection and disposal				X^6		X
Roads	X^7					X
Sewerage		X				
Social services				X^8		X
Traffic, street lighting, parking	X^9					X
Water		X	X			

1. Arts and libraries partly funded by Greater London Arts (resources from the Arts Council), partly by the London Boroughs Grant Committee and partly by the boroughs.
2. Education in Inner London provided by the Inner London Education Authority.
3. Housing mobility run by joint committee of all boroughs. All major housing functions with the boroughs.
4. Planning partly the responsibility of the Secretary of State for the Environment, partly of the London Planning Advisory Committee, partly of the boroughs.
5. Recreation partly provided by Thames Water, partly by the South Bank Board and partly by the boroughs.
6. Refuse collection and disposal by the boroughs; hazardous waste regulated by the London Waste Regulation Authority.
7. Roads partly run by the Department of Transport, partly by the boroughs.
8. Some inspection and other children's services run by the London Boroughs' Children's Regional Planning Committee; all major social services functions with boroughs.
9. Metropolitan Police fulfil some traffic functions.
10. Land drainage partly the responsibility of the Thames and Southern Water Authorities (main rivers), partly the boroughs (minor rivers etc.).

Note   Minor services have been excluded from this table, which nevertheless covers over 98 per cent of all public expenditure on local services in Greater London.

The revenue spending or turnover (as appropriate) of all of these bodies taken together was about £15 billion in 1987/8. The proportions of this total controlled by each sector were very broadly as follows:

	%	
Central government	6.5	⎫
Quangos	47 0	⎬ central government and agencies
Private company	5.5	⎭
London-wide authority/ committee	1.5	⎫
Part-London authority/ committee	6.5	⎬ elected or indirectly elected local authorities
Borough	33.0	⎭

Part II
Key Information about Organisations

In this section we seek to summarise in a succinct form the key information about almost 100 bodies currently engaged in the provision of services in Greater London. Every effort has been made to ensure that the information below is accurate and consistent. Because so many organisations are covered, many of limited size and scope, it has proved extremely difficult to be certain that all information is comparable. For example, some of the 'current expenditure' shown is given net of income from charges while other figures are gross of charges. Some institutions' expenditure is effectively spread between constituent boroughs. There has been some double-counting of staff, where they are shown both within boroughs' staff totals and as the staff of a voluntary committee.

Political control is shown as at November 1987, while information about staff, expenditure and methods of revenue raising are the latest publicly available at that time.

Finally, where some centrally appointed bodies are shown as not subject to the Audit Commission or to scrutiny by the Local Government Ombudsman, it should be noted that in many cases such institutions *are* subject to scrutiny by Parliamentary Commissions for Administration and/or the National Audit Office.

Key to Tables

How elected
A Direct elections of councillors.
B Appointment by boroughs of one or more councillors from each borough.
C Appointment by central government.
D Borough representation via local authorities' association.

Method of revenue raising
1 Precept on borough ratepayers.
2 Charge to boroughs on basis of population.
3 Part funding by Government grant, part by boroughs as a flat-rate per borough.
4 Part flat-rate per borough, part flat-rate for 24 boroughs, part in proportion to children placed.
5 Charges to boroughs for use of services plus levy on basis of borough population.
6 Levy on borough ratepayers (similar to precept).
7 Venture capital raised and invested.
8 Government funding.
9 Self-financing from sales, plus Government funding.
10 Charge to boroughs and county councils on basis of population.
11 Charges and rates paid by customers for services.
12 Part borough funding (via London Rate Equalisation Scheme), part Government grant.
13 Self-financing sales, plus rent income.
14 Flat-rate contribution per borough.
15 Charges for services.
16 Part funding by charges and part by boroughs on basis of population.
17 Contributions from boroughs in proportion to users of scheme in each borough.
18 Contributions from boroughs via London Rate Equalisation Scheme.
19 Rate levied directly on all ratepayers.
20 Charges for services, plus land sales.
21 Endowment.

1. Centrally appointed bodies

Name and Address	Telephone	Number of boroughs participating, & lead borough	How elected	Chair (1988)	Staff total (1987)	Expenditure CURRENT 86-87 (£m)	87-88 (£m)	CAPITAL 86-87 (£m)	87-88 (£m)	Method of revenue raising	Subject to Audit Commission	Public right of access to meetings	Appeal to Local Ombudsman
Central Computer Service Room 448 County Hall London SE1	633-1701	Administered by LRB who finance CCS out of charges. Transferred summer 88	See LRB	See LRB (till summer 88)	About 300 (till summer 88)	0*	0*	0	0	15	No	No	No
Dial-a-Ride Scheme c/o London Regional Transport	227-3589	Financed by LRT, out of resources earmarked by the DOT	See LRT	See LRT	100 (admin.) 250 (drivers)	5.0	6.0	0	0	Via LRT	No	No	No
Greater London Arts 9 White Lion Street London N1 9PD	837-8808	Some - Executive Committee	C	Johnathan Brill	41	9	8.5	0	0	8	No	Yes	No
Historic Buildings & Monuments Commission (London Division) Fortress House 23 Savile Row London W1	734-6010	0	C	Lord Montague	78	1.5	1.6	0	0	8	No	Part	No

Organisation	Tel	Board composition	Chairman	Type								
Home Loans Portfolio c/o Richmond-upon-Thames	633-3383	Administered by Richmond, who share any deficit or surplus with all other boroughs****	See LRB	See LRB	60–70						Yes	N/a
London Council for Sport and Recreation PO Box, Jubilee Stand, Crystal Palace Sports Centre, London SE19 2BQ (See also Sports Council below)	778-8600	1 from each plus ILEA, Govt nominees & users	P.G. Yarranton	C/B	0	0**	0**	0	—	N/a	Yes	N/a
London Docklands Development Corporation Thames House, Basin South, London E6 2QY	476-3000	0	Sir Christopher Benson	C	80 f/t 250–300 (inc. p/t and consultants)	100***	134*** See current	See current	9	No	No	No
London Regional Passenger Committee 8 Duncannon Street, London WC2N 4JF	839-1898	0	Dr Eric Midwinter	C	7	N/a	N/a	N/a	8	No	Yes	No
London Regional Transport 55 Broadway, London SW1	222-5600	0	Sir Keith Bright	C	46,291	1,060	241	N/a	6	No	No	No

* No net cost: financed by charges.   ** Financed by Sports Council (London division).   *** Total gross spending, current and capital.

**** In consequence of transfer to Richmond, this service is now more accurately described as a London-wide Local Government Body.

1. Centrally appointed bodies

Name and Address	Telephone	Number of boroughs participating, & lead borough	How elected	Chair (1988)	Staff total (1987)	Expenditure CURRENT 86–87 (£m)	CURRENT 87–88 (£m)	CAPITAL 86–87 (£m)	CAPITAL 87–88 (£m)	Method of revenue raising	Subject to Audit Commission	Public right of access to meetings	Appeal to Local Ombudsman
London Residuary Body St Vincent House Orange Street London WC2	633-6246	0	C	Sir Godfrey Taylor	2,400	622	483	70	18	5	Yes (part)	No	Yes (part)
London Scientific Services Room 755 County Hall London SE1 7PB	633-5975	Administered by L R B. Financed out of charges to boroughs and other sources. To be transferred mid 88	See L R B (till mid 88)	See L R B (till mid 88)	140	0*	0*	0	0	5	No	No	No
Manpower Services Commission 236 Gray's Inn Road London WC1X 8HL	278-0363	0	C	Sir James Munn	700 (London only)	200 (inc. capital) (London only)	N/a	See current	N/a	8	No	No	No
Metropolitan Police New Scotland Yard 8 Broadway London SW1H 0BG	230-1212	0	C	Peter Imbert (Commissioner)	44,940	826	905	45	45	1	No	No	No

Organisation	Phone	Board	C/B	Chairman		8.3 (inc. capital)		See current	N/a	12	Part	Part	Part
Museum of London 150 London Wall London EC2	600-3699	City appoints 9 members of Board		Michael Robins	400	8.3 (inc. capital)	N/a	See current	N/a	12	Part	Part	Part
Port of London Authority Europe House World Trade Centre London E1	481-8484	0	C	Sir Brian Kellett	358	0*	0*	0	0	20	No	No	No
Regional Health Authorities													
NORTH WEST THAMES as SW Thames	262-8011	0	C	William Doughty	54,829	779**	N/a	65	86	8	No	No	No
NORTH EAST THAMES as SW Thames	262-8011	0	C	David Berriman	61,265	987**	N/a	60	80.5	8	No	No	No
SOUTH WEST THAMES 40 Eastbourne Terrace London W2 3GR	262-8011	0	C	Sir Antony Driver	43,365	650	—	54	—	8	No	No	No
SOUTH EAST THAMES Thrift House Collington Avenue Bexhill-on-Sea East Sussex TN39 3NQ	(0424) 222555	0	C	Sir Peter Baldwin	61,626	848**	—	77	—	8	No	No	No
The Royal Parks Baliff of the Royal Parks Office Room C11/08 Department of the Environment 2 Marsham Street London SW1P 3EB	212-3833	0	C	N/a	673	9.27	10.47	0.37	0.40	8	No	No	No

* No net cost: financed by charges.
** Excludes family practitioner services.

1. Centrally appointed bodies

Name and Address	Telephone	Number of boroughs participating, & lead borough	How elected	Chair (1988)	Staff total (1987)	Expenditure CURRENT 86-87 (£m)	CURRENT 87-88 (£m)	CAPITAL 86-87 (£m)	CAPITAL 87-88 (£m)	Method of revenue raising	Subject to Audit Commission	Public right of access to meetings	Appeal to Local Ombudsman
Seaside and Country Homes c/o North British Housing Association South Region The Annex 38 High Street Rickmansworth Herts WD3 1ER	0923-7251581	Administered by North British Housing Association out of income from outstanding mortgages	N/a	N/a	N/a	0*	0*	0	0	15	N/a	N/a	N/a
South Bank Board Royal Festival Hall South Bank London SE1	921-0600	0	C/B	Ronald Grierson	190	9.55	11.2	1.7	1.85	9	No	No	No
Sports Council (London Division) Jubilee Stand Crystal Palace Sports Centre London SE19	778-8600	0	C/B	N/a	37	0.64	0.64	1.8	1.8	8	No	N/a	No
Thames Water Nugent House Vastern Road Reading Berks RG1 8DB	(0734) 593333	0	C	Roy Watts	8,950	373	N/a	148	N/a	11	No	No	No

Organisation													
Thamesmead Town Harrow Manor Way Thamesmead South London SE2 9XH	310-1500	0	C**	Clive Thornton	353	8.41	N/a	9.59	N/a	13	No	Part	No
Traffic Control Systems Unit Kings Buildings Smith Square London SW1P 3HQ	821-5626	Administered by the City of London, who finance the Unit out of a charge to boroughs plus a contribution from the Department of Transport.	See City	N/a	96	6.7	7.6	5.1	5.1		Yes	No	No
Trust for London City Parochial Foundation 10 Fleet Street London EC4	633-5975	Administered by City Parochial Foundation, with income from proceeds of Greater London Council disposals				0	0.5	0	0	21	No	No	No

* No net cost: financed by charges.
** Chairman and other original appointments made by L R B. Now a co-operative of Thamesmead residents and thus, more accurately, a private body.

2. London-wide local government bodies

Name and address	Telephone	Number of boroughs participating, & lead borough (if applicable)	How elected	Political control C L SLD/Oth. SDP	Chair	Staff total (1987)	Expenditure CURRENT 86–87 (£m)	87–88 (£m)	CAPITAL 86–87 (£m)	87–88 (£m)	Method of raising revenue	Subject to Audit commission	Public right of access	Appeal to Local Ombudsman
Concessionary Fares Scheme c/o London Advisory Panel Transport Services for the Mobility Handicapped	784-3020	Administered by London Regional Transport, with resources provided by the boroughs. Policy input via London Advisory Panel on Transport Service for the Mobility Handicapped					78	87	0	0	2	N/a	N/a	N/a
Greater London Employers' Secretariat for Local Authorities Services Victoria St House 191 Victoria Street London SW1E 5NE	834-8288	32 plus ILEA, LFCDA & others	B			21	0.6	0.6	0	0	14	Yes	No	No
Greater London Record Office 40 Northampton Rd London EC1R 0HB	633-6851	Administered by the City of London, with resources provided by the boroughs via the London Rate Equalisation Scheme					1.49	1.55	0.03	0.23	18	N/a	No	No

Organisation	Phone	Membership	Type	Composition	Control								
London Advisory & Consultative Committee, Room C5/16, Department of Transport, 2 Marsham Street, London SW1P 3EB	212-7022	33 plus Department of Transport	B	N/a	N/a	0	0*	0*	0	0	N/a	N/a	No	No	No
London Advisory Panel on Transport Services for the Mobility Handicapped, Hammersmith Town Hall, King Street, London W6 9JU	748-3020	Via A L A, L B A Hammersmith & Fulham	D	N/a	N/a	2.5	0.02	0.05	0	0	2	No	No	No
London Area Mobility Scheme, Devonshire House, 164–8 Westminster Bridge Road, London SE1 7RW	928-8081	33 Camden	B	14 15 3 1	Con.	55	1.8	1.8	2.5	2.5	3	Yes	Yes	Yes
London Boroughs' Children's Regional Planning Committee, Headland House, 5th Floor, 308 Gray's Inn Road, London WC1X 8DP	278-8068	33 Camden	B	13 16 3 1	Lab.	12	0.18	0.19	0	0	4	Yes	Yes	Yes

* Department of Transport pays administrative costs.

2. London-wide local government bodies

Name and address	Telephone	Number of boroughs participating, & lead borough (if applicable)	How elected	Political control C L SLD/ SDP Oth.	Chair	Staff total (1987)	Expenditure CURRENT 86–87 (£m)	87–88 (£m)	CAPITAL 86–87 (£m)	87–88 (£m)	Method of raising revenue	Subject to Audit commission	Public right of access	Appeal to Local Ombudsman
London Boroughs Grants Scheme 8th Floor Regal House London Road Twickenham Middlesex TW1 3QS	891-5021	33	B	13 16 3 1	All.	42	27	28.5	0	0	2	Yes	Yes	Yes
London Fire and Civil Defence Authority Room 200A County Hall London SE1 7PB	633-5131	33	B	14 15 3 1	Con.	8,359	166.7	182.2	4.5	10.6	1	Yes	Yes	Yes
London Planning Advisory Committee Eastern House 8–10 Eastern Road Romford Essex RM1 3PN	(0708) 45997/ 42494	33	B	14 15 3 1	SLD	21	0.4	1.1	0	0	2	Yes	Yes	Yes

Organisation	Phone	Notes											
London Recycling Forum c/o London Waste Regulation Authority	633-4045	Administered by London Waste Regulation Authority who provide resources. Involves boroughs and other interested parties						0	0	0	0	N/a	N/a	Yes	N/a
London Research Centre 5th Floor* County Hall London SE1 7PB	633-6184 735-4250 (from later 88)	*Supplementary Research:* 17 Islington *Research:* 33 Islington	B B	0 13 3 1 Lab. 12 15 3 3 Lab.	138	5.13 4.73	0	0	16	Yes	Yes	Yes
London Tourist Board Grosvenor Gardens London SW1	730-3450	33	Via London Boroughs Grants Scheme	N/a	Sir Christopher Leaver	80 (110 in summer)	1.7	1.6	0	N/a	N/a	No	No
London Waste Regulation Authority Room N174 County Hall London SE1 7PB	633-4045	33	B	14 15 3 1 Con.	86	2.9	3.13	0	0.24	2	Yes	Yes	Yes
SERPLAN 50–64 Broadway London SW1 0DB	799-2191	16 via London Planning Advisory Committee	B	N/a	Lord Sandford	15	0.37	0.50	0	0	10	Yes	No	Yes
Taxicard Scheme c/o London Regional Transport	227-3588	Administered by London Regional Transport with resources provided by the boroughs. Policy input via London Advisory Panel on Transport Services for the Mobility Handicapped	3	5.20	5.26	0	0	17	No	N/a	No

* from later 88: Parliament House, Black Prince Road, London SE11.

3. Local government bodies for parts of London

Name and Address	Telephone	Number of boroughs participating, & lead borough (if applicable)	How elected	Political control C L SLD/Oth. SDP				Chair	Staff total (1987)	Expenditure CURRENT 86–87 (£m)	87–88 (£m)	CAPITAL 86–87 (£m)	87–88 (£m)	Method of raising revenue	Subject to Audit Commission	Public right of access	Appeal to Local Ombudsman
Docklands Consultative Committee Unit 4, 3rd Floor Stratford Office Village 4 Romford Road London E15 4EA	519-5485	4 plus ILEA & parts of Tower Hamlets	B	0	6	0	0	Lab.	7	0.15	0.15	0	0	14	Yes	Yes	Yes
Greater London Enterprise Spencer House 63/67 Newington Causeway London SE1 6BD	403-0300	13	B	0	13	0	0	Lab.	70	GLE exists to invest in projects within Greater London. There was little investment in 1986/87, though investment did start in 1987–88.				7	No	No	No
Inner London Education Authority County Hall London SE1 7PB	633-5000	13	A	11	45	2	0	Lab.	64,500	1,160	1,265	16	23	1	Yes	Yes	Yes

Organisation	Phone	Members														
Lee Valley Regional Park Authority Myddelton House Bulls Cross Enfield Middlesex EN2 9HG	(0992) 717711	14 (plus 5 other non-London authorities), British Waterways Board & Thames Water	B	N/a				Con.	328	5.4	N/a	4.3	N/a	10	Yes	Yes	Yes
London Boroughs Disability Committee Rooms 92/5 County Hall London SE1 7PB	633-7107	11 Camden	B	0	11	0	0	Lab.	23	0.69	0.86	0	0	14	Yes	Yes	Yes
London Boroughs Nuclear Policy Committee 141 Euston Road London NW1 2LL	388-2484 ext. 2304	11 Camden	B	0	11	0	0	Lab.	3	0.11	0.10	0	0	14	Yes	Yes	Yes
London Boroughs Training Committee 9 Tavistock Place London WC1H 9SN	388-2041	28 (plus 12 District Health Authorities)	B	N/a				Lab.	26	0.56	0.71	N/a	N/a	14	Yes	Yes	N/a
London Boroughs Transport Committee (Lorry Control Unit) Room 411 Main Building County Hall London SE1	633-7522/ 633-6435	22	B	1	15	4	2	Lab.	32	—	0.86	—	0.53	14	Yes	Yes	Yes

3. Local government bodies for parts of London

Name and Address	Telephone	Number of boroughs participating, & lead borough (if applicable)	How elected	Political control C	L	SLD	SDP	Oth.	Chair	Staff total (1987)	Expenditure CURRENT 86–87 (£m)	87–88 (£m)	CAPITAL 86–87 (£m)	87–88 (£m)	Method of raising revenue	Subject to Audit Commission	Public right of access	Appeal to Local Ombudsman
London Canals Committee Town Hall Mare Street London E8 1EA	985-4382	9 (plus other organisations) Hackney	B	0	7	1	1	1	Lab.	0.25	0	0.01	0	0	14	Yes	Yes	Yes
London Ecology Committee 4th Floor Berkshire House 168–173 High Holborn London WC1V 7AA	379-4352	23 Camden	B	4	15	3	1		Lab.	12	0.33	0.35	0	0	14	Yes	Yes	Yes
London Housing Unit Committee 4th Floor Berkshire House 168–173 High Holborn London WC1V 7AA	379-4384	14 Camden	B	0	13	1	0		Lab.	13	0.35	0.49	0	0	14	Yes	Yes	Yes

Organisation	Phone												
London River Authority Unit 4, 3rd Floor Stratford Office Village 4 Romford Road London E15 4EA	519-8984	6 (plus Thurrock D C and other organisa- tions)	B	0 6 0 0 Lab.	3	0	0.6	0	14	Yes	Yes	Yes
London Strategic Policy Unit Middlesex House 20 Vauxhall Bridge Road London SW1	633-3724	9 Camden	B	0 9 0 0 Lab.	334	7.1	N/a	0	14	Yes	Yes	Yes
[L S P U was wound up on 31 March 1988]												
London Welfare Benefits PO Box 1119 London W3 6N3	992-5566	13 Ealing	B	1 11 0 1 Lab.	31	N/a	0.72	0	14	Yes	Yes	Yes
Technical Services Joint Committee Central Technical Unit 95–97 Wandsworth Road London SW8	735-1266	7 Hackney	B	0 7 0 0 Lab.	230	0*	0*	0	15	Yes	Yes	Yes
[C T U was wound up on 10 June 1988]												

* Financed out of charges for services.

3. Local government bodies for parts of London

Name and Address	Telephone	Number of boroughs participating, & lead borough (if applicable)	How elected	Political control C L SLD/ Oth. SDP	Chair	Staff total (1987)	Expenditure CURRENT 86–87 (£m)	87–88 (£m)	CAPITAL 86–87 (£m)	87–88 (£m)	Method of raising revenue	Subject to Audit Commission	Public right of access	Appeal to Local Ombudsman
Waste Disposal Authorities:														
East London Waste Authority Civic Centre Dagenham Essex	592-4500	4 *Administration:* Barking & Dagenham *Finance:* Redbridge *Operations:* Newham *Technical:* Havering	B	3 4 0 1	Lab.	0**	3.20	4.90	0.57	0.78	2	Yes	Yes	Yes
North London Waste Authority Town Hall Euston Road London NW1 2RU	278-4444 ext. 2016	7 Camden	B	4 10 0 0	Lab.	252	17.01	19.22	0.4	1.1	2	Yes	Yes	Yes
Western Riverside Waste Authority Town Hall Wandsworth High Street London SW18	871-2789	4 Wandsworth	B	4 4 0 0	Con.	82	8.3	9.1	0.6	0.6	2	Yes	Yes	Yes

Organisation																		
West London Waste Authority Mogden Lane Isleworth Middlesex TW7 7LP	847-5555	6	Hounslow	B	2	3	1	0	Lab.	92	9.9	9.6	0.55	0.85	2	Yes	Yes	Yes
Central London Waste Disposal Group City of London Cleansing Department Westbrook Wharf Upper Thames Street London EC4 3DT	236-9541	3	City	B	1	0	2	1	Rotates (Con./All./Ind.)	0*	0	0	0	0	—	N/a	Yes	N/a
South East London Waste Disposal Group Town Hall Catford London SE6 4RV	695-6000 ext. 3195	3	Lewisham	B	0	3	0	1	Lab.	0*	0	0	0	0	—	N/a	Yes	N/a
South London Waste Disposal Committee Public Service and Works Taberner House Park Lane Croydon CR9 3RN	686-4433	5	Croydon	B	4	0	1	0	Con.	0*	0	0	0	0	—	N/a	Yes	N/a

* All staff employed by boroughs, then recharged to Authority.

** Borough staff service the voluntary committees as part of their work. Any administrative costs are similarly borne by the lead borough(s). In some voluntary groupings, expenditure by the group may be agreed, and then recharged by one borough to the other members.

4. Local government bodies for parts of London

Borough and address	Telephone	How elected	C	L	SLD	SDP	Oth.	Control	Staff F/T (1987)	Staff P/T	Expenditure CURRENT 86-87 (£m)	87-88 (£m)	CAPITAL 85-86 (£m)	86-87 (£m)	Method of raising revenue	Subject to Audit Commission	Public right of access	Appeal to Local Ombudsman
INNER LONDON																		
City of London, PO Box 270, Guildhall, London EC2P 2EJ	606-3020	A*	0	0	0		157	Ind.	2,834	227	79.2	83.0	7.8	10.1	19	Yes	Yes	Yes
Camden, Town Hall, Euston Road, London NW1 2RU	278-4444	A	13	44	2	0	0	Lab.	7,284	965	151.8	N/a	51.4	62.0	19	Yes	Yes	Yes
Greenwich, 24–27 Wellington Road, London SE18	854-8888	A	12	42	8	0	0	Lab.	6,400	1,989	113.8	109.2	29.8	30.5	19	Yes	Yes	Yes
Hackney, Town Hall, Mare Street, London E8 1EA	986-3123	A	2	53	5	0	0	Lab.	7,743	1,376	148.6	158.2	45.7	45.4	19	Yes	Yes	Yes
Hammersmith & Fulham, Town Hall, Hammersmith, London W6 9JU	748-3020	A	9	40	1	0	0	Lab.	4,194	741	84.7	N/a	36.4	28.3	19	Yes	Yes	Yes
Islington, Town Hall, Upper Street	226-1234	A	0	36	16	0	0	Lab.	6,114	1,300	114.1	113.4	56.5	50.6	19	Yes	Yes	Yes

Organisation	Phone		Composition				Control										
Kensington & Chelsea The Town Hall Hornton Street London W8 7NX	937-5464	A	39	14	0	1	Con.	2,887	313	53.5	54.9	36.2	26.5	19	Yes	Yes	Yes
Lambeth Town Hall Brixton Hill London SW2 1RW	274-7722	A	21	40	3	0	Lab.	9,531	1,665	179.0	166.6	56.9	51.1	19	Yes	Yes	Yes
Lewisham Town Hall Catford London SE6 4RU	695-6000	A	18	41	1	0	Lab.	7,004	1,759	131.1	137.8	39.5	33.8	19	Yes	Yes	Yes
Southwark Town Hall Peckham Road London SE6 8UP	703-6311	A	7	43	14	0	Lab.	N/a	N/a	141.7	N/a	45.2	52.4	19	Yes	Yes	Yes
Tower Hamlets Town Hall Patriot Square London E2 9LN	980-4831	A	0	24	26	0	All.	6,084	818	128.0	129.9	16.3	19.5	19	Yes	Yes	Yes
Wandsworth Town Hall Wandsworth High Street London SW18 2PU	871-6000	4	31	30	0	0	Con.	4,101	1,256	97.6	107.4	50.7	59.5	19	Yes	Yes	Yes
Westminster City Hall Victoria Street London SE1 6QP	828-8070	A	32	27	0	1	Con.	5,579	464	100.1	100.4	31.0	28.4	19	Yes	Yes	Yes

4. Local government bodies for parts of London

Borough and address	Telephone	How elected	C	L	SLD/Oth.	SDP	Control	Staff total F/T P/T (1987)		Expenditure CURRENT 86–87 (£m)	87–88 (£m)	CAPITAL 85–86 (£m)	86–87 (£m)	Method of raising revenue	Subject to Audit Commission	Public right of access	Appeal to Local Ombudsman
OUTER LONDON																	
Barking & Dagenham Civic Centre Dagenham Essex RM10 7BN	592-4500	A	3	37	5	3	Lab.	4,826	2,940	73.9	79.2	11.1	10.6	19	Yes	Yes	Yes
Barnet Town Hall The Burroughs London NW4 4BG	202-8282	A	39	18	3	0	Con.	7,106	4,225	138.4	145.8	18.8	18.8	19	Yes	Yes	Yes
Bexley Civic Offices Broadway Bexleyheath Kent DA6 7LB	303-7777	A	37	15	10	0	Con.	4,763	3,887	99.9	108.5	15.3	14.9	19	Yes	Yes	Yes
Brent Town Hall Forty Lane Wembley Middlesex HA9 9HX	904-1244	A	21	41	4	0	Lab.	9,351	4,174	203.6	201.9	52.6	48.9	19	Yes	Yes	Yes
Bromley Civic Centre Rochester Avenue Bromley	464-3333	A	44	10	6	0	Con.	5,561	3,886	125.7	132.1	27.4	22.9	19	Yes	Yes	Yes

Organisation	Phone						Control									
Croydon Taberner House, Park Lane, Croydon, Surrey CR9 3JS	686-4433	A	44	26	0	0	Con.	7,516	4,928	150.2	158.1	20.7	23.3	19	Yes	Yes	Yes
Ealing Town Hall, Ealing, London W5 2BY	579-2424	A	20	47	3	0	Lab.	8,342	4,386	162.1	193.2	35.3	26.7	19	Yes	Yes	Yes
Enfield Civic Centre, Silver Street, Enfield, Middlesex EN1 3XA	366-6565	A	40	26	0	0	Con.	6,068	3,578	131.4	129.0	16.0	16.3	19	Yes	Yes	Yes
Haringey Civic Centre, PO Box 264, High Road, London N22 4LE	881-3000	A	17	41	1	0	Con.	9,495	4,843	183.7	172.3	51.8	55.2	19	Yes	Yes	Yes
Harrow Civic Centre, Harrow, Middlesex HA1 2UW	863-5611	A	32	9	18	4	Con.	4,476	3,753	100.3	106.2	23.3	13.1	19	Yes	Yes	Yes
Havering Town Hall, Romford, Essex RM1 3RD	0708-46040	A	28	20	5	10	NOC	5,772	4,045	103.9	110.1	16.0	23.1	19	Yes	Yes	Yes
Hillingdon Civic Centre, Uxbridge, Middlesex UB8 1UW	0895-50111	A	28	34	7	0	NOC	6,107	4,515	112.2	116.9	28.8	24.7	19	Yes	Yes	Yes

4. Local government bodies for parts of London

Borough and address	Telephone	How elected	C	L	SLD/ SDP	Oth.	Control	Staff total F/T (1987)	P/T	Expenditure CURRENT 86–87 (£m)	87–88 (£m)	CAPITAL 85–86 (£m)	86–87 (£m)	Method of raising revenue	Subject to Audit Commission	Public right of access	Appeal to Local Ombudsman
Hounslow Civic Centre Lampton Road Hounslow Middlesex TW3 4DN	570-7728	A	17	40	3	1	Lab.	6,209	3,497	122.3	111.9	25.5	17.7	19	Yes	Yes	Yes
Kingston-upon-Thames Guildhall Kingston-upon-Thames Surrey KT1 1EU	546-2121	A	26	4	20	0	Con.	4,237	2,512	62.2	70.1	11.3	18.0	19	Yes	Yes	Yes
Merton Crown House London Road Merton SM4 5DX	543-2222	A	29	25	0	3	Con.	3,250	1,480	77.1	81.0	17.0	17.9	19	Yes	Yes	Yes
Newham Town Hall East Ham	472-1430	A	0	59	1	0	Lab.	9,376	2,892	179.3	187.0	59.9	51.9	19	Yes	Yes	Yes

Organisation	Phone																
Redbridge Town Hall High Road Ilford Essex IG1 1DD	478-3020	A	45	17	1	0	Con.	4,820	3,495	105.1	111.6	27.0	20.2	19	Yes	Yes	Yes
Richmond-upon-Thames Municipal Offices Twickenham TW1 3AA	891-1411	A	4	0	48	0	All.	3,518	2,098	75.7	79.8	9.0	7.1	19	Yes	Yes	Yes
Sutton Civic Offices St Nicholas Way Sutton SM1 1EA	661-5000	A	21	7	28	0	All.	3,346	2,298	74.2	82.2	15.4	9.9	19	Yes	Yes	Yes
Waltham Forest Town Hall Forest Road London E17 4JF	527-5544	A	16	30	11	0	Lab.	6,844	4,907	137.0	163.1	20.3	17.5	19	Yes	Yes	Yes

PART III
Associations of Local Government Officers in London

Advisory Body of Chief Education Officers, K. G. M. Ratcliffe, Lynton House, 255 High Road, Ilford, Essex IG1 1NN (01-478 3020)

Association of Civil Defence and Emergency Planning Officers, London Branch, Major R. E. B. Morris, Town Hall, King Street, London W6 9JU (01-748 3020, ext. 2260)

Association of District Secretaries, London Branch, Mrs. S. G. Smith, Town Hall, Wandsworth High Street, London SW18 2PU (01-871 6107)

Association of London Borough Architects, K. Lund, Newham Town Hall Annexe, Barking Road, London E6 2RP (01-472 1430)

Association of London Borough Chief Librarians, J. Lowry, Greenwich Library, Woolwich Road, London SE10 ORL (01-858 6656)

Association of London Borough Engineers and Surveyors, C. E. Carter, Crown House, London Road, Morden, Surrey SM4 5DX (01-545 3050)

Association of London Borough Planning Officers, J. B. Durham, Brent House, 349 High Road, Wembley, Middx HA9 6BZ (01-900 5092)

Association of London Cleansing Officers, M. L. P. Dean, Montague Road Depot, Edmonton, London N9 (01-807 0918)

Association of London Directors of Housing, R. E. Janering, Directorate of Housing and Environmental Health, Barnet House, 1255 High Road, Whetstone, London N20 OEJ (01-446 8511)

Association of London Road Safety Officers, C. Roy Clark, Development Department, Taberner House, Park Lane, Croydon CR9 1JT (01-686 4433, ext. 2467/2189)

Guild of London Baths Managers, M. Carty, Plumstead High Street, London SE18 1JL (01-854 8466)

Local Authority Valuers Association, R. S. Gregory, Town Hall, High Road, Ilford, Essex IG1 1DD (01-487 3020, ext. 3201)

London Advisory Group of Chief Leisure Officers, D. J. Bryant, Leisure Department, Westminster City Hall, London SW1E 6QP (01-798 2236)

London Association of Directors of Social Services, A. Holden, PO Box 7, Civic Centre, Station Road, Harrow, Middx HA1 2UL (01-863 5611)

London Borough Arts and Entertainments Officers' Group, Ms M. Short, Community Services Department, 22–24 Uxbridge Road, London W5 2BP (01-579 2424, ext. 3321)

London Boroughs Security Officers Association, T. W. G. Harding, Westminster City Hall, Victoria Street, London SW1E 6QP (01-789 2738)

London Chief Environmental Health Officers Association, G. L. Fish, Environmental Health Department, Barnet House, 1255 High Road, Whetstone, London NE20 OEJ (01-446 8511)

London Chief Trading Standards Officers, J. Taylor, Trading Standards
Service, 249 Willesden Lane, London NW2 5JH (01-908 7445)

London Financial Advisory Committee, D. J. Hopkins, Westminster City
Hall, Victoria Street, London SW1E 6QP (01-798 2309)

London Government Public Relations Association, A. O'Regan, Tower
Hamlets Town Hall, Patriot Square, London E2 9LN (01-980 4831, ext. 216)

Society of Chief Personnel Officers London Region, D. E. Lawrence,
Personnel Division, Taberner House, Park Lane, Croydon CR9 3JS (01-686
4433, ext. 5608)

Society of Local Authority Chief Executives, London Branch, E. W. Dear,
Town Hall, Upper Street, London N1 2UD (01-226 1234, ext. 3139)

PART IV
London's MPs (by borough)

Barking and Dagenham
BARKING Jo Richardson (Lab.)
DAGENHAM Bryan Gould (Lab.)

Barnet
CHIPPING BARNET Sydney Chapman (Con.)
FINCHLEY Margaret Thatcher (Con.)
HENDON NORTH John Gorst (Con.)
HENDON SOUTH J.L. Marshall (Con.)

Bexley
BEXLEY HEATH Cyril Townsend (Con.)
ERITH & CRAYFORD D. A Evennett (Con.)
OLD BEXLEY & SIDCUP Edward Heath (Con.)

Brent
BRENT EAST Ken Livingstone (Lab.)
BRENT NORTH Dr Rhodes Boyson (Con.)
BRENT SOUTH Paul Boateng (Lab.)

Bromley
BECKENHAM Sir Phillip Goodhart (Con.)
CHISLEHURST Roger Sims (Con.)
ORPINGTON Ivor Stanbrook (Con.)
RAVENSBOURNE John Hunt (Con.)

Camden
HAMPSTEAD & HIGHGATE Geoffrey Finsberg (Con.)
HOLBORN & ST. PANCRAS Frank Dobson (Lab.)

Croydon
CROYDON CENTRAL John Moore (Con.)
CROYDON NE Bernard Weatherill (Ind.)
CROYDON NW H.J. Malins (Con.)
CROYDON SOUTH Sir William Clark (Con.)

Ealing
EALING ACTON Sir George Young (Con.)
EALING NORTH Harry Greenway (Con.)
EALING SOUTHALL Sidney Bidwell (Lab.)

Enfield
EDMONTON I.D. Twinn (Con.)
ENFIELD NORTH Tim Eggar (Con.)
ENFIELD SOUTHGATE M.D.X. Portillo (Con.)

Greenwich
GREENWICH Rosie Barnes (SDP)
ELTHAM Peter Bottomley (Con.)
WOOLWICH John Cartwright (SDP)

Hackney
HACKNEY N & STOKE NEWINGTON Diane Abbott (Lab.)
HACKNEY S & SHOREDITCH Brian Sedgemore (Lab.)

Hammersmith and Fulham
HAMMERSMITH Clive Soley (Lab.)
FULHAM M.H.M. Carrington (Con.)

Haringey
TOTTENHAM Bernie Grant (Lab.)
HORNSEY & WOOD GREEN Sir
  Hugh Rossi (Con.)

Harrow
HARROW EAST Hugh Dykes
  (Con.)
HARROW WEST R.G. Hughes
  (Con.)

Havering
HORNCHURCH Robin Squire
  (Con.)
ROMFORD Michael Neubert (Con.)
UPMINSTER Sir Nicholas Bonsor
  (Con.)

Hillingdon
HAYES & HILLINGDON Terry
  Dicks (Con.)
RUISLIP NORTHWOOD J.A.D.
  Wilkinson (Con.)
UXBRIDGE Michael Shersby
  (Con.)

Hounslow
BRENTFORD & ISLEWORTH Sir
  Barney Hayhoe (Con.)
FELTHAM & HESTON R.P.
  Ground (Con.)

Islington
ISLINGTON N Jeremy Corbyn
  (Lab.)
ISLINGTON S &
  FINSBURY Chris Smith (Lab.)

Kensington and Chelsea
CHELSEA Nicholas Scott (Con.)
KENSINGTON Dudley Fishburn
  (Con.)

Kingston
KINGSTON Norman Lamont
  (Con.)
SURBITON R.P. Tracey (Con.)

Lambeth
STREATHAM W.J.M. Shelton
  (Con.)
NORWOOD John Fraser (Lab.)
VAUXHALL Stuart Holland (Lab.)

Lewisham
LEWISHAM DEPTFORD Joan
  Ruddock (Lab.)
LEWISHAM EAST C.B. Moynihan
  (Con.)
LEWISHAM WEST J.C. Maples
  (Con.)

Merton
MITCHAM & MORDEN Angela
  Rumbold (Con.)
WIMBLEDON Dr C. Goodson-
  Wickes (Con.)

Newham
NEWHAM NE Ronald Leighton
  (Lab.)
NEWHAM NW Tony Banks (Lab.)
NEWHAM SOUTH Nigel Spearing
  (Lab.)

Redbridge
ILFORD NORTH Vivian Bendall
  (Con.)
ILFORD SOUTH Neil Thorne
  (Con.)
WANSTEAD & WOODFORD J.
  N. Arbuthnott (Con.)

Richmond-upon-Thames
RICHMOND & BARNES Jeremy
  Hanley (Con.)
TWICKENHAM Toby Jessel (Con.)

Southwark
SOUTHWARK &
  BERMONDSEY Simon Hughes
  (SLD)
DULWICH G.R. Bowden (Con.)
PECKHAM Harriet Harman (Lab.)

Sutton
SUTTON & CHEAM Neil
  McFarlane (Con.)
CARSHALTON &
  WALLINGTON Nigel Forman
  (Con.)

Tower Hamlets
BETHNAL GREEN &
  STEPNEY Peter Shore (Lab.)
BOW AND POPLAR Mildred
  Gordon (Lab.)

Waltham Forest
CHINGFORD Norman Tebbit
  (Con.)

LEYTON H.M. Cohen (Lab.)
WALTHAMSTOW H. H. F.
  Summerson (Con.)

Wandsworth
BATTERSEA J.C. Bowis (Con.)
PUTNEY David Mellor (Con.)
TOOTING Thomas Cox (Lab.)

Westminster and City of London
WESTMINSTER NORTH John
  Wheeler (Con.)
CITY OF LONDON &
  WESTMINSTER Peter Brooke
  (Con.)

PART V
London Boroughs Basic Data, 1987-88

	Population	Area (Hectares)	Rateable value (£m)	% Non-domestic RV	Average domestic rate bill
Inner London					
City of London	5240	0.274	273.0	99.4	631
Camden	180400	2.171	119.3	76.1	745
Greenwich	216200	4.744	33.1	43.7	467
Hackney	185800	1.948	38.6	51.2	583
Hammersmith and Fulham	151000	1.617	37.0	54.7	365
Islington	167900	1.489	55.0	62.0	552
Kensington and Chelsea	137600	1.195	73.3	46.8	522
Lambeth	243500	2.727	61.2	56.8	538
Lewisham	232100	3.473	35.3	35.8	544
Southwark	215900	2.880	61.8	63.9	487
Tower Hamlets	149700	1.973	51.8	69.4	499
Wandsworth	258800	3.491	44.4	39.3	295
Westminster	174900	2.158	327.6	83.8	733

(Outer London data appear overleaf)

	Population	Area (Hectares)	Rateable value (£m)	% Non-domestic RV	Average domestic rate bill
Outer London					
Barking and Dagenham	148000	3.419	27.0	53.1	388
Barnet	298000	8.953	62.8	34.3	555
Bexley	218500	6.065	31.7	38.7	347
Brent	254900	4.421	52.2	48.9	631
Bromley	297900	15.179	51.7	34.1	389
Croydon	321200	8.658	71.8	48.5	406
Ealing	292400	5.547	57.9	50.2	383
Enfield	263300	8.115	49.8	45.5	413
Haringey	196000	3.031	37.3	43.9	670
Harrow	201700	5.082	35.8	35.3	485
Havering	238500	11.776	38.8	38.4	408
Hillingdon	232300	11.037	60.2	61.0	477
Hounslow	200500	5.852	51.5	60.9	571
Kingston-upon-Thames	133900	3.756	29.2	47.3	409
Merton	168135	3.796	31.8	40.7	392
Newham	210600	3.637	36.6	53.3	580
Redbridge	227500	5.647	37.0	34.0	388
Richmond-upon-Thames	161500	5.525	33.3	39.2	458
Sutton	169600	4.342	30.4	39.5	412
Waltham Forest	216800	3.966	32.2	38.5	433
Greater London total	6770275	157.947	2070.4	62.1	517
South East Region total (incl. Greater London)	17322675	2722.494	3756.9	54.2	485

Index